Choosing Faith...

Choosing Faith...
AGAINST THE ODDS

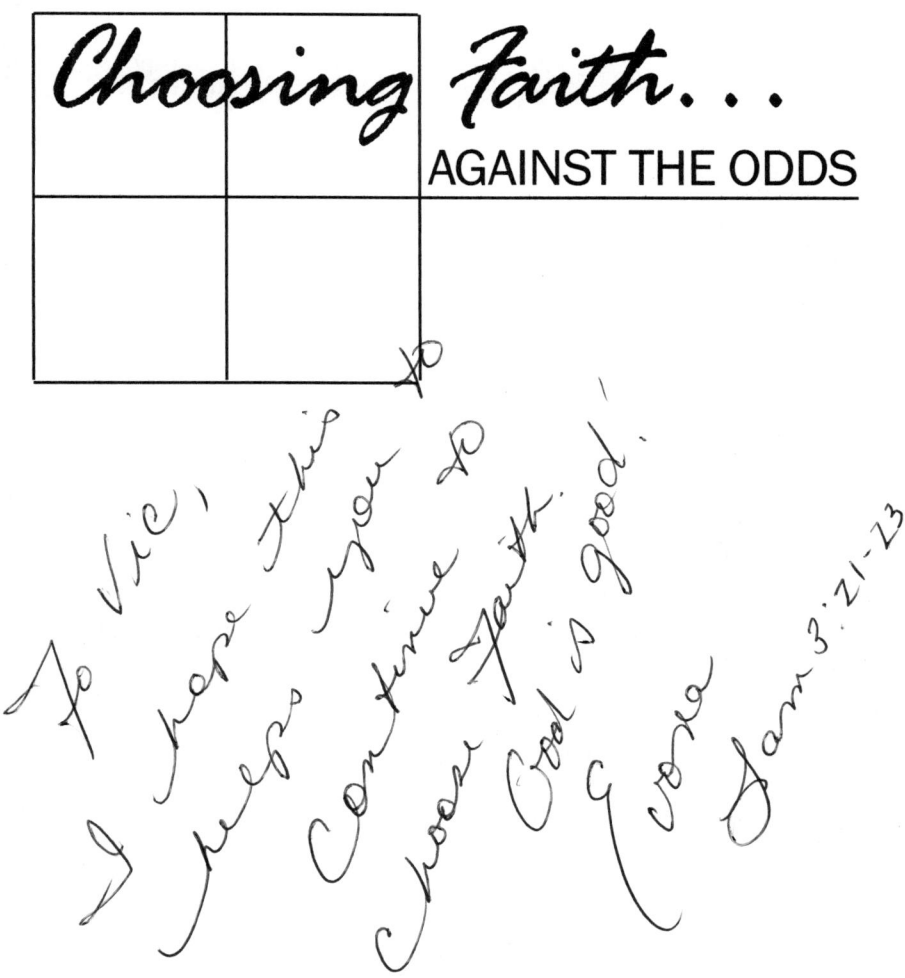

Cliff and Evona Frink

VMI Publishers • Sisters, Oregon

© 2009 by Cliff and Evona Frink

All rights reserved

Published by
VMI Publishers
Sisters, Oregon
www.vmipublishers.com

Unless otherwise indicated, all Scripture quotations are taken from the *King James* Version of the Bible.

Emphases in Scripture quotations are added by the authors.

ISBN: 13 978-1-933204-78-9
ISBN: 10 1-933204-78-8

Library of Congress: 2009921470

Printed in the USA

Cover artwork was created by Angela DiFilippo Cofield
Contact: GraphicsbyADC@gmail.com

Most of the Frink family pictures were taken by Tammy Folsom Grant

This book is dedicated to our three boys.
Micah Daniel, Caleb Nathanael and Lucas Samuel
Your steadfast faith in God has inspired many to continue to
"Choose Faith."
You are your daddy's legacy.

"For this child [these children] I prayed; and the Lord hath given me my petition which I asked of him."

1 Samuel 1:27

Table of Contents

March 2008 15
   Prologue
May 19, 2006 19
   Pastor Frink's Health (First Update)
May 21, 2006 20
   Sunday Morning Letter to our Congregation (From Mrs. Evona)
May 23, 2006 22
   Bad News but a Good God
May 24, 2006 23
   The Faith of a Child
May 26, 2006 25
   Comfort from a Stranger
May 27, 2006 27
   The Works of the Lord Are Great
May 29, 2006 29
   Marvelous Sunday at Fellowship Baptist
May 30, 2006 30
   The Cry of a Mother's Heart
May 31, 2006 31
   Our Plan of Action
June 1, 2006 33
   Another Great Day at Moffitt
June 2, 2006 35
   Simulation Success
June 3, 2006 37
   The Reality of Cancer
June 4, 2006 39
   Second Sunday Back…Can It Get any Better?
June 6, 2006 41
   A Day Together
June 7, 2006 43
   Long Day at Moffitt
June 8, 2006 45
   Second Radiation Treatment

June 9, 2006 47
   Prayer Meeting Blessings and Third Radiation Treatment
June 10, 2006 49
   An Answer to Our Prayers
June 11, 2006 51
   Praying "Republicans" and a New "Ride"
June 12, 2006 53
   Getting Ready for Another Week of Radiation
June 13, 2006 54
   Midnight Ice Cream Run
June 14, 2006 56
   How Will They Know? (From Mrs. Evona)
June 15, 2006 59
   9 to 5 at Moffitt and a Lot of News
June 16, 2006 62
   Last Night's Prayer Meeting and Today's Moffitt
June 17, 2006 64
   Hair Today…Gone Tomorrow!
June 18, 2006 67
   A Father's Day to Remember
June 19, 2006 69
   Great Father's Day at Home and Church
June 20, 2006 71
   Just When I Need Him Most (From Mrs. Evona)
June 21, 2006 73
   Last Radiation and Our Purple Pal
June 22, 2006 75
   Will the Real Curly Please Stand Up?
June 23, 2006 77
   A Day of Rest (From Mrs. Evona)
June 24, 2006 79
   Job Well Done
June 26, 2006 81
   Satan Battles but God Blesses
June 27, 2006 83
   You Have Been Discharged

June 28, 2006 85
   A Port for the Upcoming Storms
June 29, 2006 87
   An Unexpected Bloom
June 30, 2006 90
   This Is No Coincidence
July 1, 2006 92
   Platelets Down, No Chemo
July 2, 2006 94
   The Blankie (From Mrs. Evona)
July 3, 2006 97
   Pulpits and Platelets
July 4, 2006 99
   Praise the Lord, Chemotherapy Went Well (From Mrs. Evona)
July 5, 2006 101
   To Tube or Not to Tube—That is the Question
July 6, 2006 103
   Rip Van Frinkle
July 7, 2006 105
   We Will Remember the Name of the Lord (From Mrs. Evona)
July 8, 2006 107
   The Horse Did Not Get to Head to the Barn
July 9, 2006 109
   A Rough Week but a Good God
July 10, 2006 111
   Going Home…God Willing
July 11, 2006 113
   A Way Higher than Our Own
July 12, 2006 116
   Complications, Setbacks…Finally Improvement
July 13, 2006 118
   A Sticky Note I've Needed Many Times in My Life
July 14, 2006 120
   Good News for a Change
July 15, 2006 122
   A Special Surprise

July 16, 2006	125
The Fight Begins	
July 17, 2006	127
A Morning in the Life of…the Preacher	
July 18, 2006	129
Home at Last	
July 19, 2006	132
Our Dandelion of Faith (From Mrs. Evona)	
July 20, 2006	135
"We Choose Faith Rally" Planned	
July 21, 2006	138
Pecking with the Chickens or Soaring with the Eagles (From Mrs. Evona)	
July 22, 2006	141
What's in Your Closet?	
July 23, 2006	144
And When They Had Prayed	
July 24, 2006	147
I'm Back	
July 25, 2006	149
Lusting for Light	
July 26, 2006	151
A Changed Focus	
July 27, 2006	154
Power Tools, Even for Girls (From Mrs. Evona)	
July 28, 2006	156
Let's Be Childish	
July 29, 2006	158
Enduring the Thorns to Enjoy the Rose	
July 30, 2006	161
Pick Me, Lord! (From Mrs. Evona)	
July 31, 2006	164
A Day of Giving and God's Grace at Fellowship Baptist	
August 1, 2006	167
Preparing for the Battle	
August 2, 2006	171
Do the First Works	

August 3, 2006 174
    Fear? Flight? Or Faith? (From Mrs. Evona)
August 4, 2006 177
    In the Shadow of Thy Wings
August 5, 2006 179
    A Sport Not for the Faint of Heart (From Mrs. Evona)
August 6, 2006 182
    The Caregiver
August 7, 2006 184
    "We Choose Faith Rally" off to a Great Start
August 8, 2006 186
    Getting the Troops Ready for Battle (From Mrs. Evona)
August 9, 2006 189
    600 Plus Come to "Choose Faith" at Rally
August 10, 2006 191
    Great Final Service of "We Choose Faith Rally"
August 11, 2006 193
    Why, Lord? (From Mrs. Evona)
August 12, 2006 197
    We're Not Alone
August 13, 2006 199
    For Such a Time as This
August 14, 2006 200
    You Want to, Now Will You?
August 15, 2006 202
    Holding Hands in the Dark (From Mrs. Evona)
August 16, 2006 204
    Mirror, Mirror
August 17, 2006 207
    I'll Take the Good News First…Actually with God…It's all Good News!
August 18, 2006 209
    The Heavenly Taste Test (From Mrs. Evona)
August 19, 2006 212
    Seeing through Satan's Lies and Surrendering to Christ's Truth
August 20, 2006 214
    In Acceptance Lieth Peace (From Mrs. Evona)

August 21, 2006 217
   Tarceva Begins
August 22, 2006 219
   When No One's Looking
August 23, 2006 221
   We Do Not Well
August 24, 2006 223
   Packing For the Journey (From Mrs. Evona)
August 25, 2006 226
   Comfort from the Comforter
August 26, 2006 229
   The Taste Can Be Deceiving
August 27, 2006 231
   Choosing Faith One Step at a Time.
August 28, 2006 233
   The Best Pain Medicine
August 29, 2006 235
   Who is Like unto Thee?
August 30, 2006 237
   How Does Your Garden Grow? (From Mrs. Evona)
August 31, 2006 240
   I'm Sick of Cancer!
September 1, 2006 243
   Why Doesn't the Toilet Paper Fairy Come to my House? (From Mrs. Evona)
September 2, 2006 246
   Delay is Not Denial
September 3, 2006 250
   The Key is to Start on Saturday
September 4, 2006 253
   Taking it Easy on Labor Day
September 5, 2006 255
   Lucy and Ethel (From Mrs. Evona)
September 6, 2006 258
   A Heart to Heart Talk
September 7, 2006 260
   Our Time

September 8, 2006 262
   The Man Chair
September 9, 2006 264
   Songs in the Night (From Mrs. Evona)
September 10, 2006 266
   Where to Go With Your Problems!
September 11, 2006 268
   Our Forever Friend
September 12, 2006 271
   Attitude Determines Altitude
September 13, 2006 274
   A Blessing in Disguise! (From Mrs. Evona)
September 14, 2006 277
   Strength for My Soul
September 15, 2006 279
   It's All in Who You Know
September 16, 2006 281
   The Thief of Time and the Grave of Opportunity
September 17, 2006 283
   Who's 'We', Kemo Sabe? (From Mrs. Evona)
September 18, 2006 286
   Picking Priceless Pearls
September 19, 2006 288
   We Press On (From Mrs. Evona)
September 20, 2006 291
   Thanks for Sharing…I Think
September 21, 2006 293
   Double Digits
September 22, 2006 295
   Hot and Cranky in Frinkville (From Mrs. Evona)
September 23, 2006 298
   God's Unusual Care
September 24, 2006 301
   What's in a Name?
September 25, 2006 304
   Breathing…a Must in Anyone's Daily Routine

September 26, 2006 306
    Just Hold Your Peace! (From Mrs. Evona)
September 27, 2006 309
    My Ears Are in the Wrong Place (From Mrs. Evona)
September 28, 2006 312
    A Time to Weep and a Time to Laugh (From Mrs. Evona)
September 29, 2006 315
    Blessed Beyond Measure
September 30, 2006 317
    A Dry Spell
October 1, 2006 319
    A Character to Be Proud Of
October 2, 2006 321
    Life on the Border
October 3, 2006 323
    In the Hospital Again! (From Mrs. Evona)
October 4, 2006 324
    The Roller Coaster of Life! (From Mrs. Evona)
October 5, 2006 326
    Ups and Downs Are Part of Life,
    But How 'Bout a Little Smooth Sailing for a While?
October 6, 2006 328
    What Day Is It Anyway? (From Mrs. Evona)
October 6, 2006 329
    Calling Post Message from Pastor Dave
October 7, 2006 330
    Message from Brother Derryl Boyette, Evona's Dad
October 8, 2006 331
    It's Time to Live What I Preach
October 12, 2006 333
    A Celebration to Remember (From Derryl Boyette, Evona's Dad)
October 13, 2006 335
    We Will Not Be Bitter; We Will Be Thankful
March 2008 337
    Epilogue

Prologue

This morning I grabbed my coffee, hunted for my keys and counted kids as we ran out the door trying to make it to school on time. With a feeling of accomplishment, I cranked the car only to hear snickering in the back seat. I turned around with my angry eyebrows and demanded to know what the issue was this time. Due to years of experience, the older two boys deferred to the youngest (because he is too new to understand the implications of the angry eyebrows). With joy in his voice he told me my shoes were pretty! I looked to see what shoes were pretty enough for three boys to notice. *Pink fuzzy slippers!* I dashed into the house to retrieve my work shoes and we were off. What a day and it was only 6:45 A.M.

Cliff and his mom Kay and Evona and her mom Paulette in 1973

In the multitude of trials, faith can, against the odds, be given the nourishment it needs to flourish. When circumstances are humanly impossible, God gives us the grace to believe that *He* is able. If we make the choice to take one small step in the direction of faith, we know he will give us the strength to make the next step, even if our feet of faith are wearing pink fuzzy slippers!

Years ago a doctor gravely gave the news to a young couple that the odds of success were slim to none. After years of unanswered prayer, human hope was crushed. There was no place to turn but to God. Just like David the Psalmist did in chapter 62, the couple turned toward their loving heavenly father and poured out their heart to Him and He helped. This couple chose to trust God in the midst of heartbreaking circumstances and trust Him with the outcome. A friend was asked to join with them in prayer for this humanly impossible situation. Together they prayed and chose faith against the odds.

Many years later, at a bridal shower we attended, this entire story was told. The mother of the bride, never one to speak in public, stood and began to share her story of faith. As the words poured out of this mother, the room became silent. Gone was the normal chatter as all strained to hear what God had done in her life. Years before, the doctors had told her and her husband that after many complications and a lost pregnancy, that they would never conceive a child of their own. This was devastating news to the couple. Their hearts' desire was to hold a child of their own. Humanly speaking all hope was gone. Instead of giving up, they gave it to the Lord. Diligently they prayed to God to answer their request. This mother of the bride told the captivated crowd that she had asked a good friend of hers to pray for her request, not giving any details. This friend committed to pray, not knowing the specific circumstances. Years passed by, and both couples moved and changed churches and jobs. Almost 22 years later, the two couples once again were serving the Lord together at the same church. With tears in her eyes, the bride's mother turned toward the mother of the groom and announced loud enough for the entire room to hear, "I asked you to pray for an unspoken need that was breaking my heart, and you chose to join with me and choose faith against the odds, not knowing the situation. God answered our prayers by giving us a beautiful little girl of our own, whose name means "a gracious gift from God." In a few days, my husband and I are going to give that precious gift God gave us to your son for a bride." What a testimony of faith we received that day as we watched those two mothers hug and thank God for His mercy and faithfulness.

I WAS THAT BRIDE AND CLIFF WAS THAT GROOM!

GOD IS STILL ON HIS THRONE. These were six words Cliff would never forget. On a cool November morning in 1983, a dump truck hit his small Datsun B210 carrying a full load of cement. Cliff, two sisters named Kim and Julie, and their friend Vince were headed to school that morning when all their lives forever changed. While an ambulance rushed Cliff to the hospital to treat his injuries, all he could do was beg for news about his three friends who were also in the car. After an eternity, Cliff's family was able to see him. He was completely distraught and collapsed into their arms like a helpless child. Through tears his father told him that Kim was dead and Julie and Vince were seriously hurt. A message came from Kim and Julie's mom. Cliff was terrified at what her message might be. Her message was only six words: "God is still on His throne." Vince had not survived the crash and Julie was taken off life support shortly after. "How could God still be on His throne?" Cliff questioned. "How could something so tragic have invaded my life?"

God was desperately trying to reach Cliff. As a child he had heard the gospel, how Jesus Christ had paid for his sin debt on the cross, and asked him to be his personal Savior, but many years had passed and Cliff had drifted far away from the Lord. His plans were to pay his respects at all three funerals and then end his own life. The mother of the two girls, Mrs. Beverly, called and asked that Cliff do something for her. She wanted him to be a pallbearer for Kimberly. He agreed but had no idea how he would be able to fulfill this request. The verse, *"You have not because ye ask not"* (James 4:2), reminded him how he would make it through. The funerals were very sad and emotional. Later at the graveside, Cliff remembered setting the casket on the grave and feeling such despair. *"This is the end for my friends,"* he thought. But in that moment, God spoke to his heart and reminded him that this was not the end for his friends. They were beginning their eternal life with Him and it could be a beginning for him also. As a broken seventeen-year-old young man he surrendered his life to Christ. God took the broken boy and called him to be a man of God. Cliff surrendered his life to fulltime ministry and began preaching in Tampa, Florida.

We were married in 1993 and Cliff became Senior Pastor of Fellowship Baptist Church soon after. As a couple we never dreamed we would walk this valley together. We said to each other over and over how perfect our life was. We were madly in love with each other, had three beautiful boys, a lovely home and a wonderful ministry. The year 2005-2006 was the busiest and most exciting year of our ministry. Life was like a train that had left the station without us and we spent all our time trying to get back on. We loved it! It was picture perfect, we thought. Overnight our lives changed forever. On Mother's Day 2006, Cliff was in agony from severe headaches. By the grace of God he was able to preach that morning, but we knew something was very wrong. After seeing the doctor, Cliff went from his previous diagnosis of pneumonia and a sinus infection to needing an MRI that showed "several abnormalities." He was admitted to the hospital that night and there was given a series of tests. Less than a week later, Cliff and I and his parents had to hear some of the worst news a family could ever hear…cancer. It was in his lungs, bones and in his brain. What a devastating 10 minutes. However, the journey only begins there. We want to share with you our hearts and how the seeds of faith that have been planted throughout our lives have taken root and been allowed to grow. We want to give you hope that no matter what valley you are going through, God can help you to

Choose Faith…AGAINST THE ODDS.

May 19, 2006—

Pastor Frink's Health (First Update)

For those of you who did not receive the calling post call on Thursday, I wanted to update you on my health. I have had a cough which was diagnosed as pneumonia. I then started having painful headaches and was sent to have an MRI which showed abnormalities in my brain. I was admitted to University Community Hospital for further tests. A CT scan confirmed multiple spots on my brain, lungs and spine. Before I can get a diagnosis, several other tests need to be run. I want to tell you that God is in control of my life and I have faith in His goodness and His perfect will for my life, my family, and our church. I do need rest, so please understand my not receiving visits or calls, but I covet your prayers.

> *"That I may know him, and the power of his resurrection, and the fellowship of his sufferings, being made conformable unto his death; ..."*
>
> Philippians 3:10

Pastor

∞ ∞ ∞

May 21, 2006—
Sunday Morning Letter to Our Congregation
(From Mrs. Evona)

As you know, Pastor and I and our three boys received some devastating news this week. After thinking that Pastor had a serious sinus infection that developed into pneumonia, we were told his MRI was abnormal, showing several masses on his brain. This is what was causing his debilitating headaches. After further tests, we were told there are other areas that are showing spots. We have not been given any other information at this point. Pastor has been through many tests and procedures the past 3 or 4 days. The outcome of each has only brought more questions and resulted in more tests.

My heart is broken. I am scared and hurting. I hurt for Pastor, for our children, for his parents and family. However, God is the God of comfort! He has filled my heart with peace and given me grace to make it through things I had never even imagined. Pastor has been a source of comfort to me, our children and his own family. Of course he is dealing with it in his usual way…humor! He announced to me that he had "more spots than a Dalmatian!" Only he could make me laugh at a time like this. He knows that God is in control, and keeps reminding me of that fact. I have been humbled watching him minister to the nurses and staff and other patients, even in the midst of personal hurt and fear. Pastor is adamant that he is going to let God use him no matter what happens. His heart is here with you. You are our church and our family. We feel your love and support. The cards have been such a blessing and encouragement.

There are three specific ways you can pray for us:

- Pray that God continues to give us grace to face each day. Every day more information and news comes. This is very overwhelming. We need God to give us strength and grace to face each step.
- Pray that God gives His wisdom to the doctors and nurses that are

trying to find out the answers for us. God is the great physician. He can give these earthly doctors heavenly wisdom.
- Pray that through this trial our faith in God shines through to all who come in contact with us.

Pastor tried his best to talk me into sneaking him out so he could come to church today! His heart is aching because of not being able to be here with you. You can make things easier, however, if you open your heart during our Family Life Conference and let God change you for His glory. We have learned in such a dramatic way that family should be your priority. Let God help your families today.

Thank you for understanding that we need time together with our family while we make so many decisions. We would love to be able to see and visit with you all, but Pastor's strength has got to be directed toward feeling better and being well enough to make some serious decisions.

As soon as he is "set free" (as he calls it) from the hospital and is feeling well enough, he will be right back here in the pulpit, making silly jokes and preaching his heart out.

We love you all and covet your prayers. *Second Corinthians 3:5 says, "Not that we are sufficient of ourselves to think any thing as of ourselves; But our sufficiency is of God."* God will enable us to make it through this trial. He will give us what we need to make it through each day.

We can't wait to be back in our places serving the Lord.

Love,
Mrs. Evona, Pastor and boys

May 23, 2006—
Bad News but a Good God

The doctor was able to meet with us yesterday morning and go over the results of the lung biopsy. He confirmed the presence of lung cancer, which they feel has moved into some of Pastor's bones and his brain.

We now have to hear what the oncologist (cancer doctor) feels like the next course of action will be. The lung doctor seems to think that chemotherapy and radiation will be what will be in store for us. I directly asked the doctor if we have a way to fight this cancer and he said "absolutely." With the Lord's help, we will do whatever it takes.

We have begun the process of researching and consulting with different doctors to find the best treatment and the right place to take this treatment. The next step is to receive a referral to Moffitt Cancer Center and meet with the doctors there. We have so many decisions to make and it is all very overwhelming. We sincerely covet your prayers.

After being released from the hospital Monday evening, Pastor is now resting at home. He asked that you pray that he will be able to be back in the pulpit on this coming Sunday. Thank you for your understanding during this difficult time. The privacy you are giving is allowing us to spend time with each other and our three sweet boys. We feel your love and support and know you are praying. We can't wait to see you all at church and be back in our place serving the Lord.

There is hope! God is good and He is *"able to do exceeding abundantly above all that we ask or think, according to the power that worketh in us"* (Ephesians 3:20).

Love,
Mrs. Evona, Pastor and the Boys

May 24, 2006—
The Faith of a Child

Good morning. It is amazing to feel well enough to be able to write to you today. I want you to know I have read every word of every card and every email and been told of every phone call you have made. It is overwhelming to be loved as you have loved me and my family. I appreciate so much the prayer meeting last night at church for us. Evona and I could feel God's touch through you during the evening.

We had a long talk with our boys last night, and they showed remarkable faith and trust in God as we told them that Daddy has cancer and now we have to seek God's next steps in treatment. Micah said, "Dad, God's brought you through so much…the accident and other things; I know He can take us through this." I was blessed in my spirit by my own son! Caleb was quiet but he came over and hugged me gently and said, "It's gonna be OK, Daddy." I didn't know how much I needed to be home with my wife and boys until supper time and we sat around our own table and enjoyed a meal—a little bit of heaven!

Evona is a tower of strength. She has a verse God gave her from Psalms that we are steadily claiming: Psalms 30:2-3: *"O Lord, my God, I cried unto thee, and thou hast healed me. O, Lord, thou hast brought up my soul from the grave: thou hast kept me alive, that I should not go down to the pit."* Isn't that awesome? I believe God is able to heal me, either miraculously or through medicine, and this is what we are praying for. I will most likely have to go down into the grave of "human hope" before God raises me up through His "heavenly hope," but I can't see how He would get the full glory He deserves otherwise.

I do not believe God is finished with me. I have much to do! My family needs me and I feel that our church needs me. I'm willing to suffer if God asks this of me. Suffering is the "great teacher." I know there is so much I need to learn and to change.

Just so you know, I am doing fairly well. I would not say I have pain right now, only tenderness in my lower back and my right hip. The headaches are under control (thank the Lord) and the cough is still a little naggy. I am being very careful when I walk.

I want to thank God for everyone who is filling the pulpit as I'm away. You guys have outdone yourselves. I'm praying to be there Sunday and preach the wonderful Word of God. Now, don't start worrying. I will make sure I am able before I attempt it. But also understand—I need to preach to you. There's nothing like standing in our pulpit and preaching to the people of Fellowship Baptist Church. I need to do this if God will let me.

Pray that we can get a referral to Moffitt Cancer Center. Evona cannot stand waiting on insurance procedures. She's ready to get on with this fight! I married a fighter and she is up for it. I am too, by the way! I'm determined to fight "fire" with "faith!"

One last thing... *God is still good!*

I love you,
Preacher

May 26, 2006—
Comfort from a Stranger

"That their hearts might be comforted, being knit together in love . . ."

COLOSSIANS 2:2

The Lord is taking care of us in wonderful ways each and every day. After our current primary care physician refused to give us a referral to Moffitt Cancer Center, which is where we believe the Lord would have us pursue treatment, God enabled us to find a new primary care physician who will see us this morning. My in-laws, the Boyettes, have been such a help during this difficult time. They have helped with the boys and given us the comfort to know they are being well taken care of. A tremendous help has come through friends of theirs at church. Our new primary care physician agreed to take us because of his relationship with Derryl and Paulette. We are now praying to receive our Moffitt referral today. We already know some excellent doctors at Moffitt who are working on getting us in as quickly as possible. Please pray with us in this matter.

Evona's entire family has pitched in to help. We have more food in the freezer than in the history of our married life. Kevin and Jonathan added

a screen porch to the back of our house. This is very needed to help keep little Lucas safe from our swimming pool. Both of them were so tired but they kept working until it was finished. Paulette and Desiree worked in the house and even planted some new flowers in my garden. What a wonderful family we have.

We cannot say enough about the cards, letters, emails, phone messages and food you have provided our family. We feel loved and missed by you all. The special notes you have sent our children have blessed them immensely. They are doing well with all this and showing great faith in God. We had a family prayer meeting last night and all of us prayed for the Lord's healing and that He would receive glory from our lives.

Something interesting happened today that we think will bless you. We had to go to various places regarding medical records and decided to stop by Staples Office Store to get some file folders and a date planner for our upcoming treatment. There is a cashier that works there who loves the Lord and always gives a word of testimony about Christ when we see her. Today, as we went through her line, she looked at us and said, "You know, in our darkest hours, God always carries us." It was so precious to me to hear those words, knowing she knew absolutely nothing about our situation. I teared up and thanked her and went to the car. Evona went back in to get a drink for me and the cashier called her to the side and said, "God just put a heavy burden on my heart as you were checking out to pray that God would heal your husband's body." We still had not told her of my health condition. Evona said, "Well, we need it right now more than ever. His name is Cliff and our verse is Psalm 30:2-3. Pray for him every night and claim this verse for us." The last thing this caring woman said was, "Come back in and tell me when God heals him." We've heard of these things happening to others but it is amazing to live it!

We look forward to being back to the greatest church this side of heaven on Sunday.

We love you,
Preacher and Mrs. Evona

MAY 27, 2006—
The Works of the Lord are Great

We are coming to you with one of the greatest updates to date! We had asked you to pray about receiving a referral to Moffitt Cancer Center in a timely fashion. Listen to what God did for us today...

We began this morning with an appointment with our new primary care physician in hopes we could obtain our needed referral. Six other doctors were unable to help us in this matter. Seven, as you know, is God's number. As soon as we walked in, Mary Beth, who is in charge of referrals, began working on our behalf. An hour later, we left the office with our referral in hand! Isn't God good?

After lunch, Evona suggested we go on over to Moffitt, even though we had no appointment. God had impressed my Aunt Cathy to return from her vacation a day early. As you know, Cathy has been a long-time patient of Moffitt. Cathy met us at Moffitt and we began trying to determine where to start. Cathy helped us find our way to the Thoracic/Pulminary Clinic of Moffitt where we met a wonderfully helpful receptionist named Marjorie. Marjorie helped us get in contact with a doctor we knew at Moffitt who had already been trying to get us set up with the proper doctor for my type of cancer—Dr. George Simon. Because of these two doctors' relationship, we were able to leave all of my medical records with Dr. Simon's office, even though I was not yet officially a "patient."

Marjorie informed us we would have to wait on the "New Patients Department" to call us and complete paperwork before we could receive any appointments with Dr. Simon. This could take up to two weeks, waiting on the department to call and then filling out the paperwork and mailing it back. She suggested we ask the case worker on duty if there was any way to expedite things with "New Patient." We walked to the next booth, and a lady named Diane saw Cathy and said, "Cathy Jeter, what are you doing here?" Diane had been Cathy's caseworker during her cancer fight. Cathy introduced me to Diane as her nephew/preacher and asked her to help me become an official patient as quickly as possible.

Within 20 minutes, I was accepted as a patient for Dr. Simon.

Shortly thereafter, Dr. Simon's chief nurse came up (also named Diane) and introduced herself to us. The first Diane asked her to get us an appointment as soon as possible and she gave us June 14th as first available. Our hearts sank as we had hoped for something considerably sooner. This cancer is not only in my lungs, it's in my bones and my brain and I'm ready to get on with fighting it. Diane said, "There's always the possibility of an earlier appointment if we have availability." I said to her, "Thank you, Diane, we appreciate that and I want you to know I'll be praying for you as you try to help us." Listen closely now, by the time we got to the lobby of Moffitt, Diane called and told us we have an appointment next Wednesday, May 31st. *Praise God! Hallelujah! Glory to His name!* He sent one miracle after another and He did it in one afternoon! The work God is doing on our behalf is amazing and we are humbled at His goodness. He is real and He is strong!

> *"The works of the LORD are great, sought out of all them that have pleasure therein. His work is honourable and glorious; and his righteousness endureth for ever. He hath made his wonderful works to be remembered; the LORD is gracious and full of compassion."*
>
> PSALM 111:2–4

With love and thanksgiving for your prayers,
Preacher and Mrs. Evona

May 29, 2006—
Marvelous Sunday at Fellowship Baptist!

We rejoiced to return to the pulpit yesterday morning, May 28, and preach God's Word to the wonderful people at Fellowship Baptist Church! It was a Memorial Day weekend, but we packed in over 500, enjoyed the West-coast Baptist Bible College Singers and then brought a message entitled, "Hope from a Hospital Bed." I shared the great "hope" God is giving us as we take this path called "cancer."

> *"And I said, My strength and my hope is perished from the LORD:...This I recall to my mind, therefore have I hope. It is of the Lord's mercies that we are not consumed, because his compassions fail not. They are new every morning: great is thy faithfulness. The Lord is my portion, saith my soul; therefore will I hope in him."*
>
> LAMENTATIONS 3:18, 21-24

I was able to return last night and hear my dear friend, Bill Daab preach and sing in the evening service and was blessed beyond words. God is providing many men to fill the pulpit over this time and I'm thankful for every one.

Pray for our appointment at Moffitt with Dr. Simon this Wednesday. We look forward to the next phase of this fight and our faith is strong in the Lord Jesus. Remember to claim Psalms 30:2–3 for us every time you pray.

We love you and felt like we were "home" just being with you.
Preacher and Mrs. Evona

May 30, 2006—

The Cry of a Mother's Heart

I am bringing you this update today because the Moffitt Center called unexpectedly and requested that Pastor and Evona be in the doctor's office today at 2:00 P.M.

We have been praying earnestly every waking minute for a touch each day from God and claiming this Scripture: Psalm 102:1–2: *"Hear my prayer, O Lord and let my cry come unto thee…Hide not thy face from me in trouble, incline thine ear unto me: in the day when I call answer me speedily."*

I was also claiming this scripture the day that God saw fit to propel them through the "New Patient" procedure that saved them several weeks of waiting. I was there firsthand to see that "miracle of God" happen. What a wonderful God we have; He is still on the throne.

Pastor and Evona are overjoyed that the appointment for the Moffitt Center has come a day earlier than we all expected and still covet your prayers as they take one step at a time with God's loving and tender care. They are ready to get on with this fight of faith.

Please join me in praying that God will get the glory through this trial and continue to be faithful to a wonderful Savior who will bring us through this a better church, willing to do more than ever before. We will update you with any news after the appointment.

Sincerely,
Kay Frink, Pastor's mom

May 31, 2006—
Our Plan of Action

On Tuesday morning, Pastor and I awoke knowing that his appointment to Moffitt would be on the following day. Our day was going to be spent preparing for the consultation and reading everything we could get our hands on to be well-informed. God, however, had different plans! Before 9:00, He had worked another miracle. Moffitt called and asked us to be there at 1:30 that afternoon. After recovering from the shock, I jumped into action. Off we went, trying to finish collecting all the tests and records and rearranging "our" schedule. Upon hearing my anxiety over the situation, Pastor asked, "Didn't you pray that the Lord would answer our prayer speedily?" Of course I had claimed Psalm102:2–3, but I didn't expect "speedily" to come so quick! What I didn't know was that both Brother David and Mrs. Kay, and probably many others, were begging God to help the doctors to move "speedily" also.

We were able to collect all of Pastor's records (some of which were "accidentally" sent to an office they were not supposed to be sent to. This office just "happened" to be right near Moffitt enabling us to collect his tests and make our appointment on time). Our own little "tumor team" met in the lobby of Moffitt. (Aunt Cathy, the Moffitt veteran, Mrs. Kay, the mother person, Pastor, the patient, and I, the one carrying all the vital information!)

Our consultation with Dr. George Simon went beautifully. He was kind and straightforward. He spent several hours with us, going over every possible solution. After much discussion, we formulated a plan. The first step is to start the process of radiation. Pastor will go in for more scans. These will allow the doctors to target the areas of the brain in need of radiation. After a spinal MRI, they will determine if his spine and femur should also receive radiation at the same time to prevent any bone fractures. This radiation will probably entail a five-day-a-week treatment for about 3 consecutive weeks. After some blood work (which you all know is his least favorite pastime), he will also receive an infusion of a bone-strengthening medicine. We shared with Dr. Simon that we have been led of God to seek treatment under his care at Moffitt. Pastor said, "Dr. Simon, I am praying that you will be a tool in God's hands to help us." The doctor replied, "I will give you 150 percent and we will throw everything, including the kitchen sink, at this disease but it will ultimately be up to God."

The next step will be chemotherapy. Dr. Simon has planned two rounds of chemotherapy to begin with, and then a reevaluation of our situation. The chemo may last for several months. We are praying that Pastor can tolerate these treatments well and be where his heart is…in the pulpit. Only God knows what the next few months hold, but Lamentations 3:23 says that God's mercies *"are new every morning: great is thy faithfulness."* We do know that no matter what comes our way, God is still good and he is faithful.

Man does not give us much hope, but God is the one in control. We choose *hope*. We choose *faith*. *Faith* pleases God. God is a rewarder of those who diligently seek to have *faith* in *him*.

> *"Now faith is the substance of things hoped for, the evidence of things not seen"* (Hebrews 11:1). *"But without faith it is impossible to please him: for he that cometh to God must believe that he is, and that he is a rewarder of them that diligently seek him"*
>
> Hebrews 11:6

Keep us in your thoughts and prayers as we meet each new challenge.

Love in Christ and trusting God,
Mrs. Evona

Pastor's P.S.: This morning in my prayer time, I once again felt God telling me that He is not finished with me yet and we all have so much to accomplish for His glory! I know this…God never leads us where His grace won't keep us.

I love you!
Preacher

JUNE 1, 2006—
Another Great Day at Moffitt!

We arrived at Moffitt Cancer Center at 3:00 P.M. on May 31 for lab work, a bone strengthening treatment and our scheduled appointment with the Radiation Oncologist, Dr. Stevens. We were also hoping to get a spinal MRI that Dr. Simon requested. Pastor had lab work done and then headed for the appointment with Dr. Stevens, who will be administering the radiation therapy. Due to the lengthy appointment, we received the bone treatment today but the doctors reevaluated the urgency of the spinal MRI and felt safe to wait until next Wednesday.

We met with Dr. Steven's nurse, Barbara, a born-again believer on Jesus Christ who works in her children's ministry at the Bell Shoals Baptist Church. It is a blessing that the Lord continues to put us under the care of His children.

Barbara began by explaining that Pastor would undergo radiation therapy on the brain before chemotherapy and must first go through "simulation," a process to map out all the target areas for the radiation therapy. Another nurse had informed us that it may take several weeks to get the "simulation" appointment and the planning process completed. This would mean a considerable delay before radiation could begin, which would mean that chemotherapy would also be delayed.

We told her we were praying for her as she worked to help us and she immediately picked up her phone and was able to set a simulation appointment for us that day at 3:00 P.M. As she reviewed our files she commented that she has never seen a case move this fast. (Remember Psalm 102:2: "*…in the day when I call answer me speedily*").

After a wait, Dr. Stevens came in to see us and examined Pastor. Dr. Stevens is from M.D. Anderson in Texas, a leading cancer clinic in America and is a believer on Christ as well. He met with a team of doctors today where Dr. Simon (our main oncologist) presented Pastor's case. Dr. Stevens shared with us that the entire team was working diligently to come up with the best plan of attack. This is very exciting because it allows many talented doctors the ability to get involved in our case. It also broadens the potential witness of God's power to many other doctors and staff. The doctor told us that the cancer in Pastor's brain is extensive…he stopped counting at nine masses. His intentions are to speed up the simulation process and begin radiation on Monday. He added that this cancer responds well to radiation. Pastor said, "Dr. Stevens, I am praying for God to use you as a tool to help us fight this cancer." Dr. Stevens replied, "I am praying for you too." Pastor took out his wallet and showed Dr. Stevens a picture of our boys and said, "Doctor, these guys are who we're fighting for." Without missing a beat, Dr. Stevens replied, "And we're going to fight with God to allow you to see your grandchildren."

We left Moffitt with another confirmation that God is at work in our lives! He is planning something spectacular for our family and our church! When we shared these things with the boys before bed, Micah said something that touched our hearts. "Why would God waste His time doing all these miracles if He is not going to heal you, Daddy?" Oh, the faith of a child…it is a delight to the Lord Jesus.

Our morning devotion was from Psalm 3. Knowing that cancer is our enemy, ("…*how are they increased that trouble me! Many are they that rise up against me.*" v. 1), it was such a blessing to realize that God is our victor. ("*But thou, O LORD, art a shield for me; my glory, and the lifter up of mine head.*" v. 3). It is such a comfort to know that God has already "*smitten all mine enemies* [cancer] *upon the cheek bone*" and "*broken the teeth of the ungodly*" (v. 7). Cancer will not be able to take any more bites out of Pastor now!

Please pray for our simulation appointment today at 3:00. We need the Lord to guide the instruments to all the right places so that Pastor's treatment will begin on time, or should I say…"speedily."

We love you,
Preacher & Mrs. Evona

June 2, 2006—
Simulation Success!

We had our "simulation" appointment today at Moffitt at 3:00 P.M. My brain masses were targeted (that's me on the table with the "hockey mask" on), and my radiation therapy will begin on Tuesday, June 6. This will entail eleven total treatments and our prayer is that it will kill all the tumors in my brain. I will have a spinal MRI, also on June 6, to determine if radiation will be needed on my spine while they radiate my brain.

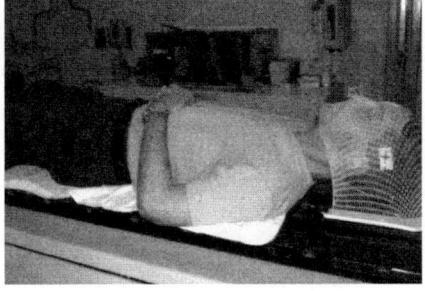

I asked the young lady who was scheduling my radiation appointments to arrange the times on the two Wednesdays so that I will be able come to Prayer Meeting. She was so kind to do this for me and I rejoice in this. I want to be faithful to our church. Wednesday Night Prayer Meetings are too important to miss! I love the scriptures in Matthew 18:20: *"For where two or three are gathered together in my name, THERE am I in the midst of them."* and Acts 4:31: *"And when they had prayed, the PLACE was shaken where they were assembled together; and they were ALL filled with the Holy Ghost, and they spake the Word of God with boldness."* When I begin chemotherapy, I may be too ill to attend our Prayer Meetings and I want to be there as much as I am physically able now. Too often we have made Wednesday night church optional in our lives and the lives of our children…let's get back to making it a weekly essential.

God is teaching me to be more aware of hurting people around us. I met a nurse when I received my bone-strengthening treatment who is heartbroken from family troubles. I told her that the Lord wanted to heal her heart and that our church is a place filled with people who would love her. She took my card and I pray she will come. I met a man as we waited for our simulation appointment named Charlie who has esophagus cancer. He spoke of trusting the Lord when he found out I am a preacher. I assured him our church would be praying for him as he fights this battle. I'm convinced we are surrounded by hurting people every day, and if we will pray for the Lord to make us more aware and willing vessels to witness and encourage them, He will provide a multitude of opportunities. Galatians 6:2 says, "*Bear ye one another's burdens, and so fulfill the law of Christ.*" Can you tell I've been out of the pulpit too much lately? I'm full of "preach" and it keeps oozing out here and there. If you were blessed, send an offering to…I'm just kidding.

Evona and I are extremely excited about all God is doing in our lives and the lives of our congregation. We are mindful that we are not "great people" trusting God, but just people trusting a "great God!" The focus in all this must remain on God's glory. We are reminded in Colossians 1:18: "…*that in all things he might have the preeminence.*"

We love you and we will see you Sunday,
Preacher and Mrs. Evona

June 3, 2006—
The Reality of Cancer

This update will be different than the previous ones. There were no tests or appointments. The kids were with Evona's parents and we spent the day together. I cannot tell you how wonderful this was. My wife and I have been going from one dramatic moment to the next and we were tired and needed the time together. I am soaking in every moment with this wonderful woman God gave me 13 years ago.

Our devotions were from Psalm 5 which says, *"Give ear to my words, O LORD, consider my meditation. Hearken unto the voice of my cry, my King, and my God: for unto thee will I pray. My voice shalt thou hear in the morning, O LORD; in the morning will I direct my prayer unto thee, and will look up"* (vv. 1–3).

The mornings are difficult because I awaken to the reality that cancer is now a part of our daily lives. I realize again that I have cancer and Evona realizes that her husband has cancer. We find comfort only when we cry out in prayer to God and look up. We realize as we pray that God is our King and our God. The reality that we serve a living God who hears and answers our prayers then overpowers the reality of cancer. His mercy is new each morning. (*"But as for me, I will come into thy house in the multitude of thy mercy: and in thy fear will I worship toward thy holy temple"* v. 7.)

Every morning we seek His wisdom as we face so many decisions involving doctors and treatment. (*"Lead me, O Lord, in thy righteousness because of mine enemies; make thy way straight before thy face"* v. 8.) We pray that God will heal me of cancer and allow me to continue to do His will in our family and our church. (*"Destroy thou them, O God; let them fall by their own counsels; cast them out..."* v. 10.) And then we claim the Psalm God gave us (Psalm 30:2–3) again and again.

We get up from our knees rejoicing and praising God for His loving deliverance and His daily provision of Himself as a shield (*"But let all those that put their trust in thee rejoice: let them ever shout for joy, because thou defendest them: let them also that love thy name be joyful in thee. For thou,*

Lord, wilt bless the righteous; with favour wilt thou compass him as with a shield" v. 11–12.)

The Word of God and prayer are sustaining us. We are finding Him faithful every day. He has done so many amazing things up to this point. I wonder what He has planned next. I believe we will see something great this Sunday at church. I cannot wait to stand in the pulpit and proclaim His Word to you. I'm anticipating what He will do when His Word is preached!

My prayer today has been the simple prayer Jesus prayed in John 12:28: *"Father, glorify thy name."* I want the name of the Lord to receive glory in all this. He alone deserves glory. We are only vessels through which He works. May His name be glorified!

Looking forward to Sunday,
Preacher

June 4, 2006—
Second Sunday Back...Can It Get Any Better?

I was able to stand in the pulpit all day on Sunday, which is one of my prayers...that I'll preach every Sunday throughout these treatments. I cannot tell you what it does for me spiritually to preach to the people of Fellowship Baptist Church. The spiritual strength I draw from preaching and our people helps me physically as well. Evona and the boys were glad to be back with the family of God and she looked "just right" on the piano if I do say so myself.

The music was especially good and I had a great time being back in my platform chair, shouting "amen," raising my hand and soaking it in. God let me sing a song with my family (Evona, Mom, Aunts Cathy and Carol and cousins Kim and Chris) that has blessed me since all this started. It's called, "I Still Trust You Lord."[1] The words to this song express what my heart is feeling right now.

I preached on the subject, "We Choose Faith," and we saw God's hand in the services. I had asked God to anoint my preaching as He had anointed my preparation and I felt His hand on me from start to finish. Christ is the best "preacher" at Fellowship so it was good to step aside and let Him have the pulpit. We're just tools in His hands anyway. He's the One who does all the work. We were blessed with 507 in attendance, one rededication, one for membership by letter and one baptized! The only thing missing was a salvation...and perhaps a millionaire giving a check to pay off our debt. We did receive a special offering of $15,000.00 from our people to pay on the debt, which is phenomenal because, believe me, we don't have any millionaires in our church. Now, we will take any who are looking for a church home so remember we are located at...just kidding. Actually, it's fun to see God bring in such large offerings with just plain, average working folks...He gets more credit that way.

Remember to pray for us as I am scheduled to begin brain radiation on Tuesday (June 6) at 2:00 P.M. as well as get the spinal MRI to see if spinal radiation is needed along with the brain radiation. I am ready for this, so don't worry about me…just pray. The Lord holds tomorrow in His hands and I'll find Him there with grace, comfort, mercy peace and power.

May God give you a fruitful and "Christ-filled" week,
Preacher

June 6, 2006—
A Day Together

As we prepare for the start of Pastor's radiation treatments, we took time off yesterday to enjoy each other. It is hard to believe that next week it will be 13 years since we stood together at the old 109th property and heard Pastor say "you betcha" instead of "I do" as we took our wedding vows. We have cherished every minute of our 13-year love affair. (I should say my 18-year and his 13-year love affair, because it took 5 years of chasing to talk him into marrying me!)

Because of the effects of the radiation treatments, Pastor will not be able to use any hair products (gel, hair- spray, etc.)! As we all know, due to the precocious nature of his hair, this is not going to be a pretty sight! So, to avoid any undue trauma for the congregation, we headed straight for the barber shop. Another side effect of brain radiation will be the total loss of Pastor's hair. This will probably happen after the two weeks of therapy has ended. I think he has it coming after all the "bald" jokes 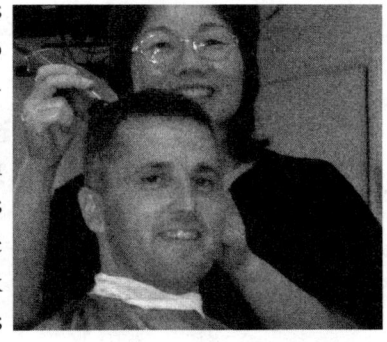 he's used on my father through the years. Pastor wanted to say goodbye slowly to his hair so he is doing it in stages! In this first stage, Pastor asked Sherry, the stylist, to only cut out the gray. This was too drastic however, so he settled for very short. He explained why he needed his hair cut short. At the mention of cancer, the barber shop fell silent as a library. He was then able to share his faith that the Lord will see us through this valley. We *Choose Faith!*

Of course, no good anniversary date can end without the customary trip to Wal-Mart! We were making a few purchases and needed some help from an associate. The associate, named Sheila, asked about one of our purchases and we were able to share our situation. She stunned us by pulling a small piece of paper out of her pocket with a Bible reference on it and handing it to Pastor. She told us that God had given her these verses and told her it would be for someone who needed it during her day. She knew we were those "someones." It begins with Psalm 107:8: *"Oh that men would praise the Lord for his goodness, and for his wonderful works to the children of men!"* Continue reading on through verse 15. This entire passage reads like it is talking about us. What a blessing and encouragement to get to the part after the afflictions (v. 10) where God brings us *"out of darkness and the shadow of death, and brake their bands in sunder"* (v. 14). And then to end with our heart's cry again in verse 15: *"that men would praise the Lord for his goodness...."* Needless to say, we had a wonderful day yesterday and are prepared to begin the first phase of this fight at 2:00 P.M. today.

With love and praise to God,
Pastor, Mrs. Evona and boys

We Choose Faith!

JUNE 7, 2006—

Long Day at Moffitt

Our day began with a phone call from Moffitt that the "radiation software" was down and they were not able to commit to our 2:00 P.M. appointment for the first brain radiation treatment. Since we also had the spinal MRI scheduled at 3:30 P.M., we went ahead over to Moffitt to see if the software issue would get straightened out and we could keep both appointments. It was a little concerning to think that I may get radiation on my brain with newly reinstalled software. This isn't a computer program we're dealing with, it's my head! But we trust the Lord to protect us through this entire process.

We were able to have the spinal MRI at 3:30 P.M. as scheduled. This will determine if radiation is also needed on my spine while they radiate the brain. I was able to talk with David, the MRI tech and to determine he is a believer on Christ. He put me on the MRI table and set up some headphones so I might listen to some soft guitar music. I took the time to talk with the Lord, and apparently after 10 minutes, I fell asleep. Now I understand why some of you sleep during the last portion of my sermons. I still believe that I should be compensated for helping some of you overcome sleep deprivation. David said, "You're done, Mr. Cliff," and I woke up after a 35-minute nap. Isn't the Lord good to give me rest during this procedure? I thought of the verse in Matthew 11:28 where Jesus said, *"Come unto me, all ye that labour and are heavy laden, and I will give you rest."* When David took me back to the waiting area I grabbed his hand and I said, "David, don't worry about me now, I've got Jesus Christ and He's all I need."

We decided to wait at radiation and see if they would be able to get the software back online and follow through with my brain radiation. After about an hour, they called my name and a man named "Jim" and we went back for our appointments. We sat together for a few minutes and I learned that Jim has lung and colon cancer, and before he came to Moffitt, he was under the care of another oncologist who unfortunately missed a spot on his lungs that continued to grow. He came to Moffitt and is now undergoing chemotherapy. I told Jim we would be praying for him and he was thankful.

They called me back to the radiation lab, strapped on my "hockey mask" and started with x-rays of my head. I let them know they should not expect to see much and it lightened the room up a little. After Dr. Stevens approved the x-rays, my first radiation began. It was a large machine that began on the left side of my head and shot two phases of radiation and then moved over me to the right side and shot two more. The radiation treatment lasted all of 10 minutes. I prayed the entire time that God would guide the doctor, the technicians, the machines and yes, the software. I claimed the "wisdom" God promises in James 1:5 for Dr. Stevens and his assistants. I claimed Proverbs 3:5–6, Romans 8:28, Philippians 4:13 and 19 and Ephesians 5:27, which asks God to present us not having "spot" or "wrinkle" or "any such thing." I would've liked to have claimed a lot more scriptures but the process was over too fast. When the technicians came back in to take the mask off I asked them, "Is that all I get for my money?" You know, you can have joy in situations like this if you'll let Jesus give it to you. Jesus said in John 15:11, "*These things have I spoken unto you, that my joy might remain in you, and that your joy might be full.*" I not only choose faith, I choose joy!

Evona and I went home to get a good night's sleep and get the second treatment tomorrow. We set up this appointment early in the day so we can be with you in Prayer Meeting tonight. God's house is the greatest place to be on Wednesday night.

We'll see you tonight,
Preacher

∽ ∽ ∽

June 8, 2006—
Second Radiation Treatment

My Aunt Carol drove me to Moffitt for my second brain radiation treatment, which was done by 7:20 A.M. We had asked for an early appointment so we could attend Wednesday Prayer Meeting and 7:00 A.M. was the only early slot available. Carol seemed a little sleepy so I reminded her of Psalm 46:5: "...*God shall help her, and that right early.*" Carol is so dear to me. I could never describe it. We have a rare heart connection and it is a beautiful thing.

Wednesday Night Prayer Meeting was wonderful! We enjoyed the singing, prayer time, preaching and fellowship with God's people. The Lord meets with us when we gather in His house and as long as I'm able...I'll be there!

We wanted to add something to a previous event that we did not know until a few days ago. In our June 6th update, we told you about the Wal-Mart associate, Sheila, giving us the passage Psalms 107:8–15 that the Lord had given her in her morning devotions. She literally took the handwritten passage out of her pocket and put it in our hands. Now, go back with me to May 28th, the first day I was back in the pulpit at Fellowship after this cancer journey began. While I was preaching here in Thonotosassa, Florida, a sister of one of our church members was visiting a church in Oklahoma and took my name to the altar to pray for me. After prayer time, the pastor of the church preached on Psalms chapter 107. After reading the update, her sister called to tell us about the Lord working in two states on my behalf. Actually, there are people praying for me, my family and our church all around the world and we are grateful for each one being offered.

In our devotions this morning, the Lord led us to Psalm 71:14: "*But I will hope continually, and will yet praise thee more and more.*" I have had a few severe pains since being home from the hospital in my shoulder and hip, and I have found that two things have helped me tremendously—pain pills and praise! When a pain comes on, I take my medicine and begin to offer God praise for His goodness, grace, mercy and love and before long, it has subsided and I am left with a lingering sense of His sweet presence.

May the Lord bless you today as you praise Him for who He is and all He's done! Pastor and Mrs. Evona

June 9, 2006—
Prayer Meeting Blessings and Third Radiation

Last night at Wednesday Night Prayer Meeting I was blessed by a special gift. I mentioned on Sunday that Evona and I did not want to become  "icons" but just be known as two people who are choosing to put their faith in God through a trial. Our Associate Pastor, David Spencer, our greatest "prankster" and worst "punster" at Fellowship, brought the Wednesday Night message. As he began speaking he said, "I know our pastor doesn't want to become an icon but I picked this up in the grocery store today and wanted to give it to him so that he will remain strong for his treatments." Proverbs 17:22 says, "*A merry heart doeth good like a medicine.*" It was good to laugh with God's people! I wouldn't have missed it for anything.

I also had another honor bestowed on me after the Prayer Meeting. Several of the men had planned to have their hair buzzed along with their preacher, and my wife took me over to the Fellowship Hall to watch as they let one of our members cut away their locks, leaving them with stubbled heads. I felt a little bad because some of them got a closer cut than I did. Radiation will take care of the rest of my hair soon enough. The Lord says in Matthew 10:30 that "… *the very hairs of your head are all numbered.*" Well, I'll soon be making it a little easier on the Lord to keep track. Perhaps I'll wear a bandana in the pulpit and call myself the "Baptist Bandana." Probably not. It blessed me that folks would do this to honor me and make me feel more comfortable. We have the greatest people in the world at Fellowship Baptist Church!

We had the third radiation treatment today at 5:15 P.M. at Moffitt. These treatments have been quick and pain free thus far and I praise God for this. I will have eight more daily treatments after this and chemotherapy is scheduled to begin on June 27 if my body is ready. We still do not know the results of the spinal MRI and are unsure if any spinal radiation will be needed so continue to pray about this for us. If spinal radiation is needed, please pray that it can take place along with the brain radiation so that chemotherapy can begin on schedule.

In our devotions this morning, Evona and I read Psalm 11 which opens with the verse, *"In the LORD put I my trust: how say ye to my soul, Flee as a bird to your mountain?"* Evona said, "The devil is taunting us and he's telling us to fly away in fear like a frightened bird." Verse 2 speaks of Satan's attack on the upright and verse 3 of the feeling the righteous get when their foundations are shaken. But when you get to verses 4 through 6, the scene changes and we look up to see God on His throne watching us, trying us through the fire that we might be made purer, and turning the tempest upon the wicked one himself. The Psalm ends in verse 7 with the righteous Lord loving and beholding the upright. Evona added, "Why would we flee like a bird to the mountains when God is watching us from heaven?" Amen! Who's the "preacher" in this house anyway?

We love you,
Preacher and Mrs. Evona

∞ ∞ ∞

June 10, 2006—
An Answer to Our Prayers

Praise the Lord! Psalm 12:5 says, "...*now will I arise, saith the Lord; I will set him in safety...*" After reading this verse yesterday morning, I should not have been surprised that the Lord was answering "swiftly" again. Pastor and Mrs. Kay went for his radiation treatment around 4:00 P.M. and started to leave and were stopped and informed that he needed to wait and meet with the doctor. I then received a call from the two of them asking me about this appointment. After checking "The Book" (our day planner with all our thousand things to remember), I told them this appointment was not scheduled. Immediately the devil whispered many alarming scenarios in my ear, each worse than the next. With my heart beating frantically, I told Pastor to call me and let me know what was going on as soon as he found out. Let me tell you, waiting at home patiently is highly overrated! I began cleaning and sweeping and dusting like a crazy woman. This only produced a clean house, not the peace I longed for. Finally I fell down on my face and cried unto the Lord to give me a peace "that passeth all understanding." God sent the Holy Spirit to comfort me and Melody (my neighbor and friend) to distract me. (Somehow we can spend hours together and get very little done, but have a great time!) After a little wait, Pastor called and said that Dr. Stevens (Radiation Oncologist) just wanted to let him know that the MRI of his spine showed that there were no spots or tumors causing any immediate concern and that the spinal cord was in good shape. This meant that no radiation was going to be needed on his spine at this time. The chemotherapy would be able to fight those areas and this would be better for his immune system and overall toleration of all the combined treatments! Praise the Lord! Funny how much time we spend worrying about things that God has under control already.

Each new day brings new challenges and concerns. Every word Pastor says and every movement gets analyzed by his mom and me. Poor man, I think we are driving him to distraction with all this mothering. A couple of days ago, he was searching for a word and I immediately began watching closely. I guess he noticed and thought it would be funny to tease me. He started saying crazy things and going on and on. However, after 13 years of marriage, I can tell the "normal" crazy from any "new" craziness. Through this entire process, one thing that has helped us make it through has been laughter. The man I married is still just as fun and crazy as ever.

Many of you have asked and have been so concerned about how Pastor is "really" doing. I am here to tell you that he is the most excited and energetic I have ever seen him. Now, part of that is the steroids, but most of it is the anticipation of wondering what God is going to do next! I told someone that he is like a little kid who knows that they are going to Disney World the next day! He is working hard and planning so many things that we all are going to need steroids to keep up with him. God is so good. We know, yes know, that the best is yet to come!

We *Choose Faith.* Faith pleases God, and he rewards those that have faith and diligently seek him (Hebrews 11). We love you and appreciate all you have done for us. Keep up the prayers. Remember…Psalm 11:1 says, *"In the Lord put I my trust."*

Love and thanks,
Mrs. Evona

June 11, 2006—
Praying "Republicans" and a New "Ride"

This past week we were told about something incredible that happened on June 6. I will relay it as it was personally relayed to me by the members of our church who were there. Five people from our church were attending a Brandon Republican Club Meeting in Valrico. The room was full of elected officials, including two state representatives, the Hillsborough County Republican Chairman, a U.S. Senate candidate and the State of Florida Chairwoman for the Republican Party. There was much tension in the room. Everyone was working to help improve the image of their chosen candidate. As the meeting began, a gentleman by the name of Richard Skinner was asked to give the invocation. He began, "You know, folks, I just have a feeling about something and I'm going to do something a little different tonight. I want to ask everyone in this room to take three minutes and think for a moment. Everyone is here because you want to support a candidate or have an agenda. I want us all to stop thinking about that and think about what is really important in life. There are people around us who are dealing with issues far more important than politics." Our church members were thinking of me, my family and our church as we face our present valley. After three minutes, Mr. Skinner said, "You know, folks, there is a preacher over there on 301, and he's very sick. I believe he's the pastor of some of you here tonight. We need to pray for him and his family and his church." Our people were overwhelmed by hearing my name in such an unlikely setting. After the club meeting, our members found out that Mr. Skinner had heard about my illness at two different Bible studies in two of our churches here in town and he felt the Lord's prompting to conduct the invocation the way he had. WOW! I knew people were praying for me in churches, Sunday school classes, Bible studies and their own personal prayer times around the world, but I had no idea God would allow a Republican Club meeting to remember me. It's a blessing to be loved and prayed for by so many. You will never know the encouragement it brings to my heart to realize people are lifting up my name, my wife and boys' names and the Fellowship Baptist Church before God each day.

I must tell you about another blessing God gave our family yesterday (June 9). I still don't quite know how to feel or how to comprehend this. Our family had gone shopping for some items for our home office as I will be working a lot from home during the cancer treatments. We met my parents for lunch when I got a call from an old friend I'd gone to school with. His name is Steve Williams and he and his family have known me since high school. Steve and his father Buster did the site work on our 301 church property. They are dear friends of mine and have helped our church many ways throughout the years. Steve gave me a man's name and phone number and asked me to call him. I asked what I was calling him about and Steve informed me he is a manager at Brandon Ford and I was to go there as soon as possible and pick out a new vehicle for my family that he wanted to provide. I was stunned and did not know what to say. I told Steve that we already have good vehicles and that we didn't need one right now, to which he replied, "Cliff, I've done many things in my life I regret and I wish I'd have done more for the Lord, but I know what's right and this is right, so please go get the car you want and drive it home today." I cried and thanked my friend and sent our boys with Mom and Dad. Evona and I went to Brandon Ford and by the day's end pulled into our driveway with a 2006 Ford Expedition. I still do not know how to feel about this except extreme gratitude to God and my friend, Steve, for letting God generously use him.

We are looking forward to another great Sunday at Fellowship. I will be preaching on the subject, "His Knock, My Heartbeat." My prayer is that the Lord will anoint the message and souls will be saved and lives changed! Pray with us to this end.

God bless you,
Preacher & Mrs. Evona

June 12, 2006—
Getting Ready for another Week of Radiation

The Lord was good to us at church yesterday (June 11). After some pretty intense pains on Saturday (June 10), we were praying I could wake up and be able to preach in the pulpit. In our Sunday morning devotions, God directed us to Proverbs 18:14, which says *"The spirit of man will sustain his infirmity…"* Then He led us to Romans 8:26, which says, *"Likewise the Spirit also helpeth our infirmities…"* I prayed immediately that "my spirit" would cooperate with "His Spirit" and allow me to preach in spite of this infirmity. The Lord answered our prayers. I preached to a great crowd on Sunday morning a sermon entitled, "Let His Knock Be Our Heartbeat." God allowed me to return Sunday evening and preach a sermon entitled, "It Matters How You Finish." What a day! To God be the glory!

When I came through the side door at the beginning of the service, I was struck by the fact that our people had gotten together ahead of time and decided to wear purple. "Purple" is the color of the "cancer survivor." The choir was all dressed in purple and the congregation was either dressed in purple or had purple ribbons on. The front row was filled with the guys who had buzzed their hair for me, dressed in purple shirts and ties. This was a huge sacrifice to some of these "manly men!" What a great group of people. They just keep pouring their love on me, Evona and our boys. The Lord must love me a lot to let me pastor people like this.

We begin a new week of radiation today. There will be seven more treatments and chemotherapy is scheduled to begin on June 27. The news that I do not need radiation on my spine is thrilling. The Lord is so good to design it so that no tumors are compromising the spinal column and no more radiation is needed right now. Praise Him, praise Him, and praise Him again!

We love you,
Preacher & Mrs. Evona

∽ ∽ ∽

June 13, 2006—

Midnight Ice Cream Run

Last month Mom and Dad told us about the cancer that was causing our dad to feel bad. We felt shocked and scared. Our dad is the coolest and best dad ever. We wondered what would happen. After we found out and talked to Mom and Dad, we knew we needed to have a family prayer meeting. It was a nice time and we know God heard us.

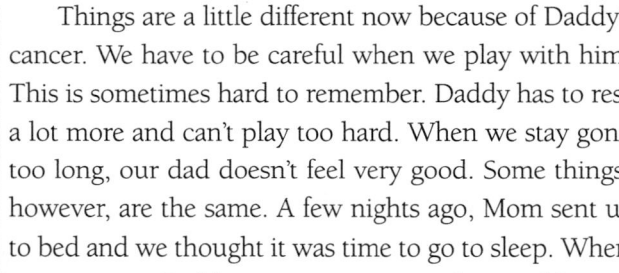

Things are a little different now because of Daddy's cancer. We have to be careful when we play with him. This is sometimes hard to remember. Daddy has to rest a lot more and can't play too hard. When we stay gone too long, our dad doesn't feel very good. Some things, however, are the same. A few nights ago, Mom sent us to bed and we thought it was time to go to sleep. When

Daddy came in to pray with us and kiss us goodnight, he was holding an ice cream scoop and said, "Midnight ice cream run!" We were so excited. Every so often, for something special, our dad takes us out for ice cream late at night. We are all in our pajamas and we just run out to the car and

go. (Of course we don't go in! We just go through the drive-through!) It was a blast. We listened to gospel music really loud and rolled down all the windows. It was so loud we might have woken up the people who live near the ice cream shop. (It wasn't on purpose; we were just having fun!)

When we get scared or worried, we like to read Psalm 77:1. It says, "*I cried unto God with my voice, even unto God with my voice; and he gave ear unto me.*" When we were younger, we both realized we were sinners and asked Jesus to forgive our sins and come into our hearts. In John 3:16 it tells us that "*God so loved the world, that he gave his only begotten Son, that whosoever believeth in him should not perish, but have everlasting life.*" We believe God's Word is true and now we are saved! Because of this, we know God hears our prayers. It is so nice to be able to take all our problems to Him.

Keep praying for our dad. He really needs it a lot. Thank you for all the great food you are sending. We especially like the junk food!

Love
Micah, Caleb and Baby Lucas

∽ ∽ ∽

June 14, 2006—
How Will They Know?
(From Mrs. Evona)

On Friday (the sixteenth of this month), it will only have been one month since we began this journey. It seems like a lifetime. I can not even remember what kind of person I was a month ago. This entire situation has changed our lives so much and believe it or not, for the better. We have heard the knock at our heart's door to have a closer, more intimate relationship with Christ, and it has changed us all. Christ has become so real to us. He is our friend we can share with and find comfort in.

As time goes by, Pastor has become more fatigued. This, coupled with bone pain, has made him have to slow down. It has been difficult for him to change his way of doing things. He has always been wound up and ready to go all the time. Now we have to plan fewer things and go a lot slower. He has been so excited to be able to be in the pulpit over the last few weeks. God has given him such grace and strength when he preaches. However, the amount of energy and effort preaching takes really wipes him out. He is so frustrated at the limitations his condition has forced on him. His desire is to be able to do everything he was doing before and more, but he just isn't able. I know many of you want to be able to sit and talk with him at church, but he can't physically handle preaching twice and then staying after. We have total faith that these limitations are temporary. God is going to do a great miracle. But as Preacher keeps telling me, "God is going to take us through this, not around it."

Our devotions have been the one place we can find peace. It is almost like God sits down, takes His pen out and writes the verses just for us each morning. Psalm 16:11 tells us that God "*wilt shew me the path of life: in thy presence is fullness of joy...*" We have longed and prayed for wisdom through this ordeal. There have been so many life-changing decisions crammed into one small month. God's promise is that He will show us the path of life. We claim this promise every single day. The place we can find peace and joy is in the presence of God. At Moffitt Cancer Center there are so many people facing many of the same battles we are facing. It breaks my heart to see the hopelessness and hurt on so many of their faces. But Moffitt is not the only place I see this hurt and hopeless look. People everywhere are hurting. Many of you are going through trials we don't even know about. It is a sin for us not to share the hope and joy we have found in the presence of God. It is not only a joy; it is a fullness of joy. This joy can be with us in spite of trials and circumstances. Not many days after we were told the extent of Pastor's condition, I was driving back up to the hospital. I was very tired and overwhelmed by this time. I was not paying close attention to the red light and did not pull out fast enough for the guy behind me. Of course, he honked his very rude horn at me. I remember just bursting into tears. I am sure he thought I needed to go to the funny farm (and maybe I did). However, this situation showed me that we never know what people are going through. We need to look for people to love and help. Whether it is the grouchy cashier at the grocery store, or the slow waitress at the restaurant or the new family visiting our church, people need love and understanding. We need to share the joy we have found in the presence of God with others. On my way out of the hospital one night, I saw a family pushing a newborn in a stroller coming from the radiology area of the hospital. I don't know why they were there, or if there was even a problem. But I wondered, "Do they feel the way I do? Has the doctor just given them the worst news of their lives? Are they scared and confused?" We have the answer many of these hurting people need. Jesus can give them the peace we have, but someone has to reach out and care. Romans 10:14 asks us, *"How then shall they call on him in whom they have not believed? And how shall they believe in him of whom they have not heard? And how shall they hear without a preacher?"* We are called to "preach" to these hurting people. How can they know the joy and peace we have unless we tell them about Christ?

We have many doctor appointments this week, getting Pastor ready to head into chemotherapy. We are ready to start this new battle, but covet your prayers. They have come out with a lot of new medicine to help lessen the side effects of the chemotherapy treatments, but it will still be a difficult ordeal for Pastor to endure. Thank you for all your love and understanding.

Remember...we choose faith! Faith pleases God, and He will reward those who diligently seek after him in faith (Hebrews 11).

Love,
Mrs. Evona

JUNE 15, 2006—
9 to 5 at Moffitt and a Lot of News

Yesterday, June 14, we went for our radiation appointment and the pre-op for the port I will get my cancer treatments through. We arrived at 9:00 A.M. and expected to be home by lunch time and get rested up for Prayer Meeting.

The pre-op for the port was first and the only glitch was when the IV nurse tried to get blood out of my left arm, it wouldn't yield any. (My thoughts were, "Well, I like to keep my blood to myself and my veins are cooperating with me and not her.") The nurse said, "That's strange, it's the biggest vein on your arm and it won't yield any blood." To which Evona replied, "He's been complaining about that hurting lately." Undeterred from her "vampirish mission," the IV girl just switched to my right arm and took liberal amounts of plasma. (I told myself, "Remember not to give her the right hand of fellowship anymore!")

We went from pre-op to radiation and as usual, the treatment was over in a few minutes. One of the radiation technicians is going to try to come visit our church with her family on Sunday. She's a great person and has been so kind to us. Our car salesman and his mother are also supposed to visit us this Sunday as God allows. It is exciting to invite people to the greatest church in town!

Before we left Moffitt, we were told unexpectedly that Dr. Stevens (our radiation oncologist) would like to see us. We were scheduled for an appointment for Thursday, not Wednesday. This, however, was not a problem so we waited to be called in. Dr. Steven's nurse, Barbara, met with us and listened carefully to all the new symptoms that had developed since we had seen Dr. Stevens on Friday. She immediately knew something more was going on and became as tenacious as a bull dog, trying to find out exactly what was happening. After questioning me thoroughly, she briefed Dr. Stevens and he came to examine me. They decided that the sore throat was from thrush, an infection that can be caused by some of the other medicines I am on. They were more concerned about the difficulty in breathing I developed this weekend and the pain in my ribs. After listening to me breathe and examining me, it was clear that I had an infection in my respiratory system and possibly a cracked rib. Dr. Stevens prescribed an antibiotic for the infection and another medicine for the thrush. They wanted me to go ahead and take a chest x-ray to make sure that the pain was really from a cracked rib. After waiting awhile and not being able to get the results, they sent us home. Because of my condition and the long day without rest, I was not able to attend Prayer Meeting. We asked the church to pray that the infection would go away quickly and that the results of the x-ray would come back soon. Right after the church prayed, we receive a call from Barbara, Dr. Steven's nurse, with the results of the x-ray. It was not a cracked rib after all, but fluid on my lung. This was something that might have gone unnoticed if they had not ordered an x-ray. Barbara was trying to schedule an appointment with Dr. Welch, the pulmonary specialist, but it was late and everyone had already gone home. This doctor would be able to do a procedure to drain the fluid and make me feel 100 percent better in my breathing. Barbara asked Evona what our schedule for radiation was on Thursday. She answered that we were going to be fit in after our other doctor's appointment. The nurse asked which doctor we were seeing. Evona answered, "Dr. Simon." Barbara shouted out "Isn't God good? Here I am worried about getting Cliff an appointment with Dr. Welsh and God already has it scheduled. God sure has his hand on this man." She told us that Dr. Welch and Dr. Simon are in the same clinic together and that it would work out that we could be seen by both when we are there today. This appointment with Dr. Simon was scheduled two weeks ago! Boy, isn't it great how God works out all the details. Please pray they are able to schedule this procedure quickly and relieve the pain and difficulty breathing I have had. I desperately want to be in the pulpit this Sunday and share what God has laid on my heart with all of you.

Another encouraging thing happened a few days ago. A woman who is visiting our church with her husband, was doing her daily devotions in Acts chapter 4 and God drew her to verse 22, which says, "*For the man was above forty years old, on whom this miracle of healing was shewed.*" The same morning, God led Evona to Judges 6:23, which says, "*And the LORD said* unto him, Peace be unto thee; fear not: thou shalt not die." You can take these two verses any way you'd like…I choose faith!

We love you,
Preacher

ɷ ɷ ɷ

June 16, 2006—
Last Night's Prayer Meeting and Today's Moffitt

Last night at our Wednesday Night Prayer Meeting (June 15) the church was updated that I had thrush, a respiratory infection and possibly a cracked rib from excessive coughing. Our Associate Pastor, Brother David, told the church that we were still waiting on the results of the chest x-ray to confirm whether the pain in my chest was a broken rib or something else.

The church began praying that we would get some good news right away. At the same time, we received a late call from our nurse, Barbara, that they had been able to read the chest x-ray and that the problem was not a cracked rib, but fluid on the lungs from the respiratory infection. Now, this is "good news" because there is nothing that they can do for a cracked rib. You just have to endure the pain and let it heal itself. Fluid on the lungs, however, can be drained and relieve the pain instantly. We called the church via one of the member's cell phones and gave them the "good news." Brother David rushed back to our man with the cell phone, instinctively knowing the call was from us and went immediately to the pulpit to share the "latest" answer to prayer God has given our church family!

Today we went to Moffitt for an appointment with our oncologist, Dr. George Simon. He is pictured with me here. Dr. Simon is a brilliant man, who I believe will be used as a direct tool of God to heal my body. He is aggressive and has a sense of humor, which are both important to me. Today he quoted most of the books of the Bible to me that he'd learned as a young man. He also said of our bodies, "We are fearfully and wonderfully made." (You've heard that somewhere, haven't you?)

After our oncologist's appointment, we took our eighth radiation treatment. I feel more fatigued now as the treatments progress, but my spirits are high and I have met so many wonderful people at Moffitt. I wouldn't trade where I am for anything. It has redirected the focus of my entire life to my family, my church and other people God allows me cross paths with. I want to touch each one with the love of God, the joy of the Lord and just plain kindness.

Unfortunately, there were no appointments to have the fluid drawn off my lungs today. We will be there at 8:45 A.M. in the morning for this 30-minute outpatient procedure. Pray that all goes well with this and that the lungs themselves aren't punctured.

In our devotions this morning, Evona and I read Psalm 18. The Psalm begins by proclaiming who God is and how personal our relationship is as His children.

Verses 1 and 2 say God is *"my strength,"* *"my rock,"* *"my fortress,"* *"my deliverer,"* again, *"my strength,"* *"my buckler,"* *"the horn of my salvation"* and *"my high tower."*

Verses 3 through 6 emphasize the power of this personal relationship with God, which gives us the privilege of calling upon Him in prayer. Verse 7 through the end of the chapter declare God's wonderful deliverance He gives His children amidst their trouble as they call upon Him in prayer.

Now, I want you to pay attention to verses 14 and 15, which say, *"Yea, he sent out his arrows, and scattered them; and he shot out lightnings, and discomfited them."* (Sound like radiation to you?) *"Then the channels of waters were seen, and the foundations of the world were discovered at thy rebuke, O LORD, at the blast of the breath of thy nostrils."* (Sound like chemotherapy to you?) "Cancer" is just another enemy God has on His list to totally destroy, either here on earth or one day completely in heaven, as His will dictates.

I love verse 19, which says, *"He brought me forth also into a large place; he delivered me, because he delighted in me."* Let's be a daily delight to our Savior that He might daily deliver us in all of life.

Please pray that I will endure the procedure and treatments well today. Also pray that God gives me extra strength and stamina. We are having our little Lucas' first birthday party tonight and I really want to be able to feel well enough to enjoy this wonderful day.

We love you,
Preacher and Mrs. Evona

∽ ∽ ∽

June 17, 2006—
Hair Today... Gone Tomorrow!

Well...it won't be long now and I'll say my final farewells to my lovely, longed-after locks. I've often joked that the only two men who had worse hair days than I've had were Samson and Absalom. One lady who cut my hair said the reason my hair is such a challenge is that it grows straight out from my scalp with several cranky cowlicks and one mean swirly on the crown. That's "barber's language" for a "head full of trials and tribulations."

In honor of this special occasion, I have rewritten a Mosie Lister classic and titled it:

"Goodbye Hair, Goodbye" [2]
(Verse)
I've told all my trusses "goodbye"
They all bit the dust when they fried
My head now seems huge
Like "Curley" the "Stooge"
I hope that my neck can support it
My hair was the joy of my life
Now it's been replaced by a shine
I'll not suck my thumb
"Uncle Fester" here I come
Goodbye, Hair, goodbye!

(Chorus)
Now don't you weep for my hair when it's gone
'Cuz it won't leave my head all alone
It'll probably take my brows when it goes
I hope it takes the hair in my nose
Gonna leave me like a bowling ball
I'll look like "Mr. Clean," just not tall

Baldness is near, please take the hair in my ears
Goodbye hair, goodbye

P.S. Don't tell Mosie

If you're looking for a new title for me when I enter the world of Baldness, you may select from one of the following:

(1) The Bald, Yet Beautiful Baptist
(2) The Chrome-Domed Reverend
(3) O, Hairless Wonder
(4) The Prophet of Baldlehem
(5) The Melon-headed Man of God

Please read this update in the spirit it is intended...to make you laugh and be of good cheer. If you can poke fun at things, they are easier to handle. I've always been this way. My Bible tells me in Proverbs 15:13, "*A merry heart maketh a cheerful countenance: but by sorrow of heart the spirit is broken.*" In Proverbs 17:22 it says, "*A merry heart doeth good like a medicine: but a broken spirit drieth the bones.*" The way I look at it, cancer can take my hair but it can't take my handsome away.

As you can tell from my hair tribute, yesterday went very well and I am feeling 100 percent better! God is so good. The procedure was painless, and in about an hour, I was feeling so much better. We were able to really enjoy Lucas' first birthday and spend time with the family. Lucas had a blast. Every new item he was given had to be taken by him on a tour of the entire room to show it off. His favorite gifts were the two ball hats he was given. He was determined to wear both of them at the same time. (This, however, is not a good com-  bination with just recently learning to walk and caused a few minor collisions.) Pretty soon, he and I will be a pair with our new hats!

Cancer has changed everything. I have slowed down and am able to spend special time with each of the boys. I have been bathing Lucas each day and we play and sing. He's getting to know his daddy better and this is blessing me to no end. I'm telling you, this baby is a joy! He's happy and smiles all the time. I love to hear his sweet high-pitched voice say "Daaaeee." I thank God every day for giving us Lucas.

With a merry heart,
Preacher & Mrs. Evona

June 18, 2006—
A Father's Day to Remember

First, let our family and church wish you a "Happy Father's Day" today. This is that special day we set aside to honor our fathers for their love, labor and living unselfishly throughout our lives so that we could have the blessings of God that most of them did not get to enjoy.

Secondly, I would like to share with you what God has done in my life as a result of being diagnosed with cancer. Cancer can get your attention and it certainly got mine! Although I am a pastor, I am first a father. The Word of God is very clear in the epistle of Timothy that if I fail to take care of my family, I am not fit to take care of the church of God (1 Timothy 3:5). I have always believed, and I believe today, that my family must come first in my life. That being said, applying this principle is harder than believing it.

I found myself letting some of the things that made our family feel "special" and that helped bond our family together slip as a result of being busy with church, occupied with personal goals and yes, even watching television. I allowed us to get away from the family being seated around the table together for nightly dinner, and many nights let the boys watch a video at the counter bar instead of sharing time with one another around a meal. I got away from the nightly prayer time that reinforces spiritual values in our family. Evona and I even started making the boys come to us during a commercial of our TV show for their kiss goodnight rather than going to their beds and lying with them and letting them tell us about their day and giving them the "end-of-the-day hug and kiss." If I as a pastor let this happen, it may have happened to others as well.

Cancer changed that! It's a shame I had to have a doctor tell me about my condition to make me realize the importance of every moment and how much family time I have wasted. We're back at the table together again. And those nightly prayer times are precious…I couldn't do without them! And we've turned the TV off and we're back to their beds to let them tell us their hearts. I could not fight this battle without my family. My wife and boys have been used of God to help me "choose faith" each day!

Now, do something for me…don't let a doctor have to tell you that you have cancer and that your time is short before you make your family your first priority. Make the most out of every moment and do it today!

Evona, the boys and I wish you the happiest Father's Day you've ever had!

Preacher

June 19, 2006—
Great Father's Day at Home and Church

What a wonderful day we had yesterday celebrating "Father's Day!" Evona and I enjoyed some awesome devotions from Psalm 20. We then woke up the gang for a family breakfast of biscuits, syrup, bacon and Brother David Spencer's "home fries." (Caleb had pizza; he has a different palate than the rest of us). The boys gave me my "Dad's Day" gift...a spectacular collection of eighty "Three Stooges" episodes! (Mom is overjoyed, as you can imagine) The boys and I are planning a "Three Stooges Marathon" the next time Mom is out for the day.

After the family left for church, I prayed in the garden for God's anointing on my throat to preach His Word in the pulpit. I asked the Holy Spirit to fill me and open my lungs to sound forth His message to our people. *He did it!* As I stepped to the pulpit, I felt His power and was able to preach with both liberty and boldness. We found out at church from a doctor in our congregation who read my chest x-ray that there is a tumor on my wind pipe, so this accounts for my trouble breathing and speaking at times. Praise God, when He wants to preach past a tumor...He does it! The doctor also told us something very exciting. He said that he has never seen a case move so "speedily" in all the years he has practiced medicine. He commented that to begin the initial examination, go through the battery of tests we were given and to finally have a diagnosis can generally take up to 6 months. God did these things in 7 days! We were then accepted at Moffitt, and now only a little over a month later from my original examination with our primary care doctor, I am almost finished with radiation! *He is so good!*

Today we will have our tenth radiation treatment. God has been good through the entire process. Evona and I cannot help but rejoice in all the blessings He has sent along the way. Pray that my body will be strong enough to begin the chemotherapy on June 27 and we can begin the second stage of this fight.

Choose faith with us as we daily place ourselves in His all-sufficient and powerful hands!

We love you,
Preacher and Mrs. Evona

∽ ∽ ∽

June 20, 2006—
Just When I Need Him Most
(From Mrs. Evona)

Have you ever noticed how you can tell the moms that have all or mostly boys from the other moms who have the sweet, delicate little girls? They are the ones who quickly grab their food at the table and eat really fast so that none of the boys have a chance to ask if she is going to finish all of her food. She is the mom who says, even if it fell on the floor, it is OK, as long as you blow it off before you eat it! Only mothers of boys understand why you always say the same two words when the boys head off to their bath…*use soap!* "Boy moms" always yell things like, "If you scream like that again, there better be blood involved;" or "Don't swing from the tree with that rope; I don't have time to go to the emergency room!" If you are wondering how I know all these things, it is because my house is full of boys. I lovingly refer to them as my "three smelly monsters." We also have an obnoxious boy wiener dog named Shakespeare and a boy hamster (we think) that is named Q-tip. However, after the last few hamster chases, we renamed him "Houdini."

Amidst all the doctor visits and hospital stays and radiation treatments, one thing has stayed the same. Life keeps going on. It still amazes me that the trivial matters of life continue to happen, even when you are in crisis. Somehow you run out of toilet paper and the dishes still pile up. There is even more dirty laundry than before or at least there seems to be. (Wet, smelly, dirty boy socks are no fun, let me tell you.) Having three "smelly monsters" keeps things lively. Yet what a comfort this has become. Folding laundry and scrubbing bathrooms makes things seem "normal." Your mind can go into neutral and enjoy serving those you love best.

Sunday evening I was not able to attend church because our "smelly baby monster" had a lovely runny nose. (For some reason other mothers don't appreciate it when you stick your sick baby in the nursery with their well babies!) This gave me time to catch up on the routine, around the house stuff. Lucas was in the bathtub, so I brought a load of towels to fold and put them in the hallway where I could see him and still get some things done. It seems that the devil chooses to send fear to my heart mostly when I am alone. I guess the old saying "divide and conquer" is one of Satan's tactics. I began to focus on my human fear. My mind began to remind me what the doctors had told us, what all the books have said, and what many people think. As soon as I recognized the fear, I began praying that the Lord would help me listen to His words of comfort and not man's words of defeat. I admit that somehow my head knew I should listen to God, but my heart and emotions had missed the memo. I closed my eyes, concentrated and prayed earnestly that God would speak His Word to my heart. I opened my eyes and focused on a piece of paper Micah had tacked up on his message board in his room. It was Psalm 71:1: *"In thee, O LORD, do I put my trust: let me never be put to confusion."* What a blessing it was to have God answer my prayer right away and through such a wonderful tool. Our sweet "smelly monsters" have grown so much with us over this past month. As a mother, it has touched my heart over and over to hear them pray with such simple trust and faith in God. This verse has helped both of the bigger boys deal with the confusion and uncertainty our valley has brought, and last night their verse ministered to me.

Faith is a conscious choice. Every time you allow God to speak His words of truth to your heart, your faith grows. Some days, choosing faith is a minute by minute decision. No matter what valley you are going through, you can choose faith. Remember…faith pleases God and he rewards those who diligently seek after him.

With love,
Mrs. Evona

PS: I believe the reality of faith that I was taught and witnessed firsthand from my mom and dad has given me the foundation to build upon and the strength to continue to trust God through the darkest valley of my life. Happy Anniversary, Mom and Dad. Thank you for your true examples of "living by faith." I love you! *"And that from a child thou hast known the holy scriptures, which are able to make thee wise unto salvation through Faith which is in Christ Jesus"* (2 Timothy 3:15).

June 21, 2006—
Last Radiation and Our Purple Pal

We finished radiation yesterday (June 20) and I received my "Radiation Graduation!" Along with this award, I lost most of my hair. Micah told me that if I were 100 pounds heavier, I'd look like "Curly." (I don't quite know how to take that, except to say "Why you, I oughta!" and give him an eye-poke).

We have a CT scan scheduled this Friday to set up a base-line to measure the decrease of cancer after the treatments. I will receive a port for the treatments on June 27 but my chemotherapy has now been changed to June 30. The chemo that Dr. Simon has prescribed is a strong one, which I welcome. If you're going to drive nails, you don't go to your tool box and get a rubber mallet…you get a big hammer. I am praying that I will tolerate the treatments well and enjoy my family and preach in the pulpit on Sundays throughout.

This morning, Evona and I read Psalm 22. This is a messianic Psalm and foretells what the Lord Jesus would one day do for us on the cross. He wore the crown of thorns and suffered as the sacrifice for all sinners, dying in our place to pay for our sins (Verses 1, 7, 8, 14, 15, 16 and 18). The Psalm also foretells Christ's resurrection from the grave and His future kingdom when He will wear the crown of glory (Verses 19–31). We were especially blessed as we read the final verse of this chapter, *"They shall come, and shall declare his righteousness unto a people that SHALL BE BORN, that he hath done this"* (Psalm 22:31). I was reminded of showing Dr. Stevens a picture of our boys in my wallet and telling him, "These boys are who we're fighting for." To which he replied, "Then we will fight with God so that you see your grandchildren." I want to live to see my boys tell their children all that God has done for their dad.

We would like to take some time and tell you about someone who has been very special to Evona and me. Her name is Cathy Jeter and she is now called "Our Purple Pal." ("Purple" is the color of the cancer survivor.) Cathy is my aunt and also member of our church. She was diagnosed with adrenal cancer five years ago. Adrenal cancer is one of the rarest types of cancer today. There are only thirty-two cases in America at this time and six here locally. There is very little research available because of the rarity of this cancer type. The best course of action with adrenal cancer is to remove any tumors that have metastasized in the body. Cathy has gone through six surgeries (three in 1 year) and a 4-year series of chemotherapies. At one point, she was told there was nothing more that could be done.

She did not give up! She claimed James 1:5, which says, *"If any of you lack wisdom, let him ask of God, that giveth to all men liberally, and upbraideth not; and it shall be given him."* Over and over again, Cathy and her husband, John, were faced with important decisions that were too big for them, but not for God. They claimed the verse and looked to the Lord for wisdom. He gave it to them every time! Today, Cathy is "cancer-free" and she is still faithful to church and singing in the choir!

Our family feels that God has provided Cathy to help guide us through this process, about which we know *nothing!* She has been there for us throughout the journey and she has given us insights about cancer, chemo, doctors, medicines, Moffitt policies and what to expect next. Micah, once again with his deep-thinking and faith-oriented mind, made the statement, "I didn't ever want Aunt Happy (what they call Cathy) to get cancer, but now that Daddy has it, I see how God has used her to help us." We agree wholeheartedly.

This is a picture of me and Cathy, her husband John and her two kids, Kimberly and Chris.

Cathy, you're one of our special blessings. You encourage us as we travel this road you've already taken. You are truly, "Our Purple Pal"!

We love you!
Preacher and Mrs. Evona

June 22, 2006—
Will the Real Curly Please Stand Up

It's all gone but the shine! I have been so particular about my hair for all these years...making the cowlicks lay down...making the part stand up...making the sides blend in, that the Lord decided He would alleviate all my hair problems completely this week. (Even Dr. Howard, Dr. Fine, Dr. Howard couldn't help me! Stooges humor for those of you who are confused!) It's hard to believe that even a marine has more hair than I do now. This was good for me! I needed a "pride-zapping" like this. (No offense to those who already wear their head this way. "Bald" is in now. In fact, our church has so many bald men in it, that when we pray the dismissal prayer and everyone disperses at the close of the service, it looks like someone just broke in a pool game.) As I was saying, I may be a preacher but preachers need to have their pride broken just like everyone else.

Pride is the original sin of Satan (Isaiah 14:12–15) and of Adam and Eve (Genesis 3:1–6). It has plagued man since the fall (Psalm 73:6; Mark 7:21, 22; 1 John 2:15, 16). God hates pride (Proverbs 6:16, 17; 8:13; 15:25). God judges pride (Proverbs 11:2; Proverbs 16:18; 29:23; Daniel 4:37; James 4:6; 1 Peter 5:5). Last night (June 21) I had to walk in our church for our Wednesday Night Prayer Meeting and let my pride go with my hair. Our people were so good and even funny. They all said they "loved it!" and I "looked great!" But the funny thing was that so many tried not to look up at my head. It's like when you have a sore in your mouth and you tell your tongue it's not going to touch it but it keeps finding its way back to that irresistible spot. I laughed out loud more than once by our sweet church member's attempts not to notice ("nyuk, nyuk, nyuk"). I thank God for doing this. He's teaching me that He is the "giver" and He is the "taker away" and everything I have belongs to Him!

God wants us to have the mind of Christ in all matters of life (Philippians 2:3-11). He wants us to realize He *owns* all of us and we *owe* everything to Him. He has given us more than we deserve in saving our souls, yet He continues to shower His blessings upon us each and every day we live. We're never "victims of circumstance." I'm learning to focus on all He has done and is doing for me, not the things I think He should have done or should be doing for me.

They tell me that I will lose all my hair when I go through chemotherapy. I sure wish I could keep my eyebrows (you need them for something, I'm sure of it). Perhaps I'll draw on different eyebrow styles each Sunday for our people to guess who I'm imitating. I'll start with "Groucho" and work my way to "Bella Ligosi's Count Dracula." (Our church is used to my sense of humor so don't worry about them). One thing is certain…I will *not* let Satan steal my joy through this and I *will* endeavor to let God use my life to get the complete glory! *God is good all the time!*

Lovingly lacking locks,
Preacher

June 23, 2006—
A Day of Rest
(From Mrs. Evona)

As you well know, as a wife there are very few phrases as satisfying as "I told you so!" However, this time it wasn't as fun as it usually is to say that phrase. (Of course I still said it. You can't pass up these kinds of opportunities.) Pastor has enjoyed being finished with his radiation and that, combined with the steroids, has made him become the "energizer bunny!" I constantly have to remind him that I am not getting any medications, and he has to slow down for me! On Wednesday morning I knew we were in for a busy day. He woke up singing and talking a mile a minute. He already had worked in his home office for several hours, even before I woke up. I did the routine "you need to take it easy" speech, to which he smiled and just shook his head. (This in husband language means…"I am going to do what I want as soon as you leave; I am just humoring you!") By the end of the day, he was wiped out. (This is where the "I told you so" came in.) He realized that even though he feels like "Superman," he needs to pace himself and go slower, more like "Underdog." It has been a difficult adjustment for Pastor. Going slow and taking it easy have never been things he was very good at.

Because of overdoing it on Wednesday, we took the day and rested on Thursday. It was a great time together with the boys and each other. We spent time playing in the pool with the boys. (His ulterior motive was to get just a little color on the new shiny white head before Sunday!) The guys watched several episodes of "The Three Stooges"! I know it is a lost cause with the big boys, but I am determined to shield poor Baby Lucas from such bad entertainment.

Our morning devotions were from Psalm 24. We were greatly inspired by verses 1 through 5, which stress the importance of maintaining holiness before the Lord. This includes outward holiness ("clean hands") which reflects an inward holiness ("pure heart"). This is required if we desire God's blessings on our lives.

Preacher had personal devotions in his garden and was blessed by his daily reading from *The Read through the Bible in a Year*. The passage 1 Chronicles 5:18-20 records the story of God's deliverance of His people in a battle they were facing. Acts chapter 5 also encouraged him as it told of the early church's powerful impact on their entire city and how they overcame persecution as they trusted the Lord. Both of these passages together emphasize the victory we have in Christ through the battles we face. In Psalm 24:8 it says "...*the* LORD *mighty in battle*." What a comfort to know that Christ is in the battle with us and through Him we have the victory.

We are going for a doctor appointment and a CT scan today. This is a scan the doctors will use to determine, after two sessions of chemotherapy, if the medications they used are working. If not, they plan to change to different medications and try again. Preacher still has a very sore throat. The doctor will decide if it is still the thrush infection or a side effect of the radiation. Either way, they will give him something to make if feel better so he continues to eat and keep up his weight. One great blessing through this trial has been that Preacher has been able to eat anything he wants. He has worried about his weight for so many years that he is in heaven, eating whatever he takes a fancy too, any time of the day!

It has taken cancer to make us slow down and return to the basics. God's Word has become so dear and comforting to us. We now evaluate each and every activity and know every day, every hour, every minute needs to count for Christ. Make this the way you live your life. Don't wait until you are in the midst of a valley to return to the basics. Do it now! Plant your small seed of faith and watch it grow. Choose faith. Faith pleases God and he will reward those who diligently seek after Him!

With love,
Mrs. Evona

JUNE 24, 2006—
A Job Well Done!

Thirty-nine days ago today, our doctor sent us for that fateful MRI of my brain. During this short time, we have been privileged to meet some of the finest doctors and nurses around. It has been humbling to see the tireless effort and great sacrifice many of these professionals give. The concern and emotional investment they have shown us has been overwhelming. We have met so many which not only feel that the medical field is a profession, but also a calling. They are using their God-given gifts to help needy people all over.

We want to take a minute to thank the entire staff at the Moffitt Cancer Center Radiation Department. They have befriended and helped us from the moment we began radiation. We appreciate their willingness to work with our schedule. Many times they worked us in, to help shorten our time at the hospital. They moved our appointments so that we could be at Prayer Meeting and made it possible to have the baby's party as scheduled. The technicians were kind and considerate. Some would even come out and check on Evona, just to make sure she was doing all right. We would not have had such a fantastic experience if it were not for two wonderful people: Dr. Stevens and Barbara Bertel, his nurse. We would not have even been able to get in to see a doctor until June 15 if Dr. Stevens had not been willing to stay late and fit us in on top of all his regular patients. He has the rare ability to appreciate my humor, and was very easy to communicate with. Barbara, Dr. Stevens' nurse, has been a constant delight and encouragement to us. She has fought to get us squeezed in and moved mountains to make things work out for us. Barbara took the time to listen and find out why I was not feeling well. She made sure they worked until the problems were found and solutions were decided upon. *Thank you for a job well done!* Dr. Stevens is on the left and Barbara is on the right. Yes, I know I am in a dress in Barbara's picture, but she assured me that it didn't make me look fat!

We are now headed for the next hurdle. Chemotherapy! Yesterday I had blood work done and a CT scan. This will be what the doctor uses to make a comparison after we have had two chemotherapy treatments. We  are praying that the first combination of chemotherapy medications are the perfect ones and great improvement is seen (or total healing, which is my personal choice!). Next week begins the process. We have many doctor appointments, a procedure to put in a port and on Friday, June 30 my first chemotherapy treatment. (The date was changed so that I didn't have to have the procedure and chemo on the same day!) Pray that all goes well and I am able to preach on that following Sunday.

In Psalm 25:20–21 the scripture says, "*O keep my soul, and deliver me: let me not be ashamed; for I put my trust in thee. Let integrity and uprightness preserve me; for I wait on thee.*" We know every- 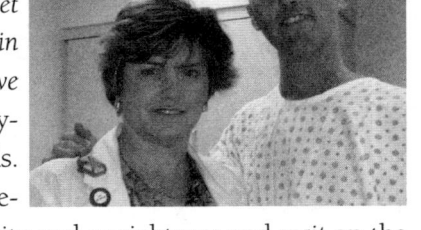 thing is in the Great Physician's hands. He will keep our souls, deliver and preserve us. Our job is to walk in integrity and uprightness and *wait* on the Lord. He is worthy of our trust.

In Christian love,
Preacher and Mrs. Evona

June 26, 2006—
Satan Battles but God Blesses!

We had a wonderful day at Fellowship Baptist Church yesterday (June 25) in spite of Satan's attack. Whenever the Lord is working, the devil is hard at work to thwart God's plans.

When I was getting ready for church in the morning, I had a nosebleed that was persistent for several minutes. I finally got it stopped and finished dressing and headed to church. On the way, I prayed and asked the Lord to prevent any further nosebleeds. When I arrived at church, I went to the side room to prepare my heart to stand in the pulpit and deliver God's Word. With the cancer, I have to come in just as the service is beginning so that I might conserve my energy for the preaching. It's not the way I've done things all these years but it is necessary right now.

I came out during the opening music and then came to the pulpit to pray and welcome our people. I finished the prayer and began the welcome and my nose started to bleed. I finished the welcome and went back to the side room. My thoughts were, "Lord, I asked you to prevent this. You are the One who called me to preach. Why would You allow this to stand in the way of fulfilling Your calling?" My heart smote me. I felt like Job when he questioned the Lord and God answered, *"Where wast thou when I laid the foundations of the earth?"* (Job 38:4). Who am I to question anything God does? He made my nose and if He wants to let it bleed when it's preaching time…that's His business.

Then something else dawned on me…this is an attack of Satan. The Bible calls the devil a *"roaring lion, who walketh about, seeking whom he may devour"* (1 Peter 5:8).

Satan attacked Job's body (Job 1) and I believe he was attacking mine…specifically…my nose! I remembered that the book of Micah speaks of God rebuking the devourer for His people's sake (Micah 3:11), so I prayed this prayer. After a few minutes of holding my head back, the nosebleed stopped. Praise the Lord…I can preach now!

After the final solo, I walked to the pulpit and began my sermon,

"Behind Our Mask." I had no sooner got into the message when the nosebleed started again. I took out a tissue and held it up to my nose and debated whether I should continue or not. God spoke to me and said, "Preach anyway!" I apologized to the congregation if this made them uncomfortable, but I was going to preach the message God had given me. I held the tissue and then an ice towel on my nose for 30 to 40 minutes and preached the Word!

Now, listen closely...the last point of my sermon was "Are You Wearing a Mask of Personal Strength to Project an Image of Perfection and Power to God and Others?" I spoke of how we try to impress others with our own strength, but it is just a mask to hide our weaknesses and that we need to let the Lord strip away our masks and confess our weaknesses and then let His strength shine through us so that He gets the glory in our lives and not ourselves.

I think that the Lord overruled Satan's attack and illustrated the truth of this sermon by showing my weakness before our people and God's strength to preach His Word. It definitely was not me who delivered the sermon that morning.

When Satan battles...God blesses! Our First Grade Sunday School Class sent this picture reminding me that *together* we are choosing faith in God. Caleb, our middle son, is the excited on in the middle. We were blessed by God with a great attendance of 461, an anonymous gift to our debt of $100,000.00, two for church membership and one for believer's baptism! I'll have a nosebleed every service for that! *Praise his name!*

This week is filled with appointments, which we will keep you updated on so that you can pray for us. God bless you, and it is a joy to rejoice in all God has done and is doing!

Basking in His blessings,
Preacher and Mrs. Evona

June 27, 2006—
You Have Been Discharged!

Today I went to my last appointment with the radiation oncologist, Dr. Stevens. He addressed any concerns about the effects of my medicines and the radiation treatment, including the nosebleeds. Dr. Stevens feels that after examining me, the nosebleeds could be the result of sinus problems (which I've had all my life), certain medicines I am taking which can often inflame the nasal lining or the radiation which sometimes dries out the nasal cavity. He informed me that as far as he was concerned, I was ready to be discharged to the care of our thoracic oncologist, Dr. Simon, who will conduct the chemotherapy treatments. Dr. Stevens and his nurse, Barbara, have been a great blessing through the radiation process, and Evona and I thank them for their wonderful care. One of the last things Dr. Stevens said to me yesterday as he shook my hand was, "This is all in God's hands, not ours." What a great closer! Reminds me of God's closing to His Word in Revelation 22:21, *"The grace of our Lord Jesus Christ be with you all. Amen."* I've often told people that this is proof that God is a southerner because He uses our southern term "you all." No offense to our northern brethren…heaven is located in the sides of the "north." (Isaiah 14:13).

We will get the "port" today at 7:00 A.M. through which all my blood work and chemotherapy can be given. It is ironic that a guy who hated to get stuck with needles and give blood and who had a problem swallowing a pill all these years is being stuck multiple times each week and swallowing up to ten pills a day. God has a way of humbling us, doesn't He? I am rejoicing for this port because it will simplify things. I'm not rejoicing as much about the pills yet.

Please pray for a young man and his wife named Rick and Ruby Velez. Rick grew up at Fellowship and was in my youth group as a teen. He surrendered to preach and went to Hyles Anderson College in Hammond, Indiana. He and his wife have been a fantastic couple for God through these years and God has blessed them with three beautiful children. On Sunday (June 25), Ruby went to pick up their four-month-old, Damaris

Maria, from the church nursery and the baby had stopped breathing in her crib. She was rushed to the hospital but the doctors were unable to revive her. I spoke with Rick yesterday and he and Ruby are experiencing God's grace in a powerful way. He said, "Brother Cliff, the Lord giveth and the Lord taketh away, blessed be His name. His will is perfect and we are heartbroken but we accept it." What a testimony of trusting God when you face your darkest valley. They have chosen faith and God is pleased and He will reward it. I covet your prayers for them on Thursday as they have Damaris's funeral.

Our devotions were from Psalm 28, which begins, *"Unto thee will I cry, O LORD my rock..."* God is the only solid foundation upon which to build our lives. Plant your feet on Him...you will never fall!

Rejoicing in His goodness,
Preacher and Mrs. Evona

June 28, 2006—
A Port for the Upcoming Storms

All went well yesterday at Moffitt Cancer Center. We arrived before seven in the morning, ready to meet the day's challenges. My surgery for the placement of the port went pretty well. I ended up having some localized hemorrhaging where they placed my port, but other than taking a little longer than expected there are no lasting issues. This port is going to make my chemotherapy treatments so much more comfortable. Many healthcare professionals have encouraged the placement of a port. It will allow me not to have an IV every time we have a treatment and the actual medications are much less uncomfortable going in the port, where there is a larger vein. When I came out of surgery, Evona was disappointed that I wasn't groggy or showing the effects of the twilight sleep medication. She said after the last procedure that I was given this medication, I was highly entertaining. She found out much information that under normal circumstances I would not have disclosed!! The Lord is good. Sometimes a man needs a few well kept secrets…even from the love of his life. (Most of these secrets deal with certain meals I don't care for that she makes and a dress or two that are not my favorites! Don't spill the beans.)

We are so excited about the future that it is sometimes tedious dealing with the day to day issues of my illness. God has laid so many things on my heart and new projects and directions for our church. I just want to jump up every morning and rush to meet the day and get it all accomplished. However, my immediate focus has to be fighting this cancer with the help of God and the infamous Cisplatin/Taxotere chemotherapy. Much to Evona and my mother's dismay (Mom is my secretary), I can cram a lot of work into the small windows of opportunity I find. I call this being a good steward of my time, like the Bible teaches. Evona calls this sneaky. Either way, I seem to get a good amount accomplished in spite of my limitations.

Every morning we beg God to feed us from His Word, yet we are always surprised how personal the passage becomes. I guess we forget that the beauty of God's Word is that even though it was written thousands of years ago, it can minister directly to us if we will allow it. Psalm 28:7-8 says *"The LORD is my strength and my shield;"* (He will give us the power and protection we need.) *"my heart trusted in him, and I am helped:"* (Our faith is based on Someone who not only cares about us, but One who can do something about our situation!) *"Therefore my heart greatly rejoiceth; and with my song will I praise him."* (Our hearts are comforted and our joy is full and comes out in songs of praise to him.)

Music has always been very dear and special to me. Because of the difficulty I now have breathing I am not able to sing like I want to. This has not stopped me from trying. (My family isn't all that excited about the results, but it is a joyful noise!) One song that has been especially comforting has been Horatio Spafford's hymn, "It Is Well with My Soul."[3]

Verse one addresses the Christian's current circumstances:

When peace, like a river, attendeth my way,
When sorrows like sea billows roll;
Whatever my lot, Thou has taught me to say,
It is well, it is well with my soul.

Even amidst the trial, we can know it is well. Not, it will be well, but it is well. If you study the story of Elisha and the Shunemite woman in 2 Kings 4:8–37, you will see the roots of this great hymn of the faith.

Verse four helps us remember that one day we will understand the things that we have to receive by faith during this life time:

And, Lord, haste the day when our faith shall be sight,
The clouds be roll'd back as a scroll,
The trump shall resound and the Lord shall descend,
"Even so," it is well with my soul.

All is well with our souls,
Preacher and Mrs. Evona

June 29, 2006—
An Unexpected Bloom

Yesterday (June 28), I awoke early after a night of little sleep. To be honest, I was feeling some discouragement about our previous night (June 27). We had gone to Moffitt and I had received the port, which was a good thing. We got home and I put my exhausted wife to bed. She has been the one who has had to take up the slack during my illness, which includes our household, her ministry responsibilities (she is our church pianist) and my appointments and medications. She lies in bed with me at night unable to sleep because she is listening to my breathing, trying to make sure I am OK. She has been a remarkable testimony to me of grace under fire, strength under pressure and faith through the valley.

About an hour after she lay down to rest, Moffitt called with some alarming news. I had a CT scan performed last Friday, and apparently they had discovered some clots in my lungs on Tuesday (June 27), and I needed to come in within the hour and get a shot of blood thinner to prevent further clotting. I looked at my poor wife, who was so tired and finally had settled into a well-deserved rest, and at first I thought that I would just leave her sleeping and go take care of this alone. Then I realized that if I went to the hospital alone that when she woke up she would kill me and the shot wouldn't matter. I gently tapped her and gave her the bad news. She shrugged off her weariness, got dressed and off we went to Moffitt. On our way, she called the nurse to confirm everything and the nurse told her something that I had missed earlier. She said, "This is serious; it can be potentially life-threatening." Evona gulped and said, "We're on our way, get the shot ready." This is my wife. She becomes a tenacious fighter when it comes to her husband. It is the Lord who gives her the strength she needs and I thank God every day that I married a fighter like her when we face trials like this!

I received the needed injection and was informed that this will become part of my daily regimen. Now I've told you how much I "love" needles, so this was some of the most unwanted news I could get. We went back home and after an evening with the family, we were hit with something worse than the day's already discouraging events. I was walking into our bedroom when my nose started bleeding for no reason. I put the cold pack on it to stop it, and then the place where I received my injection started bleeding shortly thereafter. I called for Evona, who brought me a towel to put pressure on the blood flow at the injection site. I could see the fear in her eyes. We called the doctor on call, who informed us that this is a side effect of taking a blood thinner. Because of whole brain radiation, my platelets are low and this can cause bleeding also. If we could not stop it ourselves, we would have to go to the emergency room. If we could stop the bleeding, we could discuss it with our oncologist at our scheduled appointment the next day. I'm not a big fan of waiting around for hours with an ice pack on my nose and a towel on my stomach in an emergency room, so we worked for about half an hour to stop the bleeding. Evona stopped the injection site bleeding with a pressure bandage and we were able to stop the nosebleed with a gauze and petroleum jelly nostril pack. This was not how we planned to spend our evening and to be honest, I didn't get much sleep.

The next morning (June 28) I woke up early to go out and pray in the garden about this disturbing "clot" situation. As I sat on the bench, I cried out to God, "Lord, You know my heart and You know I'm discouraged right now. I need to fight this cancer with the chemotherapy this Friday and we don't need anything to interrupt that." (As if God doesn't know what's going on in my body). I continued, "I need something Lord. I need something to encourage my heart." I opened my *Read through the Bible in a Year* that I read in my garden in the mornings and the portion devoted to the Proverbs was Proverbs 19:27, which says, *"CEASE, my son, to hear the instruction that causeth to err from the words of knowledge." This is what I need to do,* I thought, *I need to shut out the words of discouragement the devil was speaking to me and grab hold of the Word of God that will fill my heart with faith.* I began claiming scriptures like Proverbs 3:5, 6; Jeremiah 33:3; Philippians 3:10; 4:13, 19 and 1 Peter 5:7. I looked down at a plant I had recently added to my garden. It was a bromeliad with pink blooms. I looked closer. I could not believe what I saw…the middle bloom had opened up at the top and produced a purple flower. You know by now that "purple" is the color of the cancer survivor. I wept. God gave me an unexpected bloom. He knows just what we need and when we need it.

We went to our appointment at Moffitt with Dr. Simon and discussed the clotting situation, and he addressed all our concerns with his capable medical wisdom. The clots that are already in the lungs will dissolve themselves and the daily injection will prevent future clotting. We had to wait for blood work to determine if I could receive the blood thinner injections because my platelets were low, which is a common side effect of whole brain radiation. My platelet number had been going down each time we had blood work done. Dr. Simon felt like it might still go even lower, and this could affect my ability to take chemotherapy on Friday. We prayed together and Dr. Eric Capaci asked his church to pray by sending out a call post for this special request. Miraculously, after two sets of blood work, we were told my platelets had increased and I was given the approval for the injection. We will be administering these shots ourselves, and my "fighter" wife learned how to give me my shots. I'm not sure how she feels about this, but I am sure of one thing…"I" got the point. We will go in on Friday and have more blood work done and determine if the platelet number is still going up. If it is still on the rise, I will be able to receive my first chemotherapy treatment as scheduled.

We arrived home late and were unable to attend Prayer Meeting. I feel my church's prayers for me though and I feel all of yours too. Thank you for your love, support and prayers…they are an unexpected bloom to me each and every day.

Watching for the blooms God sends our way,
Preacher and Mrs. Evona

June 30, 2006—
This Is No Coincidence

We use the word "coincidence" in life to describe something that happens by chance or accident. With the believer there are no coincidences, only God-ordered steps (*"the steps of a good man are ordered by the* Lord*..."* Psalm 37:23). Believers have divine appointments set up by the Lord every day that work all things for our ultimate good and His ultimate glory (Romans 8:28).

There was a youth conference this week in Gatlinburg, Tennessee, sponsored by the Calvary Baptist Church, where my family, the Greens, attend and serve in the ministry. My cousin, Lisa Green, had taken her baby, Gracie, outside the services to keep her from disrupting the preaching. She met another lady holding her baby outside the services for the same reason. The two mothers began to talk. In a few moments, the mother Lisa had met began to share with her about an illness that she had had in the previous year. It was a life-threatening, skin-deteriorating disease that was working its way to her heart and she was unaware of it. Her husband is a pastor in Arkansas. The Lord gave them a particular Psalm to claim for her healing. Lisa asked what Psalm God had provided them and she replied Psalm 30, specifically verses 2 and 3. Lisa began to cry and was unable to speak for several minutes. When she regained her composure, she told this pastor's wife about my illness and God giving Evona and me Psalm 30:2-3. The two women cried and praised God together. After nearly dying and God raising her up, this dear woman's husband preached a sermon how that God not only gave her life back, but put a new life inside of her, the baby she was now holding. They named the baby "Gloryann" after the last verse of Psalm 30, which says, *"To the end that my glory may sing praise to thee, and not be silent. O* Lord *my God, I will give thanks unto thee forever."* This pastor and pastor's wife are none other than Eric and Carolann Capaci, one of the pastors who will be preaching in our upcoming "We Choose Faith" Rally on August 7th, 8th and 9th!

Again, there are no coincidences with the Lord, only "divine appointments." Look for them each day and be blessed.

Allowing Him to order our steps,
Preacher and Mrs. Evona

JULY 1, 2006—
Platelets Down, No Chemo

We arrived for our lab work at Moffitt yesterday (June 30), which determines my blood levels and whether or not I can receive my chemotherapy. The main numbers that the doctor is looking at are my platelets. Typically, platelets go down when you have whole brain radiation and then will go up again as your body gets better. When they go high enough (in the 100s) you can take chemotherapy.

As we have seen so many times throughout our fight with cancer, the Lord has done things, both spiritually and physically in my life and body which have both amazed and shocked Evona and me. On Wednesday my platelet count had gone from 85 to 94, which was up! When we did the labs yesterday, my count had gone back down to 88. This meant no chemotherapy.

My reaction was that God is in control of my body and my blood. He knows when I will be ready to begin chemotherapy and He has charge of my platelets. As we were waiting today for results, Evona began reading Psalm 31. She got to verses 9 and 10 and said, "Cliff, look at this…you're not going to believe this." She gave me her Bible and I read the verses, which say, *"Have mercy upon me, O LORD, for I am in trouble: mine eye is consumed with grief, yea, my soul and my belly. For my life is spent with grief, and my years with sighing: my strength faileth because of mine iniquity, and my bones are consumed."* "Sounds like cancer, doesn't it, honey?" I asked my wife. "Yes, but I love the way it ends…*"O love the LORD, all ye his saints: for the Lord preserveth the faithful, and plentifully rewardeth the proud doer. Be of good courage, and he shall strengthen your heart, all ye that hope in the Lord."* The Word of God always has something for us when we turn to it with an open ear and open heart.

We know that God is in control, and due to the postponing of the chemotherapy I will be able to be in the pulpit on Sunday. This is my heartbeat and my love. I was disappointed about the platelet number but excited at the same time. I have been concerned that taking chemotherapy late in the week would make it impossible for me to preach on Sunday. God knows our hearts and what is best for us and all things work together for our good.

Pray that my platelets will go up into the 100s this weekend so that I can begin chemotherapy early Monday morning (July 3). This is a lot to ask, but we are asking the God of gods, the Lord of lords, the King of kings and the Christ of Calvary!

(Jeremiah 33:3; Matthew 7:7–11, Philippians 4:6–7, 1 Thessalonians 5:17–18, James 1:17, 4:2, 5:13–18)

Coming boldly unto the throne of grace,
Preacher and Mrs. Evona

JULY 2, 2006—
The Blankie
(From Mrs. Evona)

After living through these past few weeks, I should immediately remember that all our supposed "coincidences" are really just miracles sent directly to us from God. But being human, it always takes me a little while to recognize God's divine intervention for me. It is probably because I am a scatterbrain and can't do two things at one time. I have always had difficulty focusing on more than one thing at a time. It was so bad when I was a teenager that when I finally passed my driving test, my parents gave me a "few" rules concerning driving. The main rule I had to live with until Cliff and I got married went something like this:

"*Never, ever, under any circumstances* chew gum, eat, try to listen to the radio or wave at pedestrians while driving! (Luckily for them, and everyone else on the roads and walking on the sidewalks, cell phones were not as popular as they are now!)

Every day I try and make it a point to notice what God has done for me that day. A few weeks back, I was reviewing how gracious God had been to Pastor and me concerning our children. We are so blessed to have both sets of parents living locally and able to help us out with the kids. During the first two weeks after finding out about Pastor's illness, the children spent a lot of time with my parents. Cliff's parents were with us at the hospital. I was so torn, being a stay-at-home mom, over not having the kids with me most of the time. The baby, Lucas, was not even a year old. It was very upsetting. I knew that there was no choice because of the situation, but that didn't help the "mom feelings." However, God sent one of those "divine coincidences" (as Preacher calls them) to us during this time. One month before we found out about Preacher's cancer, I surprised him and took him on a birthday getaway. It was so much fun. We were gone only one night and two days. After we returned, Lucas decided he didn't want to nurse anymore. He loved his sippy cup, and that was that! I was so upset. The doctor told me that it would be best for him to nurse until he was a year old. It was several months too early to stop! I "discussed" this with Lucas, but to no avail. Sippy cup it would be. Praise the Lord, God sees what lies ahead! How difficult it would have been for all of us if I were still nursing during the time we found out about Pastor's cancer. As it turned out, Baby Lucas did great and it was sure a lot easier to send the sippy cup than try to keep up with nursing.

During this time of separation, however, Lucas became very attached to his soft blue blanket. He liked to sleep with it, sit on it to play, hold it in the car seat; he even tried to talk us into letting him lay it in his lap while he was eating! It became a real comfort to him. Even when we were switching him from "Honey" (what they call my mom) to "Gee" (what they call Cliff's mom) to our neigh-  bor and friend Melody and back home, one thing was constant...the soft blue blankie! Typically, I am not a great fan of the whole carry-the-blanket-with-you thing. However, during this stressful time, I even considered getting my own blankie. It seemed to be such a help to Lucas, maybe it would help me! We all began calling the baby "Linus" after the Peanuts cartoon character that always carries his blanket.

Those of you who have had babies who love a blanket or stuffed animal know where this story is headed. Disaster struck! One grandma had the baby, and the other had the blanket! After the mad dash across town to retrieve the blanket, we all decided it would be a good thing to have more than one blanket. "Gee" was on a mission. Twenty-five stores and two weeks later we were stuck! There were no identical blankets in town. Not ever having had a baby who likes a certain blanket, I naively told "Gee" to just get one that is made from the same material. Oh no, this did not work. Lucas took one look at the soft green blanket and would have nothing to do with it. Well, try number two was a not so soft, blue blanket. No luck. Lucas smiled and ran to grab the "new" blanket and then immediately threw it down. It didn't feel the same. Blanket after blanket has been rejected. None of them are the "real" thing. We still have the same, not so nice looking soft blue blanket dragging around after baby "Linus" everywhere he goes.

This drama made me think about the search we all are on to find comfort. We look to doctors to say the right things, to give us comfort. We turn to others, hoping to hear the words that will comfort us. Just like Lucas, we run to grab the "new blanket" hoping it will comfort us and we are disappointed. Some people try to use drugs or alcohol to block out the need for comfort. The "grandmas" and I tried to trick Lucas into using a different blanket for comfort. He knew the difference between the real thing and a counterfeit. The devil is trying to convince us that he can offer us comfort. He wants us to forget that in Isaiah 51:12 God says, "*I, even I, am he that comforteth you:...*" If we try to find comfort and help in others, we are believing the devil and not God.

There are going to be times when troubles come. We will have circumstances that cause us to need comfort. We have to go to the One who can offer us true comfort and a hiding place. In Psalm 32:7 it tells us where to go to find true comfort. "*Thou art my hiding place; thou shalt preserve me from trouble; thou shalt compass [cover] me about with songs of deliverance.*" Don't try to turn to the blanket that is the same look, but made from different material. Don't talk yourself into believing that the blanket with the same "feel' but different look is just as good. Go to the genuine blanket—the blanket of grace that God gives us in times of need. (2 Thessalonians 2:16–17: "*Now our Lord Jesus Christ himself, and God, even our Father, which hath loved us, and hath given us everlasting consolation and good hope through grace, comfort your hearts...*")

Comforted by God's blanket of grace,
Mrs. Evona

∽ ∽ ∽

July 3, 2006—
Pulpits and Platelets

As you know, my chemotherapy will start this morning if my platelets are 100 or higher. We were told from the beginning, that after whole brain radiation, platelets typically go down and then up again. So it was not a surprise, just a disappointment that we could not get on with the treatments.

Since the chemotherapy was changed to Friday (June 30), I was able to travel to the "Impact Your World Youth Conference" in Gatlinburg, Tennessee on Thursday (June 29) and give my testimony to over 1,600 teenagers in seventy-eight youth groups from seventeen states. This conference is sponsored by the Calvary Baptist Church in Chattanooga, Tennessee, pastored by Brother Steve Roberson and the Gospel Light Baptist Church in Hot Springs, Arkansas, pastored by Brother Eric Capaci. Young people tend to think they are invincible and that they will live forever. I went to this conference to tell them otherwise.

James 4:14 says, *"Whereas ye know not what shall be on the morrow. For what is your life? It is even a vapour, that appeareth for a little time, and then vanisheth away."* All of us need to realize the brevity of life and the importance of living every moment as if it is our last. The Lord has a plan for all of us and we must devote ourselves wholly to it.

We experienced an awesome moving of God! Many teens began coming forward to pray before I finished my testimony. Brother Ralph Sexton Jr. gave the message shortly thereafter and hundreds of young people poured down the aisles, making decisions for Christ. The estimated number of teens who surrendered to full-time Christian service was seventy to eighty, with twenty-seven of those surrendering to preach the gospel. I saw one young man with his face touching the concrete floor of the convention center; he was so humbled before the Lord. *Praise god!* I've only been in a few of these type services where the Holy Spirit moved in a powerful way and I am so blessed to have witnessed this one!

We enjoyed great services at Fellowship on Sunday (July 2) with stirring patriotic music and honor being given to our country and flag. I was able to be in the pulpit both morning and evening. We rejoice that we had one young man get saved after the morning service. The sermon on Sunday morning was entitled, "What Does God Have to Say to Us Today?"

Praying for pleasing platelets,
Preacher

∞ ∞ ∞

July 4, 2006—
Praise the Lord, Chemotherapy Went Well!
(From Mrs. Evona)

Isn't it funny how circumstances change our perspective? As children, we were made to take naps and hated every minute. As adults, we beg to take naps and never get the time. It is all in your perspective. If you had told us two months ago that we would rejoice that Pastor would be able to take one of the strongest chemotherapy medicines available, we would have thought you were crazy. Yet here we are, praising God that his platelets went up enough to take his first chemotherapy treatment! What a change in perspective. We were so blessed to get a good friend of our Aunt Cathy's to give Preacher his treatment. This was such a comfort and help. Just having someone who cares help us through this difficult process was wonderful. Everything went very well, and we pray that God can guide the strong medicine to the exact cancer cells and make it very effective. Chemotherapy is very subjective. It takes different mixtures at different doses for different individuals. We pray that God gives our doctor wisdom as he chooses the correct dosing and mixtures for Pastor.

After preaching all day Sunday, Pastor was very tired. This caused him to have a very difficult night right before his chemotherapy. He had become increasingly more short of breath over the weekend. His cough had also worsened. This made for a stressful night, not sleeping well, waiting for chemotherapy. It was so concerning that we felt like he needed to be evaluated before taking chemotherapy. We headed to Moffitt and spoke to his doctor. Preacher's blood work had improved over the weekend and made it possible to proceed with treatment. The doctor had a chest x-ray ordered to find out about the shortness of breath and excessive coughing. This x-ray showed a problem with the left side of Pastor's lungs. We were told that it had a small collapsed spot near the bottom. The attending physician felt that it would be safer to keep Preacher overnight to watch his breathing. As low as his oxygen levels were early Monday morning, it is a miracle that he was able to concentrate and preach with such clarity and power! It truly amazes me every time he gets in the pulpit. God seems to come down and cover him, enabling him to preach with physical power that is not present at any other time. We will wait to speak to the doctor after a new CT scan is taken. We pray for wisdom concerning the direction we need to take to correct Preacher's breathing issues.

Perspective is everything! I don't think I would have ever been able to foresee a day that I would be pleased to have a doctor let us know that Pastor needed to stay overnight in the hospital. However, after listening to him suffer and cough, struggling to breathe all night long, wondering if he needed medical help the night before, I was glad the doctors would be close by to oversee his breathing last night.

We have had a change in perspective due to Pastor's illness. Everywhere we look, we see hurting, needy people. Jeremiah 5:21 sums up how most of us live our lives day after day. *"Hear now this, O foolish people, and without understanding; which have eyes, and see not; which have ears, and hear not;"* We look around us and don't really see people. We talk to others and don't really hear them. We know that people need the comfort only God can give, yet we sit by and let them suffer alone. Yesterday, for the first time in over 12 years of marriage, Pastor was put in time out! His nurse jokingly put him in "time out," because after instructing him to rest and conserve his energy, he kept talking and praying with other patients around him. Perspective is everything. We can choose to see the illness or the ministry opportunity. We can see pain or a chance to show God's grace in the midst of trials. We can see fear or an opportunity to choose faith! Our prayer is that we can see this world through the eyes of a loving God that wants to seek and to save all who are lost.

With a change in perspective,
Mrs. Evona

∞ ∞ ∞

July 5, 2006—
To Tube or Not to Tube—That Is the Question

Yesterday (July 4) was Independence Day. We celebrated it at Moffitt. There was much to celebrate as God answered our prayers, and even though my platelets were only 92, Dr. Simon allowed me to take my first chemotherapy treatment on Monday. This was another blessing from God that only came through so many of God's people praying. Acts 4:31: "*And when they had prayed, the place was shaken...*" The chemo treatments themselves are not as daunting as your mind conceives them to be. You are basically in a comfortable chair for the length of time it takes to receive your medicines. You can eat, drink, read, watch television, and listen to music. Basically anything else you can do in a chair, you are allowed to do while you wait. (Now that is an interesting assignment...what can you do in a chair while you wait for the last drip of your I.V.? Email us your answers and we'll include them in a future update). The difficult part comes over the next few days as you experience the side effects of the treatment.

The side effects of my treatment can be nausea, fatigue and a low immune system, which can make me vulnerable to getting sick easier. Another side effect is hair loss. Obviously, that is no longer an issue with me. (I wonder if my hair will return beautiful, blond and curly.) I ask you to pray that the Lord will see fit to minimize my side effects, that I may spend quality time with my family as well as preach on Sunday. We know that this is all up to the Lord, so we simply ask you to pray.

As you know, after my chemotherapy was complete, they decided to keep me overnight to monitor my breathing. The x-ray showed a small part of my lung was collapsed. The doctors wanted to take another x-ray and make sure it was not continuing to collapse further. The x-ray on yesterday morning caused the doctors to feel like the collapsed area was increasing. This led to a decision we (and the head thoracic surgeon) had to make. To tube, or not to tube! After much discussion, the doctors felt like it was in my best interests to have a small tube inserted and inflate the collapsed area of my lung. Obviously, due to my "many issues" (as Evona calls them), it was a difficult decision to make. We prayed together and claimed James 1:5: "*If any of you lack wisdom, let him ask of God...and it shall be given him.*" We also claimed our tried and tested verse in Proverbs 3:5–6: "*Trust in the LORD with all thine heart; and lean not unto thine own understanding. In all thy ways acknowledge him, and he shall direct thy paths.*" A helpful bit of information that assisted us in making this decision came by way of our thoracic surgeon. He informed us that he had been performing this procedure for almost as long as Evona has been alive (since 1972). He also said that being a doctor is called the "practice of medicine," and he has had a lot of practice doing this procedure. We decided that the procedure was needed and we had to trust the Lord with the outcome. The procedure went very well, and when the doctor called back after seeing the latest x-ray, he was extremely pleased. His comment to me was that, "We got the tube exactly where we wanted it and the lungs are inflated again. We had some invisible help today, guiding my hands." To which I replied, "We both know who that "invisible help was." Praise the Lord!!

All is well here at the hospital. So far I have not been put into "time out" again, but I did receive several warnings. Because of my weak immune system, and my shortness of breath, they don't want me to receive visitors. However, you can visit the throne of grace for me often over the next few days. I would greatly covet your prayers. Each day brings new challenges and great opportunities.

Trusting God,
Preacher and Mrs. Evona

∞ ∞ ∞

July 6, 2006—
Rip Van Frinkle

After having a very difficult night, it was a blessing to finally begin feeling some relief. The chest tube successfully inflated my lung, which improved my breathing. It is a necessary evil when dealing with these types of lung complications. There was some discussion as to the cause of the small collapsed area of my left lung. Yesterday, the various doctors' consensus was that a blood clot that was already in my lung caused this complication. Having had many x-rays and another CT scan, they have not seen any new clots. This means the medicine to thin my blood is working. Praise the Lord!

Dr. Simon (our main oncologist) came to see us unexpectedly early yesterday morning. We asked how he was able to get free during a day he is tied up seeing regular clinic patients. He and his nurses laughed and said they were "taking a field trip." We had a scheduled appointment with him during that time, and he was thoughtful enough to come to us to put our mind at ease. The hospital nurse taking care of us said that this was very unusual and we normally would not have been able to see him until very late in the day. Dr. Simon concluded that the blood clot was the cause of the collapsed portion of my lung. He told us that normally this type of complication is not detected until it becomes an emergency situation. He stated how fortunate it was that it was detected on the x-ray. We know however that the Lord has his eye on every little detail. Matthew 10:29–31: *"Are not two sparrows sold for a farthing? And one of them shall not fall on the ground without your Father. But the very hairs of your head are all numbered. Fear ye not therefore, ye are of more value than many sparrows."* (Since the Lord doesn't have to keep track of the hairs on my head anymore, He's keeping a close eye on my many x-rays!)

Another wonderful, fantastic, exciting piece of information Dr. Simon and his nurses brought with them today dealt with the side effects of the chemotherapy. They felt like I had passed the point in time when most patients experience the extreme nausea from this type of chemotherapy.

What a blessing! Contemplating dealing with extreme nausea and a chest tube at the same time was not a pleasant thought. Ruth 2:16 speaks of God blessing us with "handfuls of purpose." This was a very welcome handful. The only side effect I have experienced has been overwhelming fatigue. This fatigue has earned me a new nickname…"Rip Van Frinkle"! I think I have slept more today than I have in the last two weeks combined.

It seems as soon as Evona leaves the room, a message goes out to all the doctors to make their rounds right away. Hummm? Could they be avoiding my pretty, little inquisitive wife? Last night soon after she left, the thoracic surgeon came by and let us know that the x-ray of my lung looked so good we could go ahead and have a pleurodesis. This procedure fuses the linings where the air and fluid have been accumulating. This should prevent further collapse of my lungs and keep fluid from building up. This was a surprising but pleasant turn of events. They will keep the tube in for another day and take a few more x-rays. If everything looks good, they will be able to take out the chest tube on Friday and possibly send me home. This is very good thing since Evona has probably not fed my sweet wiener dog, Shakespeare, since I have been in the hospital.

One last blessing to share with you came through a comment from one of our nurses. It was amazing to him to see procedures that normally take much more time and scheduling go with such speed, as well as the speed of my physical progress with each procedure. Remember the verse my mother has claimed over and over during this trial, Psalm 102:2: *"Hide not thy face from me in the day when I am in trouble; incline thine ear unto me: in the day when I call answer me speedily."*

Resolved not to sleep in church,
Preacher

∽ ∽ ∽

July 7, 2006—
We Will Remember the Name of the Lord
(From Mrs. Evona)

I remember when…this phrase brings back some of my fondest memories as a little girl. Grandpas seem to have the corner on the market concerning this phrase. My Grandpa, Poppy to all of us, told the best stories. He would sit on his green couch, twiddle his thumbs and start his story with…"I remember when." Of course hearing about gas costing only a dime a gallon didn't really make much of an impression until I had to start paying $2.50 a gallon. Poppy remembered when he had to support his entire family as a young teenager picking oranges. He remembered falling in love with my Nana and talking her mother into signing the paper so they could get married when Nana was only 15 years old. Poppy looked back at his life and remembered hard work, good friends, a great family and a faithful God. I look back and remember seeing faith in action every morning when we would stay at their house. Nana would be sitting at the table reading her Bible, writing letters and poems to encourage those around her. Poppy would lovingly call Nana "Mommy" and get her anything she wanted. I remember when I would ride to church with them in their light green car Poppy had been given when he retired from TECO. I thought we would never get there because he didn't drive over 30 mph the entire way to church. My Nana would let me play with a plush monkey that was the size of a two-year-old. I would dress it and carry it around all day long. My youngest brother, Jonathan, was so glad Nana let me play with the monkey, because it made me leave him alone!

Memories can be the very thing that will help us make it through a deep valley. Stop long enough to let your current circumstances fade away and remember. Remember that the Lord is in control. Remember that "nothing happens that hasn't already passed over His desk." *"Some trust in chariots, and some in horses: but we will remember the name of the LORD our God"*(Psalm 20:7). We as children, beloved children of God, have the right to remember. I have fond memories of Nana and Poppy because we were family. We are God's family. I chose to remember the name of the Lord yesterday. The name I remembered was JEHOVAH-RAPHA. This means the Lord who heals. Exodus 15:26: "...*for I am the LORD that healeth thee.*" Some people we meet in the halls here at the hospital are trusting in doctors; some are trusting in their own strength. These things are chariots and horses. Good things, but not the way to win the battle, "...*for the battle is the LORD's...*" (1 Samuel 17:47). We must remember the name of the Lord. His name will comfort and meet our needs. There are days that the only thing that will help is remembering. What name do you need to remember? JEHOVAH RAPHA, the Lord who heals or JEHOVAH-SHALOM, the Lord who gives peace, JEHOVAH-NISSI, the Lord who is my banner and protector, JEHOVAH-JIREH, the Lord who sees and provides, JEHOVAH-TSIDKENU, the Lord who is our righteousness, JEHOVAH-SHAMMOAH, the Lord who is there, and there are many others.

Remembering the healing name of the Lord has helped us through a week that has been difficult. There have been times that the obstacles have seemed insurmountable, but praise the Lord, we hope to be headed home soon. After an early morning x-ray (we hope), they should remove the chest tube today. Preacher will have to walk around and make sure that he is breathing fine and all is well, and then we will be sent home. So far the pleurodesis (fusing of the linings of the lungs) seems to have worked. He was taken off oxygen and has been doing fine since yesterday. Pray that the chemotherapy will work "speedily" and there will be fewer complications to deal with. I told Pastor that he has had every complication of his condition that I have read about—all in less than a month! He swiftly told me not to read any more medical books. If we have had them all, then I should stop reading now!

Take comfort in the name of the Lord that meets your need. Remember that "the battle is the Lord's!"

Remembering Jehovah-Rapha,
Mrs. Evona

July 8, 2006—
The Horse Did Not Get to Head to the Barn

Sometimes, you are just glad when the day is over! We were so hopeful to have the chest tube removed and skip around the halls for a few hours showing our perfect breathing skills and head home. However, best laid plans don't always pan out. During Thursday evening, I began not feeling the best. This became an understatement by morning. Chemotherapy is very hard on your body and different organs. We took chemotherapy on Monday, when I had several other issues that my body was dealing with. Dr. Simon came in to see us last evening and said that we could not have waited for perfect conditions to start chemo. We needed to start fighting the cancer now. However, it was very hard on my body. I told him that starting to fight this evil was a good thing, even if it was hard on me. We laughed and said, just like there is no "perfect" time to start having kids, chemotherapy is the same. Sometimes you just have to go for it!

Needless to say, they did not let me go home. My sodium levels dropped and my kidney functions took a beating from the chemotherapy. These are things they want to monitor before I can head home. They were able to take the chest tube out and I am feeling much better. Pray that my body will catch up with my desire to fight this cancer. We seem to take one step forward and two steps back each day. It is a good thing the Lord is the one in control.

Our devotions were so sweet in Psalm 35. Verse 27 talks about all of you who are standing together with us as we all "choose faith." It says, *"Let them* [that is all of you!] *shout for joy and be glad, that favour my righteous cause;* [choosing faith] *yea, let them say continually, Let the* LORD *be magnified,* [we will give God the glory] *which hath pleasure in the prosperity of his servant."* Our promise to God is in Verse 28: *"And my tongue shall speak of thy righteousness and of thy praise all the day long."*

Looking forward to the day we see the miracle gives us hope. We know that Psalm 35:18 will be what we will be able to do. "*...give thee thanks in the great congregation: I will praise thee among much people.*" This verse means that we all will give thanks to God at Fellowship (great congregation) and all of you reading this will have to come be with us to help us give thanks!

Trusting God every day,
Preacher

∞ ∞ ∞

July 9, 2006—
A Rough Week but a Good God!

This past week has probably been one of the toughest I have had since we started this fight against cancer. But I wouldn't compare it to a day in Job's life. I have often referred to Job 1 as the worst day a man had on earth. However, for spiritual peons like me this defiantly qualified as one of my toughest weeks. Even though we were happy to get the chemotherapy on Monday, we were not expecting the series of complications we would face over the following few days. Dealing with four or five major complications can give Satan the home court advantage when it comes to discouragement. I woke up this morning to find that Satan was working overtime to use my circumstances to discourage me. The human side of me wanted to focus on the complications, the setbacks and pain rather than the goodness and power of God. I began praying, endeavoring to "choose faith." I also began claiming scriptures and the Lord clearly spoke to me saying to my heart, "I am doing my part supernaturally, now get up and do what you can do naturally." I said to myself, I have chosen faith in God's power, now I must choose to fight with God's strength! I looked at the two pictures I have on my cell phone. The first picture is of Evona and me, and the second is of Evona, me and the three boys. I never thought I would thank God for a camera phone. But the prayers I was praying, verses I was claiming, and the faces of my family ignited that desire to fight. I got up out of the hospital bed, changed into fresh clothes and sat in a chair beside the bed. It winded me but it was a welcome change. About that time my mom and Aunt Cathy came in and were overjoyed to see me out of bed. Mom was delivering a message from a close friend of mine in the church, Robert Anders, saying that God had laid me on his heart. He wanted me to know that he loved me and was praying for me. Mom immediately called him back and let him know that at the time he was praying for me, God had given me new strength. Isn't it wonderful how God puts us on the hearts of other believers to pray for us, just when we need it most? Philippians 1:3–4: "*I thank my God upon every remembrance of you, Always in every prayer of mine for you all making request with joy…"*

During the course of the day, we received much good news. My blood test showed that my sodium levels had not dropped any further, and my kidney functions were near normal. These are things that they will need to continue to monitor. However, each area seems to be headed in a great direction. We still covet your prayers. We know that God hears us when we pray. An interesting side note is that the platelet levels you all prayed so diligently about have stayed considerably higher than expected!

I'll miss you today in church but pray that these encouraging reports will lead to my coming home soon.

Praying for you as you are praying for me,
Preacher

∽ ∽ ∽

July 10, 2006—
Going Home... God-Willing

Even though I could not be in church Sunday (July 9), the reports of both morning and evening services were wonderful! Our people are being faithful and it encourages my heart to see it! We praise God for the couple who joined our membership Sunday and the testimonies of our teens from their trip to the WILDS this past week! We had four saved and many life-changing decisions this year! God is still moving on the hearts of young people...praise the Lord.

They found a way to allow me to be a part of the services on Sunday night by having me call in over the sound system and greet the church. I offered prayer for the evening message and it made me feel a part.

Lord willing, we will be discharged tomorrow after a long week in the hospital. I cannot wait to be in our home with my family. I hate to quote Dorothy but it just seems appropriate, "There's no place like home." In God's Word, the family is God's first divine institution. It is sacred, it is special and it is a gift from God (Proverbs 31:10–11: *"Who can find a virtuous woman? For her price is far above rubies. The heart of her husband doth safely trust in her..."* Psalm 127:3: *"Lo, children are an heritage of the Lord..."*). After being away from Evona during the times she went home to be with the boys and being away from my three sons, I will cherish coming home to my family. Pray that nothing prevents this from happening.

The upcoming two weeks leading up to my next chemotherapy treatment will be critical. I will have to rest and conserve my energy to regain my strength so that I can take the treatment again as scheduled. During this time it will be very important for us all to pray about several things:

- Pray that my blood work continues to look good and no other complications arise.
- Pray for wisdom for Dr. Simon (my oncologist) as he decides what mixture of medicines to give in the next treatment.

- Pray that many people's lives will be impacted through our "Choose Faith Rally" coming on August 7, 8, 9.

Prayer is our way of "pulling the rope that pours the blessings from the windows of heaven."

Let us all "pray without ceasing!"
Preacher

July 11, 2006—
A Way Higher than Our Own

Many times while on vacation, the famous struggle between husbands and wives rears its ugly head. It sounds a lot like this…

> WIFE: "Are we lost?"
> HUSBAND: "Of course we're not lost; I am just not sure where we are!"
> WIFE: "Stop and ask that nice man over there for directions to show us the way."
> HUSBAND: "We don't need to ask for directions, I'll find the way eventually!"

Finding our way seems to be a lifetime pursuit. We tend to struggle throughout our lives, trying to figure out which way to go. We spend a lot of time telling the Lord our own desires and not much time listening to His directions.

From the time we are small children, we do not like to take directions from others. Lucas is our littlest boy and our third baby. You all know what happens to the "baby." Preacher has missed the boys terribly. We thought it would make him feel better to see a video of the three boys at home. We all laughed at Lucas as he chased the dog with the plunger. (The plunger was clean of course!) When we tell Lucas, "No, No," and make him sit down as punishment, he puckers up his face and lets out a wail. None of us like to take directions! However, this is how we find our way. Isaiah 55:8–9 says, *"For my thoughts are not your thoughts, neither are your ways my ways, saith the L*ORD*. For as the heavens are higher than the earth, so are my ways higher than your ways, and my thoughts than your thoughts."* Today we were headed home, we thought! But the Lord had different plans. His "way" was definitely not our way. Shortly after our call into the church service Sunday evening, we noticed some swelling around my chest and neck. I had been having some tightness in my neck earlier but we hadn't noticed any swelling. After seeing the swelling the nurse paged the doctor on call. This led to several doctors examining me and yet another set of chest x-rays. We were awakened around three o'clock in the morning by the thoracic surgeon telling us there was still a leak in my lung. This leak was sending air to my chest tissues and causing the swelling. We were told a chest tube was needed to fix the problem. We asked the doctor for a few minutes alone and held hands and prayed claiming wisdom from James 1:5. We felt peace that the chest tube was needed and the rest was up to God. (We are trying to win the award for the most surgical procedures done in a normal hospital room.) There is no way to tell you how disappointed I was at this setback. I was so looking forward to going home. In my heart I thought, *I can't stay another day! I must go home and be with my family.* In the moments we prayed, God gave us peace that inserting another chest tube was the right decision, and we must follow His "way." In Psalm 18:30–33 the Word of God declares, "*As for God, his way is perfect: the word of the* LORD *is tried: he is a buckler to all those that trust in him. For who is God save the* LORD*? Or who is a rock save our God? It is God that girdeth me with strength, and maketh my way perfect...*" Knowing this verse is true, we believe that we are in God's perfect "way," still here at Moffitt once again waiting. The doctors will continue to monitor the chest tube and the air leak. Please pray that all leaks are sealed "speedily" and we can be discharged to come home.

This has been a very difficult week on my wife. She is emotionally tired and very sleepy. Another side effect of chemotherapy I have experienced has been a constant ringing in my ears. This has made it difficult to hear everything that is going on. Last night after the drama, I awakened to hear what I thought was sobbing and crying from my wife's bed. I thought to myself, *Bless her heart, she is over there weeping and praying for me.* Wanting to comfort her, I very slowly inched my way in her direction all the while holding my newly inserted chest tube carefully. I struggled to peer over my bed rail and finally caught sight of her. She was not weeping or praying...she was snoring up a storm! Nevertheless, I was glad for her to get some much needed rest.

Satan is attacking us. He knows that "choosing faith" is a lot easier when you are heading into the trial than when you are actually in the midst of that trial. But we know that Job 23:10 is true. *"But he knoweth the way that I take: when he hath tried me, I shall come forth as gold."*

Happy Birthday, Girls! God has richly blessed me with a wonderful friend and sister, Susan. I am so glad

the days of calling you a blister instead of a sister are over. You have been an encouragement and you were always there to defend me. Even if you had to use a broom! I love you.

Trusting God so that we come forth as gold,
Preacher

Choosing Faith Against the Odds

July 12, 2006—
Complications, Setbacks... Finally Improvement

Part of our Christian walk is realizing that life is not all victories and mountain tops. Amidst the wonderful blessings He gives, there are complications, setbacks, valleys and burdens. These trials are meant to teach us some great spiritual truths. First of all, our life should be all about bringing glory to Jesus Christ and not ourselves. Paul teaches this in 2 Corinthians 4:6–11:

> *For God, who commanded the light to shine out of darkness, hath shined in our hearts, to give the light of the knowledge of the glory of God in the face of Jesus Christ. But we have this treasure in earthen vessels, that the excellency of the power may be of God, and not of us. We are troubled on every side, yet not distressed; we are perplexed, but not in despair; persecuted, but not forsaken; cast down, but not destroyed; always bearing about in the body the dying of the Lord Jesus, that the life also of Jesus might be made manifest in our body. For we which live are alway delivered unto death for Jesus' sake, that the life also of Jesus might be made manifest in our mortal flesh.*

Secondly, our suffering has a deeper purpose. God allows us to suffer so that He may give us comfort, that we might comfort others who are suffering. Second Corinthians 1:3–4 says,

> *Blessed be God, even the Father of our Lord Jesus Christ, the Father of mercies, and the God of all comfort; who comforteth us in all our tribulation, that we may be able to comfort them which are in any trouble, by the comfort wherewith we ourselves are comforted of God.*

And finally, no matter what happens, God is always good, whether we suffer or succeed.

Not that I speak in respect of want: for I have learned, in whatsoever state I am, therewith to be content. I know both how to be abased, and I know how to abound: every where and in all things I am instructed both to be full and to be hungry, both to abound and to suffer need. I can do all things through Christ which strengtheneth me.

PHILIPPIANS 4:11–13

If you have been keeping up with the updates, you are aware of the many setbacks and complications we have faced this past week here at Moffitt. God gave us peace about a second chest tube that has extended our hospital stay and delayed my much anticipated homecoming. Satan has been trying to use setbacks to discourage us and weaken our faith. But just like in Genesis 50:20: *"But as for you, ye thought evil against me; but God meant it to good..."* our faith in God has been strengthened through these setbacks, rather than weakened.

Yesterday I woke up feeling better than I had in over a week. Brother David, our associate pastor at Fellowship, said he knew I was feeling better because of all the projects I sent him through my secretary (my mom). Throughout the day I was able to get out of the bed more, be taken off oxygen completely, taste food more that I have in a while, take a stroll around the nurses station and find out that the leak in my lungs is becoming smaller each day. We will now be waiting on the leak in my lungs to close up and then we will be able to have the chest tube removed. We learned that the procedure I received last week (pluerodesis) is an ongoing process that may take a while to complete. Having been on steroids for a while has slowed the process down some. The doctors are confident that it will eventually work. I wanted to help this process any way I could and so I asked the doctors what I could do to hasten things along. The doctors said that there was nothing we could do to hasten this process. But we do know one thing that will work...*prayer!* Please pray that my lungs will do their job and do it well!!

Breathing easier by God's grace,
Preacher

∽ ∽ ∽

July 13, 2006—
A Sticky Note I've Needed Many Times in My Life

We are still at Moffitt in a holding pattern. The air that has been leaking in my lungs is dissipating slowly. I have a chest x-ray every day to note any changes in the air leak. Yesterday the doctors said there was no change, but there was no increase either. We take this as good news. The Lord is teaching us to accept the path He gives us each day with grace.

We have received so many wonderfully encouraging emails from all over the world. Several have come from the sister of our associate pastor, Sharlene Ruland. I have known Sharlene since I was a boy at the Good Shepherd Baptist Church in Tampa, where we both attended. Sharlene was a young single lady who had a passion for souls and worked in a ministry winning Air Force boys to Christ. As a child I always looked up to her.

Years later, I was a young single guy serving the Lord in my church. Our present associate pastor, David Spencer, was a young single guy serving the Lord in his church. We became friends when we both attended a nightly Bible institute held at Fellowship Baptist Church where I was serving as the youth pastor. It was then that I discovered that David was Sharlene's brother. One day David invited me to go with him to visit Sharlene and her family. I was very excited to see Sharlene again. We had a rough trip with some car issues, but we finally made it there. Sharlene was just as I remembered her—friendly, jovial and always smiling. After supper and some conversation, Sharlene took me to where I would be sleeping for the night. Apparently it was the room where she had her devotions. There were sticky notes all over one wall. Each one had either a Bible verse, inspiring quote or some Bible truth she had learned written on it. I sat on the bed and began my Bible devotions. In a few moments something strange happened. One of the sticky notes detached and fluttered down from the wall and landed right on my open Bible. I picked it up and read it and this is what it said. "God never uses men greatly until he has hurt them deeply." As unbelievable as this seems now, I have never forgotten that sticky note. There have been so many times throughout my life that I have needed the message on that sticky note, especially in recent days. God has allowed cancer to invade our lives and hurt us deeply; however, we pray that we will be found faithful so that he can use us greatly.

> *"I am the true vine, and my Father is the husbandman. Every branch in me that beareth not fruit he taketh away: and every branch that beareth fruit, he purgeth it, that it may bring forth more fruit."*
>
> JOHN 15:1–2

Abiding in the vine to produce more fruit,
Preacher

JULY 14, 2006—
Good News for a Change

After many days of waiting for the leak in my lungs to stop so that we can have the chest tube removed and make sure that all is well with my body and hopefully go home, the Lord gave us some encouraging news today. Our doctor's physician's assistant came in and had viewed yesterday's (July 13) chest x-ray and said that the air leak at the bottom of the lungs had stopped. She was all smiles and she even did a happy dance. She did say that there are two small air pockets in the tip of each of my lungs that they will watch but are not a major concern. When I was up walking later in the day, we saw one of my doctors who had also viewed the chest x-ray and confirmed the leak had stopped. *Praise the lord—some good news for a change!*

You get so much bad news, you find yourself hesitant to accept good news. You can't help it, you're heart just says, "Something else will go wrong." Whether this "good news" we received today will pan out tomorrow, we'll wait and pray and trust the Lord in the morning.

There is some good news that I can share with you that will never falter or go wrong. It is the greatest news I have ever received in my life. It is the good news that Jesus Christ, God's Son, loved us enough to leave heaven and come to earth to die for our sins (John 3:16). In dying on the cross, being buried and rising from the dead, Jesus paid the penalty for our sins, a price we could not pay (Romans 3:23 and 6:23). We can be saved from our sins by simply trusting God's Son, Jesus, as our personal Savior (Romans 10:13).

As a boy, I was raised in a Christian home and went to church throughout my life. I heard this good news preached every Sunday. I knew that I needed to trust Jesus but I was afraid to walk the aisle of our church. One night my mother came to tuck me in bed. (Moms should still do this…and dads too! Trust me, I would love to be home and be able to do this for my boys.) She said, "Son, some of your friends got saved tonight and I hope that you will too." I replied, "Mom, I want to go forward every service but

I'm afraid to walk the aisle." Mom said, "You don't have to get saved at church, you can get saved any time and any place if you'll just trust Jesus as your Savior. You can get saved now, if you will." I said, "I will, Mom, one day." Now my mother is a tricky lady. She knew I was ready but I was putting it off. Procrastination is one of Satan's greatest tools to prevent us from doing what God wants us to. She went to the piano in our home and played a song called "One Day Too Late." The song lyrics speak of the man who waited too late to get saved. Jesus came back and he was left behind. (If you know about the popular *Left Behind* series today, you know about the rapture, when Jesus returns and removes only believers from the world.) The words of the song pierced my heart and I thought, "*What if I wait too late?*" I trusted Jesus as my Savior that night in my bed. I have never regretted receiving that good news! I want you to consider receiving this good news today. It's available to everyone.

We enjoyed a visit from my boys today at the hospital. All three of my rug rats were here! The baby calls me "Daaaeee" now and I heard a big one as they opened the door and he saw me. He sat with me for a good while but he's not one to stay in one place for too long, especially when he sees his mother eating. It was a delight to see my family and we have something extra special planned for the update tomorrow that my boys surprised me with. (Don't miss it! Same bat time…same bat channel. I'm sorry I can't get the classic TV out of my system). You really won't want to miss this. The second grade Sunday school class of the Cross Roads Baptist Church sent us a postcard to tell us they are praying for us and they all signed their names. The teacher wrote in a little box, "We talked about prayer and fasting, and Jacob said he gave up an ice cream to pray for you while his brothers ate their ice cream." That is precious and we thank God for such love, prayer and sacrificial fasting. Thank you Jacob…we love you!

Basking in the good news,
Preacher

July 15, 2006—
A Special Surprise

We told you in the last update we would be sharing with you a special surprise that our boys brought me when they came to see me in the hospital. I will tell you this; you could not buy this gift with any amount of money.

After the boys arrived, they handed me a CD. I asked, "What is this?" To which Caleb quickly answered, "It's a special surprise that we've been working on for you."

We got the laptop and inserted the CD and heard my children singing "He Ain't Never Done Me Nothing but Good."[4] This song says how we feel. God has done only good in our lives. Some days we have a difficult time seeing how circumstances can be for our good, but that is why we just have to trust God and have faith. The second song was so special because they chose it for me because of my love for meeting Jesus in my garden: "In The Garden."[5]

The tears streamed down my face as I listened to my boys and our associate pastor and his wife's children, Savannah and Jackson Spencer, singing songs they had recorded just for me. I want to say thank you to all four kids for this wonderful surprise. Evona and I also want to thank David and Melody Spencer for all they have done in helping us care for our children during this unexpected and lengthy hospital stay. They both have gone beyond friendship to help us in such an important area of our lives…our baby and our boys. We also want to thank Mrs. Paula Jones and Brother Dale Bowe for helping our children prepare this special surprise. You all gave me a blessing that cannot compare with any I've received.

There are so many blessings my sons bring to my life each and every day. I am pained that we cannot be together as a family right now, but I have accepted the fact that we must get this air leak fixed completely before we go home. Evona and I realized that our plan was not God's plan. Apparently, the Lord means for us to get started on building myself up for the next chemotherapy treatment while the air leak problem is getting fixed. We are working diligently to build up my body through nutrition. I didn't mention this before but early on in this hospital stay, I lost my desire to eat. I never thought that would happen to me. I've always had a great appetite, but nothing appealed to me. My family brought me everything I liked and more and I just had no desire for it. That changed a few days ago and I am eating better now. Because of a throat infection I must eat softer foods and we are supplementing it with "Boost." Have you heard of this? It tastes like vanilla or chocolate flavored pond water. It is not something I would choose in a vending machine in any millennium. Each day I drink four Boosts, and as I sip I say my boy's names because I am building up my strength for them. It's always neat to see which name I end on when I hear that delightful slurpy sound which indicates I've taken my last swallow. Motivation comes in many ways and my family motivates me to fight and build up my body.

In Genesis 45 we are told the story of Jacob discovering that his son Joseph, whom he thought was dead, was indeed alive in Egypt. Listen to the words of Genesis 45:25–28:

> *And they went up out of Egypt, and came into the land of Canaan unto Jacob their father, and told him, saying, Joseph is yet alive, and he is governor over all the land of Egypt. And Jacob's heart fainted, for he believed them not. And they told him all the words of Joseph, which he had said unto them: and when he saw the wagons which Joseph had sent to carry him, the spirit of Jacob their father revived: And Israel said, It is enough; Joseph my son is yet alive....*

My aunt Carol drove down from Chattanooga, Tennessee to see me and I said, "That was a long way to drive." She replied, "Not when it was to see you." We are motivated to see those we love. I wonder. How motivated are we to see our Lord? We do love Him. He is our Savior. He is the One Who died for us. Do we long to see Him? I believe this can be one of the greatest motivators of life...the longing to see the Lord. I know that it says in 1 John 3:1–3:

> *Behold, what manner of love the Father hath bestowed upon us, that we should be called the sons of God: therefore the world knoweth us not, because it knew him not. Beloved, now are we the sons of God, and it doth not yet appear what we shall be: but we know that, when he shall appear, we shall be like him; for we shall see him as he is. And every man that hath this hope in him purifieth himself, even as he is pure.*

We need to long to see Jesus in our daily lives through personal devotions with Him and a daily fellowship with Him that we allow to permeate our day. I have learned that you can pray and praise God in many of the situations you're in. Each day I have a chest x-ray and there is time when I wait to get my x-ray and when I wait to be taken back to my room. I use this time to pray and praise the Lord. I sing to Him, I claim scriptures in His name and I pray.

We need to long to see Jesus when He comes again. There will come a day when He will split the eastern skies and take us home to heaven to Himself and our loved ones we've said good-bye to down here. That will be a blessed day and we need to long for it in our hearts.

Looking for Jesus,
Preacher and Mrs. Evona

July 16, 2006—
The Fight Begins

Well, we were off and running (well, sort of shuffling) yesterday! I determined that yesterday would be the day to begin the fight to get in shape for the next chemotherapy treatment. Since I have been off oxygen for several days, moving around is much easier. We began the day eating a healthy breakfast and drinking our "pond water" Boost. (I use the term "we" loosely here. I was drinking pond water and Evona was sipping a white chocolate mocha coffee from Starbucks.) The doctor came in and said things were looking great with the leak. It seems to be slowing down, and it would be OK to take short walks around Moffitt. So off we went, down to a beautifully landscaped outside sitting area. We sat in the sun until a security guard came and asked us to move. Evidently my head was reflecting the sun so brightly; it was bothering some of the patients on third floor! (Some of you can relate to this problem.) It was so hot outside it prompted me to move all of you who work on roofs and AC units to the top of my prayer list. We moved into the shade and enjoyed time together away from the hospital room. We spent the rest of the day resting, eating good meals and taking a few more walks.

Philippians 3:14 says, *"I press to the mark for the prize of the high calling of God in Christ Jesus."* We are in a physical battle with cancer that requires all of our God-given energy working towards building up my body for the next chemotherapy treatment. Likewise, we are in a spiritual battle everyday with Satan. He desires to plant small cells of sin and weights in our lives that can grow like cancer and keep us from a healthy relationship with God. We must determine to fight Satan daily with the weapons God has provided in His Word. Just like we have used radiation and chemotherapy to fight my physical cancer, we must utilize these tools.

One of these weapons is the power of prayer. We have the privilege to come boldly before God's throne and petition Him for strength for the battle, wisdom for the way, comfort for the heart, grace for the soul, mercy when we need forgiveness and power to overcome. It has been said that

"Satan trembles when he sees the weakest saint on their knees." Another weapon from God is the filling of the Holy Spirit. We can yield daily to the Holy Spirit's control of our lives. This is not a difficult task. It only requires confession of all known sins, asking him to control every part of your life and then yielding control (Ephesians 5:18). After we have given the Holy Spirit control, we are ready to put on the whole armor of God (Ephesians 6:14–18): the girdle of truth protecting our loins; the breastplate of righteousness protecting our heart; the gospel of peace protecting our feet; the shield of faith protecting us from the fiery darts of the wicked; the helmet of salvation protecting our minds and the Sword of the Spirit (The Word of God) wielded like the two-edged sword it is, to fight Satan. I have some "war verses" in my wallet that I use when I know the devil is attacking me that I pull out and read to the devil when he rears his ugly head.

So let the fight begin against the devil and let's press toward the mark, which is Christ getting all the glory in our lives every day.

Fighting for the victory,
Preacher and Mrs. Evona

∞ ∞ ∞

July 17, 2006—
A Morning in the Life of...the Preacher

Eyelids..."Good Morning" (This is not morning, it's 4 A.M. I open my eyes to see several nurses). "I'm here for your morning labs" (Oh, you must be looking for someone else. I have a dachshund not a lab.). "And I'm here for your vitals" (The blood pressure thing again. How can you keep putting that on a guy's arm without eventually reducing his arm to a string?). "I'll begin drawing your blood, Mr. Frink" (You vampires never get enough of my blood). "Let me get this on your arm" (Let me get this on your neck and we'll be done with at least one of you. That won't work; they'll just send another one in your place.). "I just need one more vial of blood, Mr. Frink" (Leave me enough to enjoy the day, will you?). "Thank you for the blood, Mr. Frink" (That is rhetorical, right, because you never asked me for it to begin with). "Now for your temperature" (Let's see, will it be the ear one or the mouth one? I prefer the mouth one in case my ears are dirty. Rats, it's the ear one..."). "Thank you, Mr. Frink; have a nice day" (Oh good, I'll sleep some more...eyelids, again...) "Good Morning, Mr. Frink, I'm here for your breathing treatment (I thought I'd come at 4:30 A.M. today if you don't mind...).

This is dedicated to all the nurses and techs who have blessed me during my stay in the hospital and the above is only meant as a joke. All of you (even the vampires) have blessed me with your care and service. Evona and I thank you from our hearts.

The doctor came in this morning (July 16 while Evona was at church of course!) and examined the chest tube, had me cough and said, "The leak has stopped and I feel we can remove the chest tube today." I was shocked. I wasn't sure I'd heard him correctly (my hearing has been affected by the chemo), so I said, "Did you say you want to pull the chest tube today?" The doctor nodded yes. "Did you look at today's chest x-ray?" I asked. "Yes, and it shows the leak has stopped. I believe this is an opportune time to remove it so that it does not contribute to any future air leaks," the doctor answered. After he graciously submitted to the intense questioning by my feisty wife over the phone, he was able to proceed. And so around 12:00, after our people prayed a few minutes earlier that the leak would stop and the tube could be removed soon, the doctor pulled the chest tube out. I felt no pain and it was odd to be able to walk somewhere without carrying my "Little Buddy" as I called the 12" by 12" by 4" little box I'd been carrying for days now. It went so quick I almost forgot to thank God for allowing it to be removed. Don't worry, though, I remembered and I praised Him to the high heavens. This is one step closer to home!

I did a call in to the Sunday Morning Worship Service (July 16) and was able to speak over the sound system. I greeted our people and told them how much I miss them. I told them that the doctor wanted to pull the chest tube and to pray that Evona and I would take every step in the will of God. I told the people that there is one step that I know is the perfect will of God and that is the step into our car and on our way home! Hallelujah, glory to God, praise Jesus, can I get a witness? Then I prayed over the service and said "amen." It felt good to be a part of the services. I've been out two Sundays and I miss our church. We had a great day with 467 in attendance and a tremendous spirit in the services! It makes me happy to know our church will remain faithful when I am unable to be there. We have great people at Fellowship Baptist Church.

In 2 Corinthians 1:8–10 Paul talks about a situation he and his fellow workers endured. It was a serious set of circumstances, even to the point of impending death. I love his response and know this type of faith is what God is longing to see in our lives.

> *For we would not, brethren, have you ignorant of our trouble which came to us in Asia, that we were pressed out of measure, above strength, insomuch that we despaired even of life; but we had the sentence of death in ourselves, that we should not trust in ourselves, but in God which raiseth the dead: who delivered us from so great a death, and doth deliver; in whom we trust that he yet deliver us;...*

We are not trusting in ourselves but in God, and "He will yet deliver us!

Praising God and loving life tube free,
Preacher

JULY 18, 2006—
Home At Last!

Yesterday (July 17), our thoracic surgeons came in and gave us the thumbs up to go home. We would not allow ourselves to get excited, though, because our primary doctors must also be comfortable with my going home before they would agree to my release. Our primary doctor came in and after examining me, felt I was ready to be discharged.

By early afternoon we were released from Moffitt and on our way home. To be in our car and riding down Fletcher Avenue was something I'd thought about constantly for a week. Evona reached over and grabbed my hand. "We're going to see our boys and our baby," she said. All I could do was smile.

We went by Target to pick up some gifts from us to our boys. They have done remarkably with such a difficult situation. We wanted to let them know we're proud of them and we love them. Of all things, the boys wanted foot lockers and cordless drills. So, guess what they got? You guessed it…foot lockers and cordless drills. The baby got a huge ball and a hat (he loves hats). Our arrival home was surreal. Our neighbor had arranged that the boys be home and playing upstairs and the baby sleeping. Caleb (our middle boy) met us at the door. He heard us bringing the foot lockers and he thought someone was playing basketball so he came down to check it out. His eyes fixed on me and his face lit up. He said, "Daddy, you're home." He wrapped his arms around me and I melted. Next was Micah, who came down the stairs and threw his arms around me and whispered in my ear, "Thank God you're home." What more can a man ask for than this? A loving family to welcome you home with open arms. But there was still one more to go…Baby Lucas. While the boys began charging their drills and filling their foot lockers, Evona and I rested until the baby woke up. When Evona realized he was awake, she brought him to me and I soaked up his beautiful smile and that sound that is music to my ears…"Daaaaeeeee." We put Lucas's hat on and played with his huge ball until dinner. Then we sat down for family dinner for the first time in two weeks. I looked around our table at my wife, my boys and my baby and thought, *"Am I in heaven?"* After dinner, Evona and the baby and our neighbor went grocery shopping and the boys and I watched "The Three Stooges" and played UNO. When Evona got home, we made sugar cookies. When it was time to put the baby to bed, believe it or not, Lucas wanted me to put him down. We put the boys to bed with prayer. Then Evona and I drank coffee together and talked about how wonderful it was to have our family all sleeping under one roof. Even the dog (William Shakespeare Frink) would not leave my side all night. Frank Capra could not have written this day any more perfect than it was, though I doubt he would include the Stooges. As we drifted off to sleep, we thanked the Lord for blessing us so richly and answering a prayer we'd been praying for a week.

In the book of Ruth when Naomi returned home to Bethlehem-Judah, she was a broken woman from the trials her family had faced in Moab. The people gathered around her and she said, "I went out full, and the Lord hath brought me home again empty: "I must say the opposite: "I went out empty (knowing I was going to chemotherapy and might return sick and fatigued) and the Lord hath brought me home again full." There is nothing that fills your heart quite like your family.

Here are a few lessons Evona and I learned while we were in the hospital:

- Realize that God sometimes has a different plan than we do. His plan is perfect and what we need to do is submit to His perfect will, rather than resist it.
- There is nothing more shocking than a cold potty chair in the middle of the night.
- Be kind to everyone, even if they are not kind to you. They have a story. If you'll ask the right questions and listen, their attitude toward you will change.
- There is no good time to get a shot.
- Never touch the red button!
- Take the down time (x-rays, waiting on doctors) to pray and praise the Lord.

- Never try to blow up one of those rubber surgical gloves when you are low on oxygen.
- Keep your hospital room bright and happy; your atmosphere will affect your attitude.
- That plastic container in the bathroom is not for ice.
- Let the Lord use you to encourage others while you are in the hospital. Even a patient can show patience, love, tenderheartedness and kindness.

Happy to be home,
Preacher

JULY 19, 2006—

Our Dandelion of Faith

(From Mrs. Evona)

Strangely enough, people don't believe me when I tell them I am a country girl at heart. (Maybe it has something to do with being obsessive about always having my lipstick on, or the sixty-something pair of shoes in my closet?) My Grandpa had a farm and we loved to spend time with him. I actually know how to milk a cow and have spent many an hour being chased by chickens while I tried (usually unsuccessfully) to gather eggs.

My parents raised me and my two brothers in Odessa. This was before there was even a grocery store anywhere near. We packed a lunch to go anywhere because it took so long to get where we were going. Our home was on Lake Keystone. My friends were all jealous of my lovely tan when I was a teenager. Little did they know that the wonderful tan came from having to pull weeds from the beach area of the lake every weekend. One of my favorite pastimes as an elementary age kid was playing in the backyard with my little brother, Kevin. Our yard was so much fun to play in. It grew the best weeds. (Please don't tell my parents I said that! Their yard definitely doesn't have weeds now, of course!) My favorite weed was called "Sour Doc" (at least that is what we called it!). This is a weed that tastes good if you chew on the stem. The top part of the stalk has fuzzy little flowers and little black seeds. The reason it was my favorite weed revolves around the fact that it is the job of every big sister to torture her little bother. Kevin would put the "Sour Doc" in his mouth to chew on, and I would sneak up and pull the stem and make all those little flowers and seeds go right into his mouth. You would think after a few times he would learn his lesson and beware. But he wasn't very bright, and I was able to play this game every time he decided to chew on the weed. (I am sure he won't appreciate this story, especially since he is now an "Executive Vice President of Something or Other" at a Web based company! He was obviously a late bloomer!) We also had a lot of dandelion flowers (weeds really) in our yard. These flowers turn into the coolest fluffy powder puff after they mature. We would pick them and blow on them and send all the fluffy seeds all over the yard. There was no way to know where the seeds flew to until a new patch of "weed flowers" would grow. Our neighbor didn't appreciate our love for blowing the powder puff, because many times the seeds landed in his yard!

In 1 Thessalonians, Paul is writing a letter to a church with a wonderful testimony of faith. Chapter one verse three says, *"Remembering without ceasing your work of faith, and labour of love, and patience of hope in our Lord Jesus Christ, in the sight of God and our Father."* This church had a love for others and a faith in Christ that was put into practice. We see the words "work, labour and patience." These are all action verbs. Their testimony was one of faith in action. Paul commends them for being examples to those in their immediate area and around the world. Verse 8 is such a blessing. *"For from you sounded out the word of the Lord not only in Macedonia and Achaia, but also in every place your faith to God-ward is spread abroad; so that we need not to speak any thing."* They were such true examples of faith that Paul and Silas didn't even have to tell about them, their testimony spread on its own. Just like the dandelion after it is blown and the seeds fly all over, there is no way to know just where or how far the seeds have gone; our faith can be just as far reaching. So many times we only hear the negative side of this principle, and justifiably so. Our words can cause much hurt and damage when spoken in anger and haste. However, what an overwhelming motivator it is to know we as Christians can impact the world with a consistent faith put into action. We have an awesome responsibility to show other Christians, and unsaved people, that the hope we have is based on a faith in God that can move mountains. The seeds of the dandelion fly all over carried by the wind. Our seeds of faith can fly all over carried by the Holy Spirit. You may never know how deciding to "Choose Faith" in your own life will affect others. Sometimes you don't get to see where the seeds land and you may never get to enjoy the actual flower. However, the effects are still there. The seeds may be planted in your children's lives, in others that see your attitude as you deal with your own personal valley, or in the life of someone who has just heard about your faith. We can spread faith all over by "our work of faith, and labour of love, and patience of hope in our Lord Jesus Christ." Take your dandelion of faith and blow, knowing that God will use you to inspire others to rise up and "Choose Faith."

We are basking in the comfort of finally being home together. Yesterday was very restful, not having to run from one place to another. We ate and napped and ate some more! Preacher is doing well, getting his strength back and resting. He was not too tired, however, to plan a lively game of charades. The kids thoroughly enjoyed watching me try to act out "Q-tip the hamster, running on his wheel" and Preacher acting out "dancing ballerina." Life is good.

Striving to blow my dandelion of faith,
Mrs. Evona

July 20, 2006—
"We Choose Faith Rally" Planned

Some weeks back, the Lord put an idea for a special meeting at our church on my heart. I felt the Lord impressing me that this battle our family has faced with cancer and our daily decision to choose faith was not only our battle and our decision to choose faith, but our entire church's. We at Fellowship Baptist Church are a family. First Corinthians 12:26 says it best when it speaks of the church as a "body" and it says, "*And whether one member suffer, all the members suffer with it . . .*" Then I thought of all the people around the world who are praying for our family and our church and their commitment to "choose faith" with us for my healing.

The special meeting will be called the "We Choose Faith Rally." It will let everyone who is listening know that as a family and as a church, we have chosen faith for God's healing. I asked the Lord whom we should have as our speakers and I felt impressed to invite four men: Dr. Johnny Pope, Dr. Eric Capaci, Dr. Steve Roberson and Dr. John Bishop. I knew it would be impossible to get these men on short notice and in the same meeting. I asked Dr. Steve Roberson if he would consider helping me and he did! He got all four men for August 6, 8 and 9, 2006. Dr. Pope will preach for us Sunday Evening Worship, August 6; Dr. Bishop and Dr. Capaci will preach on Tuesday, August 8 and Dr. Roberson and Dr. Bishop will preach on Wednesday, August 9. These four men of God are some of the finest preachers in America today. This promises to be one of the greatest revival meetings we have ever had as a church. I am so blessed to be a part of something I feel God is going to use so powerfully. Please pray for each night of the meeting and if you are in the area, please come and be a part of it!

There will be a special prayer meeting at Fellowship Baptist for my healing on July 22, 2006 at 6:30 P.M. I am told that over fifty preachers and many of their people are coming. I know our church family will be there also. I cannot tell you how this makes me feel. To know that such a group of God's people will unite in prayer in God's house for me and my family is overwhelming. The Lord is too good to me.

Our devotions began today in Psalm 42:1: "*As the hart panteth after the water brooks, so panteth my soul after thee, O God.*" My thoughts go back to the hospital when I was struggling to breathe because of the collapsed lung, and they put me on oxygen. I have never struggled to breathe until this lung cancer. As they put the oxygen in my nose, I felt a sudden relief. Before that I was panting and struggling for air, but then the oxygen instantly gave me relief. The Lord said the hart (deer) pants after the water in the brook. He is thirsty and he knows his relief is at the brook. He pants the whole way there until finally he arrives and drinks in the refreshing and sustaining water. The verse says that we must pant (desire above all other desires) after God to refresh and sustain our souls. I needed that oxygen and until I received it, my body was without relief. We need the Lord and until we desire Him over all other desires, our souls will remain without relief.

When will we realize that God is the only One who can fill the needs of our soul? We pant after so many things, yet we find them empty and non-fulfilling. It is God and His Son Jesus Who alone can ultimately fill the longing of our soul.

God fills the need of the soul for salvation through Jesus Christ's sacrifice on the cross for our sins. Faith in Christ as God's Son and His work on the cross and His resurrection from the dead brings salvation to the soul with its by-product—eternal life (John 3:16).

God fills the need of the soul for a fulfilling life through a daily walk with Christ in prayer and God's Word and the filling of the Holy Spirit (yielding daily control to God's Spirit). He promises abundant life (John 10:10) and blessings through God's fullness (Ephesians 5:18–6:4).

God fills the need of the soul for comfort through the Holy Spirit of God. The Holy Spirit is the third member of the Trinity who comes to dwell permanently in every believer from their salvation until we meet the Lord (1 Corinthians 3:16; 6:19, 20; Ephesians 1:13–14). The Holy Spirit's other name is the "Comforter" (John 14:26–27) and He will come alongside and give you comfort as you face life's trials and valleys (John 16:5—7).

We need to get to the place where our souls pant after God like I panted after oxygen and the deer panted after water. It is a spiritual thirst that we need every day. When we realize that God is our only source of relief and satisfaction for our souls, we will desire Him above all other desires.

We had a good day as far as my health-building. I am eating a lot, walking and exercising, resting and getting the good medicine of being with my family. I get fatigued as the day goes on so I have to pace myself. Pray that my feet will stop swelling and I will overcome this chest cold I left the hospital with. These are important factors in being ready for the next chemo treatment (July 24). We love you all!

Panting after God,
Preacher

JULY 21, 2006—
Pecking with the Chickens or Soaring with the Eagles?
(From Mrs. Evona)

For some time now, I have been worried about a medical condition I have. Due to the seriousness of Pastor's illness, I have put off following up on my issue. However, after a great doctor's visit for Pastor and a few days down time, I feel able to tackle my problem. OK, here it is. I talk to myself...a lot! I have for most of my life. Many people have tried to make me feel better by telling me that it is fine to talk to yourself, but when you start answering yourself, you are in trouble. Well folks, I am in trouble.

Maybe many of you can relate to my problem. Don't be embarrassed, let it out. Tell the world. Believe me; it makes you feel so much better. Well, it doesn't really make you feel better, but doesn't that psychological stuff sound smart? If you are like me, talking to myself has not been a big worry. I am not the one who will have to deal with me when or if I truly go crazy. It will be my three wonderful, sweet, smelly boys who will have the problem. I will be happy as a clam (because I will be crazy!). Now, being the mother of three boys (who I lovingly call my "smelly monsters") has given me a new perspective on this issue. I have it on good authority (the two oldest smelly monsters) that if you are a boy, having a slightly strange mom is cool. So I am in great shape. I do feel sorry for those of you who don't have boys, though!

However, I have great news for all of us. I have been reading in Psalms a lot lately and found something very interesting. King David talked to himself all the time. Now imagine that. A musician, warrior, king of a very large nation and a man after God's own heart talked to himself. Well, aren't we in good company? Better yet, he even answered himself many times. In Psalm 43:5 David asks himself a question and then answers in the same verse. *"Why art thou cast down, O my soul? And why art thou disquieted within me? Hope in God: for I shall yet praise him, who is the health of my countenance, and my God."*

Have you ever felt like David? We can all get discouraged and stressed.

This is when the self pep-talk begins. It sounds something like this: "What is wrong with you? You know God is still in control. Has He ever let you down? See? Don't get all worked up over stuff you can't change. Rest in God's peace."

On and on it can go. This is what David was doing in this verse. He was taking an honest look at his heart and acknowledging weakness. The words "cast down and disquieted" mean discouraged and stressed. Sound familiar? Yep, me too! Having normal human emotions is OK because that is the way God made us. How we deal with these emotions is what God is concerned with.

I have a theory. Are you ready? Now bear with me, I have truly given this much thought (even though it may not sound like it!). We are like birds. There it is—my epiphany. I know, you really do think I am crazy now. When trouble comes we react like different types of birds. Some of us are like the ostrich. We see the problem and then bury our heads in the sand and hope it goes away. Now, believe me, I am not criticizing you. I see many benefits to this approach. But unfortunately, most of the time when you finally have to come up for air, the problem is still there or even larger. Others of us are like the common blackbird. We swoop and squawk and make things much worse than they were to begin with. There are those of you sweet, even-tempered doves who just stand back and let whatever happens happen. Even if the other birds eat all your seed, you just wait and let it all work itself out. Now, I tend to be more like the messy chicken. I make a lot of noise and rush around pecking and trying to fix things myself. (I feel sorry for you if you are married to a chicken! Just ask the preacher.)

Strangely enough, God's Word tells us which bird's behavior to emulate. Isaiah 40:31: *"But they that wait on the Lord shall renew their strength; they shall mount up with wings like eagles, they shall run and not be weary, and they shall walk and not faint."* It sounds a lot better to be soaring with the eagles than hiding with the ostrich, screeching with the blackbird, ignoring things with the dove or pecking around like a chicken with its head cut off. We can regain our strength, soar with the big birds and not give in to the stress. David put it so clearly when he finally got to the good part of his pep talk: *"Hope in God: for I shall yet praise him, who is the health of my countenance, and my God."* (Psalm 43:5b).

So many people have asked us "How can you choose faith?" My answer is always the same: "There are two choices, and faith has a much better outcome!" I am a "do-it-yourself girl." I am always starting some project or another. Many times I bite off more than I can chew. (Please don't bring this up with the Preacher; it is a sore subject!) The other day I decided to move the large antique dresser I was refinishing into the garage by myself. I tried and tried to no avail. Finally, I had to ask for help because I could not do it on my own. That is what we are dealing with as we go through this valley. It has nothing to do with our own strength "choosing faith." It is all about knowing we need help and going to the One who can give us His strength to do something we could not do on our own. It is not a difficult decision. We can not do it ourselves, so we have asked for help. David said, *"Hope in God..."* It is not hard to have faith in Someone who made the world with the spoken word, made our bodies and as it says in verse 5 of Psalm 43, *"who is the health of my countenance."* Who better to trust?

We had a wonderful day yesterday. Preacher's doctor's visit went very well. All his blood work is back to normal and the chest x-ray looked good. The wounds where the chest tubes were placed are healing nicely. The doctor asked us to wait a few days and let Preacher get stronger and then take his next round of chemotherapy. It is scheduled for next Thursday, July 27. We are praising God for good news. We left Moffitt as quickly as possible after the good news so that no one could read any new reports or order more tests!

Two chickens trusting God to help us soar like eagles,
Mrs. Evona

July 22, 2006—
What's in Your Closet?

First Peter 5:5b says: "...*and be clothed with humility*..." This is not a garment we run to our closet and throw on with excitement so that people will admire what we're wearing throughout the day. In fact, most of us rarely don this garment until the Lord dresses us in it through various "pride-pounding" situations He allows to get our attention when we need an ego adjustment.

It seems that God uses hospitals to humble me. I have had more humbling experiences through hospital visits to our church members than just about anything else.

One day, Evona and I went to visit a sweet little lady that was attending our church. When we got to the room, she was not in her bed but her neighboring patient was sitting in a chair beside her bed. My thoughts were, *I've come this far to see this lady and I don't want to have to drive back. Besides, she will be very encouraged after I talk to her. I'll ask this other lady to help me find her.* (A bit prideful, don't you think?) As I went to the other lady, I could feel Evona's grip on my arm tighten. I ignored it and asked, "Do you know where the other lady in this bed went. I came to see her and I'd like to track her down." The lady, now red-faced, replied, "Uh, no...I don't... she's gone...uh...I'm not sure..." Evona's grip now was as tight as a boa constrictor. I thought, *What is wrong with my wife? Doesn't she want me to do the work of the Lord?* I asked the lady, "Do you know if she went for tests, or when she'll be back?" The poor woman in the chair answered, "I...uh...I really don't know...I'm sorry . . ." Then like someone snatching a sweater on sale amidst a mob of greedy shoppers on Christmas Eve, Evona whisked me out of the room.

"What is your deal?" I demanded.

"Did you notice what the problem was in there?" Evona replied.

I shrugged and said, "I was trying to get some help from that lady in the chair."

Evona breathed a sigh of frustration, "That was not a regular chair she was in, it was a potty chair!"

"Well, how am I supposed to know that?" I asked with a shrug.

"Maybe the Charmin roll in her hand! That seemed like a tip-off to me. I snatched you out of there before you gave her a tract with the church name on it or one of your cards."

I left wearing "humility" from head to toe.

Another time, I visited the hospital with two of our men from church. We were going to see a man on the ninth floor and were waiting for the elevator. My thoughts were, *I'll show these two men how to make a hospital call the Lee Roberson way: "Be Positive, Be Brief, Be Gone."* The elevator opened and probably the largest person I have ever seen was being transported to the ninth floor as well. You know how you say these little catch phrases and you don't even realize you've said them? I said, "Is there room for us in there?" The two men from church were mortified. We got on the elevator and they didn't look up for nine floors. I feared that the "plumpatious" patient was going to eat me for nine floors because of my insensitive remark. We got through our visit and the men with me never asked to go with me again. Another dress-up day with "humility."

One last time, I went to see one of our seniors who was so sick she could barely lift her head from her pillow. She smiled and said in her sweet old lady voice, "Oh, Brother Cliff, thank you for coming. I've been so lonely." Feeling like the only one who had compassion in the world and wanting to make the visit a big success, I said, "Oh, look, you got some flowers." I pushed the little tray over towards her and she mustered all her strength to lift herself up and see the flowers. "Oh, how pretty. I didn't know I had flowers!" As I pushed the flowers up to her bedside, I realized from the card that they had been delivered to the person in the next bed, who was not in the room at the time. Now what do you do? Do you destroy the card? Not good publicity for a preacher. Do you splash water on it and feign ignorance? Not very honest for anyone claiming to be a Christian. So, I swallowed my pride and put on the extremely bright garment of "humility" and admitted I'd made a mistake. It was the worst sight ever to see our dear saint slump back into her bed. I think she might have strangled me with her oxygen tube if she'd had the strength.

So, here I find myself in the hospital during this stay in my lovely hospital gown, wearing my support stockings to reduce the swelling in my feet, applying cherry Chapstick to my lips and looking for moisturizer for my head. I'm either extremely in touch with my feminine side, or I am wearing the garment of "humility" that the Lord has provided! I'm glad that He did. No one can humble us quite like the Lord. He sees our hearts and He knows when we think and act in pride. I've always prided myself in my good health, my personal strength and my image as "the guy with no problems." Cancer took care of all that! This two-week hospital stay stripped me of my pride and brought me to the place where all I could do was pray to God for help. There were times when I had no appetite and had to pray that I could eat. There were times when I had to endure some things that took my dignity away. And I still endure two of the side effects of the chemo: a hearing loss and neuropathy in my hands and feet. This is part of the Lord's humbling me so that I will realize I am nothing without God but I can do all things through Christ which strengtheneth me. God cannot bless pride, but He always blesses humility. James 4:6b says, "...*God resisteth the proud, but giveth grace unto the humble.*"

There is another way to forsake our pride and replace it with humility. Remember the scripture said, "...*be clothed with humility* . . ." (1 Peter 5:5). In verse 6 it says, "*Humble yourselves therefore under the mighty hand of God, that he may exalt you in due time.*" Awake each morning and go to your prayer closet and ask God to purge you of all pride and clothe you with humility. How much easier it is to start in the right clothes each day than force the Lord to redress you through His pride-breaking means. There is grace beyond measure waiting for us when we humble ourselves before God. Start out the day wearing the right outfit and you won't be able to count the blessings God sends your way.

Yesterday (July 21) was a great family day. We spent the day together and enjoyed each other immensely. I am feeling better than I have in weeks. Tonight the church will sponsor a prayer meeting for me. It starts at 6:30 P.M. and everyone is invited. I am honored that folks would come and pray for me, my family and our church.

Determined to be clothed with humility,
Preacher

July 23, 2006—
And When They Had Prayed

"For where two or three are gathered together in my name, there am I in the midst of them."

Matthew 18:20

"And when they had prayed, the place was shaken where they were assembled together; and they were all filled with the Holy Ghost, and they spake the word of God with boldness."

Acts 4:31

Last night (July 22) there was a prayer meeting for me, my family and our church. We had almost 400 people fill our church, which included thirty-seven pastors from other churches, their church members, friends and our own people at Fellowship Baptist. One Pastor friend, Gene Gouge, drove from North Carolina to be in the prayer meeting. It was overwhelming to have so many people come to pray for my health and healing. Not to mention all God's people who are praying for me around the United States and the world. The Lord always hears the prayers of His people. The Lord always answers the prayers of His people. Jeremiah 33:3 says, *"Call unto me, and I will answer thee, and shew thee great and mighty things, which thou knowest not."*

The prayer meeting began with the inspiring hymn, "Faith Is the Victory." I came out after this and greeted the people and thanked them for coming. I gave them a short summary of how this journey began for our family and how the Lord had changed our initial reaction to my diagnosis from shock and fear to faith in God. I told the crowd that our family as well as our church had adopted a slogan— *"We Choose Faith"*—and that we are believing God for my complete healing.

Some of our men opened in prayer and blessed my soul. God has been so good to us in sending men who can preach to our church before this cancer ever struck my body. These same men are filling the pulpit with messages that are blessing our people and I thank God for providing them.

After this, our founding pastor, Brother Scotty Drake, introduced two men who would bless us in a very personal way. One of them is Pastor Dick Riley, of the Immanuel Baptist Church in Ft. Myers, Florida. Brother Riley is 70 years old and has been in the ministry over 40 years. Fourteen years ago he was diagnosed with cancer and given 6 months to live. He went through chemotherapy and has had the cancer return three different times in different places in his body. Each time God used chemotherapy to put his body into remission. Brother Riley said that he would ask God to allow him to finish projects at the church, such as completing a building or paying off the church debt. God allowed him to complete each one! He turned to me and said, "Cliff, get you a project and go to town!" I looked at my wife and my boys and I thought, *I have a project right there…raising my family and being a godly husband and father.* Then I noticed one of our men was pointing to the picture we have on the wall of the church of our future auditorium, which we plan to build as God allows. What greater projects than these two: building a godly family, and building a growing church.

Next, Brother Scotty brought up Mark Campbell, pastor of the Bible Baptist Church in Bradenton, Florida. Brother Campbell is 36 years old and 12 years ago was serving as a youth director, with a three-year-old and a one-month-old baby. He was diagnosed with cancer all over his body. He went through radiation, chemotherapy and surgery to remove a tumor the size of a grapefruit. Today, he is a pastor and he is "cancer free." Both Evona and I wept as we thought of the day when I could stand and testify of God's healing power and give Him the glory for making me "cancer free!"

The prayer meeting closed with people gathering around the altar while three pastors prayed, which included Brother Gene Gouge, Brother Mickey Carter and Brother Dick Riley to close. It was a tremendous moving of God's Spirit and Evona and I left both encouraged and filled with faith.

There is no way to adequately express our family's and church's gratitude for your prayers. We believe this is the key to my three-fold request of the Lord being granted. I have asked God to allow me to grow old with my wife, to raise my three boys into men of God and to pastor Fellowship

Baptist Church until Jesus comes back. Pray with us diligently about this. Claim the verse God gave us for my healing with us (Psalm 30:2–3). God is able to do this and our prayers are the key. Our associate pastor said tonight, "Through this satanic attack on our preacher, God has gotten our attention. Now it's time to pray and get God's attention."

Grateful for your prayers,
Preacher and Mrs. Evona

∞ ∞ ∞

July 24, 2006—
I'm Back!

I rejoice in being able to return to the house of God yesterday (July 23). Even though it has only been two weeks that I've been out, it seems like a month. There are so many things that I missed. I missed our lively music and the sweet spirit that flows through our church. I missed our people and the love I see in their eyes. I missed hearing my wife play the piano. I missed praying in the Lord's house. There's just something about praying amidst God's people in His house. I missed preaching in the pulpit, although I did not preach this Sunday. That privilege was reserved for our founding pastor, Brother Scotty Drake.

We dedicated this past Sunday to honor Brother Scotty and his wife, Mrs. Barbara. God used Brother Scotty to start Fellowship Baptist Church in December of 1984. Mrs. Barbara was right there by his side building our church into the great ministry it is today. The Lord blessed us immensely under Brother Scotty's leadership. We saw hundreds of souls saved, new converts baptized, lives changed and families find a church home. We saw a great missions endeavor (H.E.L.P. Ministries) founded, which sends millions of dollars around the world to spread the gospel. We love this dear couple and could never adequately thank them or express how deeply we are indebted to them. They are like a second dad and mom to me, and I personally want to thank Brother Scotty and Mrs. Barbara Drake for pouring their lives into mine and loving me through many difficult "growing pains." Our church also wishes to thank Brother Scotty and Mrs. Barbara for leading us in the right direction for 11 years and giving of themselves to make Fellowship one of the greatest churches in our state! *We love you!*

We went back to church tonight. Again, it was wonderful to be in the house of the Lord. The music lifted my soul and Brother Dick Riley, our good friend from Ft. Myers, preached the evening sermon. The title was "The Reason You're Sick Determines When You'll Get Well." Brother Riley spoke about sin in our lives and how God will sometimes use sickness to bring us to repentance (1 Corinthians 11:29–30). Then he spoke about

God allowing our sickness to humble us that we may be used for His glory (2 Corinthians 12:7). Thirdly, Brother Riley spoke about God's allowing sickness in our lives so that He might give us comfort to comfort others who are walking the same valley as we have walked (2 Corinthians 1:4). Finally, he spoke about how God permits the devil to afflict us even when we are right with Him to purify us and use us in a greater way than He ever has before (Job chapters 1, 2 and 23:10). It was just what we needed as a church.

Today we have to go to Moffitt to get an injection to build up my hemoglobin. Then Thursday (July 27) is the next scheduled chemotherapy. This chemo cocktail will be about 3 percent less potent thus minimizing the side effects on my body. Pray for the treatment and pray I will be able to enjoy my family and preach on Sunday.

Fighting this cancer through God's power,
Preacher

∽ ∽ ∽

July 25, 2006—

Lusting for Light

"*Thy word is a lamp unto my feet, and a light unto my path.*" (Psalm 119:105) This week my father-in-law shared with my wife some thoughts about this wonderful, well-known verse from the longest chapter in our Bible. He pointed out that a "lamp" is for our day-to-day use and that a "light" is speaking more about our future. In both cases, we need light and in both cases the light comes from God's Word.

During one of the hurricanes a few years back, we found ourselves without power for an extended period of time. This meant no water; no way to cook (this is considered a blessing from heaven in some houses…not ours, of course); no air-conditioning (this should be considered criminal in Florida); no television (can you imagine?); no pump to keep the pool from turning green; no washer and dryer to keep the boy's clothes from turning green (after they peel their clothes from their sweaty, smelly bodies, a process begins similar to stagnation and an immediate wash and dry is called for); no blow dryer and curling iron (which is a "National Emergency" by the third day) and last but not least…NO LIGHT! This turned out to be one of the worst consequences of losing our power. We weren't as prepared as we should've been. We had four flashlights, only one of which had batteries and we had a double-pack of apple cinnamon candles. The house smelled great, even though it was like being in a cave. You can only entertain the boys with a spelunking outing once before they get tired of banging their ankles on barstools and end tables. We could hear across the way the noise of a generator. We peered out our window to see one of our neighbors on the next street basking in their AC, enjoying microwave popcorn as they watched a DVD and going wherever their hearts desired in a fully-lit house. "That's disgusting!" I said, to which Evona replied, "Those people should be shot." This, of course, was three days of no power talking; we repented later, I promise. The problem was not our neighbors (even though they did seem to flaunt their possession of power during our power outage); the problem was that we had not prepared adequately for this storm and the loss of power we would experience. We found ourselves lusting for light in our darkened abode.

The Word of God prepares us to handle life's challenges, whether they are day by day or regarding our future. The light of wisdom God provides us for these areas of our lives is exactly what we need to prepare ourselves for that particular day or for our unknown future. God is omniscient (all-knowing) and He sees everything ahead of us. He will use His Word time and time again to show us how we need to prepare for today, tomorrow and the rest of our lives. Second Peter 1:3 says, *"According as his divine power hath given unto us all things that pertain to life and godliness, through the knowledge of him that hath called us to glory and virtue."* It's all there for us so that when we find ourselves "in the dark," we will have plugged into God's light before the storm hits, or whatever it is that surrounds us with darkness.

In many ways, Evona and I were prepared for cancer, as far as the future is concerned. God had planted our feet on a firm foundation so that we were not shaken in our salvation and other important core beliefs. We did lack preparation, though, when it came to dealing with cancer day by day. I think that both of us got as much light as we needed from God's Word to fashion our Sunday School lessons and my sermons. We have come to realize that we not only need the light for our future, we need the lamp for each step of our daily walk. I have had several days of pain and shortness of breath. This brings with it confusion and discouragement. We have relied on God's light to guide us through managing the pain and bring us to the place where I can say today that I feel much better and feel fairly confident God will allow me to preach on Sunday. I wouldn't trade "this little light of mine" for all the lighthouses in the world.

Keeping our lights trimmed and burning,
Preacher and Mrs. Evona

July 26, 2006—
A Changed Focus

We had a wonderful day yesterday (July 25). We went to see our family, the Greens, across the bay where they are vacationing. It is a beach condo with a pool. The boys and the baby loved both the pool and the beach. The baby ate a lot of sand. I guess you could say, "He savored the beach." The boys played in the pool, went surfboarding at the beach and had a squirt gun fight (I wish they had waited until all the other condo guests had cleared out).

I was able to get in the pool because Evona put water-proof band aids over my chest tube incisions. Both incisions are healing nicely but we don't want to take a chance and get chlorine in them. My presence in the sun began a discussion about my head and how we must be careful not to let it get sunburned. My wife and my cousin Lisa imagined what I would look like with my white, skinny body and a sunburned bald head. My wife suggested I would look like a match stick. My cousin suggested I would look like a cherry lollypop. Other suggestions from this "hilarious" duet were a thermometer, a stop sign and a plunger. I swam away from these comic queens and spent my time more wisely squirting water at others through the space in my front teeth.

After a lot of fun and some good exercise in the pool, I went back up to the condo to rest. One thing I am not used to is the fatigue that chemotherapy causes. I find that I must take naps each day. I also have limited strength in my legs and upper body. This is probably due to being in a hospital bed so long. I did not start walking until the second week because I was so sick the first week. I don't like to be restricted in my activities. This has been hard to accept. It also bothers me when I cannot help and my wife has to do things I have always done. We are working hard each day to get bodily exercise to build my strength. I'm still drinking my Boost and trying to take in as much protein as I can. Between these things we pray I will be strong enough for the next chemo treatment on July 27 (this Thursday).

I still have some lingering effects from the last chemotherapy. My hearing is still muffled by thousands of katydids or a house alarm going off in my head. Sometimes I imagine I'm walking under beautiful oaks when the katydids visit and then when the house alarm goes off, I imagine a thief broke in the house and I zap him with a tazer gun. It's a nice diversion. I also have neuropathy in my hands, which makes them cramp up at times and get suddenly cold, then suddenly warm. It's kind of like having mood hands, if you remember the "mood rings" we used to have in school. They were supposed to change colors with your mood. My hands don't change colors (I'm grateful for that) but they change temperatures. I haven't decided what mood I'm in when they change but I'll let you know. I thank God that my side effects are as minimal as they are. Some folks have extreme nausea (of which the Lord spared me…praise His name!) Others have long-standing effects on major organs. God was very good to me through this, even though we had the ongoing problem with the air leak in my lungs. There are so many people who deal with pain all the time. I have had no pain to speak of. There is a man our family met at Moffitt who will be in the hospital for three months getting ready for a bone marrow transplant. How can I complain when others are dealing with so much more pain than I?

Philippians 2:4 says, "*Look not every man on his own things, but every man also on the things of others.*" I believe if we can force our attention off ourselves and on to others, God will make our burdens lighter. A very important thing I learned while in the hospital was that people are longing to be heard, and those who are willing to listen will find God's relief through focusing on others. There were several folks at Moffitt who were not engaging and seemed detached. I sensed there were problems beneath their stoic exteriors, and God gave me some questions to ask them that prompted them to tell me their stories, which were heartbreaking and sad. Once they had shared with me the heartaches behind their public façade, I would promise to pray for them and there was such a bond between us. God really does use others to get our eyes off self and on to the needs of people. I have often recommended to a grieving widow to get involved in a ministry that will allow her to reach out to others who are hurting. We have shared this scripture with you before but it is so appropriate: 2 Corinthians 1:4: *"Who comforteth us in all our tribulation, that we may be able to comfort them which are in any trouble, by the comfort wherewith we ourselves are comforted of God."*

I will never forget the change that God wrought not only in others, but in myself, as a result of getting my focus right. It doesn't have to take a hospital bed to accomplish this in your life.

Looking on the things of others,
Preacher

∞ ∞ ∞

July 27, 2006—
Power Tools, Even for Girls!
(From Mrs. Evona)

When we decided to move out by the church, we sold our home and purchased property. After many setbacks and dead ends, the Lord led us to self-contract our home. This was only accomplished through the help of several of our loving friends with backgrounds in building. During this time, Preacher and I learned that many overwhelming and seemingly insurmountable projects can be accomplished by diligence and a lot of white caulk. (The workers taught me that most mistakes can be covered up with a large amount of caulk!!) This love of "doing it ourselves" has carried over to help us through building the church buildings and helping friends on their homes. When a friend of mine started on her home, she and I had lofty plans for her custom tile work. After much teasing and many "helpful manly tips," we completed all her tile work. The excitement of a job finished prompted me to want to branch out. I decided that trim work looked rewarding. The problem I faced was talking someone into actually teaching me to use the large miter saw that was needed to do really nice trim work. One carpenter friend (to remain unnamed, but he knows who he is) actually laughed at me when I asked for help! The response I got (and am still getting) is that girls should not use such powerful tools. (Something about not being able to walk and chew gum, and needing all ten fingers for playing the piano have also been mentioned.) I keep fussing but so far have not found anyone willing to take on the responsibility of teaching me to use such a big, bad saw. "Girls should not use such powerful tools," my foot! They are just afraid I am going to show them up with my lovely trim work!

This little controversy has reminded me how important it is to use the right tool for the job. There is no use trying to use a hacksaw to make the beautiful angled cuts needed to trim in a window or a door. You might be able to make the cut, but believe me no one wants the results actually hanging in her home. We have a very powerful tool given to us (even the girls!)

by God—prayer! Prayer is the way we can come before the Almighty and talk to the King of kings and know he will hear and answer us. Hebrews 4:16 says, "*Let us therefore come boldly unto the throne of grace, that we may obtain mercy, and find grace to help in time of need.*" God wants us to come to Him with the boldness that comes from knowing that we are his loved and cherished children. He looks at us and sees Christ's righteousness. Second Corinthians 5:21 says, "*For he hath made him [Christ] to be sin for us, who knew no sin; that we might be made the righteousness of God in him.*" What a blessing to know God trusts us with such a powerful tool. God allows us to not only use this tool, He promises to hear and answer our prayers. Job 22:27: "*Thou shalt make thy prayer unto him, and he shall hear thee.*" In Psalm 34 it speaks directly to those of us who need to use our power tool of prayer because of our broken hearts and the valleys we are facing. Psalm 34:17–18: "*The righteous cry, and the Lord heareth, and delivereth them out of all their troubles. The Lord is nigh unto them that are of a broken heart;…*"

Even if circumstances seem to set limits on your ability to complete the job set before you (your own trial), know that God has given you the "power tool" of prayer. You can reach heaven and acquire the strength needed to finish your task (even those of us of the more beautiful gender!)

Brother David Catlin shared with us in Wednesday Night Prayer Meeting Joshua 3:4–7: "*…that ye may know the way by which ye must go: for ye have not passed this way heretofore. And Joshua said unto the people, sanctify yourselves: for to morrow the Lord will do wonders among you… that they may know that, as I was with Moses, so I will be with thee.*" He challenged us as a church family to sanctify ourselves (confess our sins) and pray that tomorrow (chemotherapy treatment day) the Lord will do wonders among us. What a great time to power up our tool of prayer and boldly come to the throne of grace asking God to do wonders among us.

As you read this we are probably in the middle of our second chemotherapy treatment. Pray that the medicine will target the cancer cells and kill them all! We are also praying that this mixture will have no side effects and Preacher will be able to be in the pulpit on this coming Sunday.

Using my power tool of prayer,
Mrs. Evona

July 28, 2006—
Let's Be Childish

We praise God for the successful chemotherapy treatment that I was able to take yesterday, July 27. My anti-nausea medicine worked wonderfully and I had no sickness. Dr. Simon changed the chemo cocktail from Cisplatin/Taxotere to Carboplatin/Taxotere. The previous treatment was very hard on my body and caused complications that we can not afford to have repeated. The new medicine is in the same family but doesn't have the extensive side effects that were so detrimental to my body. I was so surprised and pleased when the nurse told me that after only 2½ hours my treatment was finished. We were expecting to be there for around 5 hours like the last time. Due to the change in medicine, this treatment went much faster and did not require the time consuming IV fluids. I felt so good after my treatment that we went to the food court and ate lunch together, celebrating a successful chemo treatment. (I wanted oriental fried rice for the thousandth time since my illness!)

In Matthew 18:1–4, Jesus uses a child to teach us an important truth.

At the same time came the disciples to Jesus, saying, Who is the greatest in the kingdom of heaven? And Jesus called a little child unto him, and set him in the midst of them, and said, Verily I say unto you, except you be converted, and become as little children, ye shall not enter into the kingdom of heaven. Whosoever therefore shall humble himself as this little child, the same is the greatest in the kingdom of heaven.

Christ is teaching us that greatness in heaven comes only when we humble ourselves as little children. We saw this truth in action when we received a call from Brother Mike Higgins of Hope Children's Home. This is a ministry very close and dear to our hearts. We as a church support their work and personally have spent much time preaching and ministering at the home with the kids. Brother Mike, the director of the home, called and shared how concerned the children have been over my recent condition. They have continually prayed for me, my wife and especially my boys. He relayed that the kids wanted to not only pray, but also help out in some other way. Several times a year the home has a large yard sale and the proceeds go for some extracurricular fun activity for the children. This year they prayed and felt led to take the money from the yard sale coming up this weekend and give it to our family. We were so overwhelmed at the faith in action of these prayer warriors. It was such a blessing to see the kids learning to focus on others and allow God to work through them to be a blessing.

Another lesson we learned through children is their uninhibited faith. Recently we received an email from one of our church ladies (Dr. Laurie Barclay) relaying that our missionary to Ethiopia, Brother Elijah, has been praying for my healing with his son, Stephen (who is six years old). Stephen's prayer each night is "I am going to bed now God, but please heal Pastor Cliff." Every night after this prayer, Stephen asks his father, "Is Pastor Cliff healed yet?" This past week he became ill with the flu. Brother Elijah reminded Stephen that they needed to pray that he would get well. Stephen agreed but said, "I want to pray for Pastor Cliff's healing first!" The dear member who relayed this story brought Stephen before our church during Wednesday Prayer Meeting. That night our church prayed for little Stephen. By the time Dr. Laurie got home, she had an email waiting that said Stephen was so much better he was up and about and back in school. Just like Job was healed when he prayed for his friends, we can see this same faith demonstrated in young Stephen.

Our hearts were so moved to see this same faith in our middle son Caleb. In family prayer time he closed his prayer saying, "Thank you, God, that my daddy is almost cancer free!" We can all learn from the humble sacrifice and uninhibited faith of children. Oh, that our hearts would embrace these "childish" truths.

Seeking to come as little children,
Preacher and Mrs. Evona

JULY 29, 2006—
Enduring the Thorns to Enjoy the Rose

Yesterday (July 28) was one of the best days I've had. I felt great! I had a day of much activity, good nutrition intake and best of all...it was spent with my family. I did have to get an injection at Moffitt to boost my white cells. The injection on Monday (July 24) was to boost my red cells. Why don't they get these guys together and make them pink cells and we can just get one shot? There has to be at least one thorn on every rose and shots have always been thorns to me. I think if you enjoy shots, you need help. I have to take a blood-thinning injection every night. Evona administers it to me. I still can't tell if she enjoys it or not, but the same rule holds true—if you enjoy giving shots, you need help. All in all, it was a wonderful day.

There was another "thorn" that I experienced every day (all 14 days) that I was in the hospital, and that was the daily chest x-ray. The chest x-ray was on the schedule each day, but I never knew when it was to take place. It could be early in the morning, later in the morning, in the early afternoon or even late in the day. There was no advance warning. I would hear them say, "Transport is here to take you to your x-ray." I then had to get up and get in the wheelchair and head to the x-ray lab. Most of the time, I would wait in the hallway outside of the lab for them to get ready for me (i.e. finish their coffee). If I didn't take a blanket I could get cold in the hallway and sometimes I drifted off to sleep. One morning a Moffitt worker nudged me and asked if I was alright. I replied, "I'm fine," but I thought, *What...the sight of a pale, bald man slumped over in a wheelchair bothers you?* The x-rays were more difficult at first because I was very weak on my feet and we had to carry a portion of the chest tube with us. There were two positions I had to get in for my x-rays: a full chest shot from the back and a side shot with my arms held out straight in front of me. One day the chest x-ray was very early and I was exceptionally weak from being in bed all night long. It was all I could do to get in and out of the wheelchair and then go over and make the two positions to be x-rayed. When I got back to my chair I was out of energy and so glad it was over. The x-ray tech went to develop the x-rays as usual and then return to take me to a hallway to await transport back to my room. On this morning, though, he returned and said that the x-rays were not usable because he failed to get all my lungs in the shot. Apparently, I have long lungs. They go very high up in my torso and if you aren't careful, you'll cut the top off in the x-ray. I could not believe it! I didn't think I could do it again but I prayed and we took the shots again. I will admit this to you, as I got up from the wheelchair for the second round, I did contemplate how I could trick the tech into staying in the room and getting a little "x-ray exposure." It was a fleeting thought, don't worry. From that point on I'd always say to the x-ray techs, "I've got long lungs; make sure you get 'em all in the picture."

Some thorns are necessary for advancement. The chest x-ray was necessary to check the progress of the air leak in my lungs. There was no gauge to measure it without that daily glance at my gizzard. Trials are like this. God allows them to test our faith and determine if we are growing to be more like Him. The Lord says in 1 Peter 4:12–13:

Beloved, think it not strange concerning the fiery trial which is to try you, as though some strange thing happened to you: But rejoice, insomuch as ye are partakers of Christ's sufferings; that, when his glory shall be revealed, ye may be glad also with exceeding joy.

He says in 1 Peter 1:6–7:

Wherein ye greatly rejoice, though now for a season, if need be, ye are in heaviness through manifold temptations: That the trial of your faith, being much more precious than of gold that perisheth, though it be tried with fire, might be found unto praise and honor and glory at the appearing of Jesus Christ.

Our fiery trial is cancer. Your trial may be another illness, a broken relationship, a financial crisis, loss of a job, loss of a loved one, wayward children, problems at your church or something that cuts your heart so deep you cannot even speak about it. Trials hurt but they should be expected in the life of the believer. Satan is real and he will do anything God allows him to do to us to bring us down. God allows Satan to put us through trials, and God Himself sends us trials to bring about His ultimate purpose in our lives. This will bring about our ultimate good and His ultimate glory.

God's motivation in sending trials is to make us more like Jesus (Romans 8:28–29). Satan's motivation in sending trials as he is permitted by God is to weaken and destroy us (2 Corinthians 12:7). If we will realize that it is not who sent the trial that matters as much as the ultimate result of the trial being to be more like Jesus and bring God the most possible glory we can, our trials transform from adversities to opportunities.

I know that cancer has given Evona and me many open doors of ministry since it invaded our lives. Doors we never would have walked through otherwise. The great news is that God promises our trials are for "a season" and that they will yield eternal rewards that are more precious than gold that perisheth. Don't give in when facing trials…look up!

Rejoicing in the fiery trials,
Preacher

∞ ∞ ∞

July 30, 2006—
Pick Me, Lord!
(From Mrs. Evona)

Some people peak physically and mentally in their twenties, others in their thirties. There are the few and the proud that never peak, they just keep getting better and better as the years pass on. I, however, am not one of those blessed souls. I was contemplating this thought the other day. I really believe I peaked physically (possibly mentally also) in the fifth grade! I mean, I could throw farther, run faster, hit the ball longer, and generally outdo everyone in the entire fifth grade. (All forty-three of us, boys included!)

We always played softball during recess in fifth grade. We performed the awful ritual every day of choosing teams. Now in general, the boys disliked me greatly, because even at eleven, it is not cool to be beaten at anything by a girl. (And I had a nasty habit of reminding them that I was better!) However, when it was time to pick teams, they swallowed their pride and picked me. One fine day, we had chosen teams and were playing a very intense game of softball. Unfortunately for me, on this particular day, my team was losing. I have always been a very competitive person (to a fault). I absolutely hate to lose or come in second. (Preacher is still working on helping me become a good loser! It is not working, by the way.) On this day, I figured I would help my team win. Instead of playing harder, I thought it would be easier to trip the boy rounding third base, who was going to be the winning score. This worked beautifully! He fell to the ground and I put on the most innocent, angelic face possible. Everyone believed that it was just bad luck on the runner's part that he fell, except the actual runner of course. While my team was jumping around and rejoicing, he headed towards me on third base. The actual events are kind of fuzzy from this point on, but evidently "Johnny," the runner (name changed to protect the innocent), decided he would take things into his own hands. I remember finding myself flat on my back, having to pull my now very dirty dress back down from over my head and looking into the startled faces of my entire fifth grade class. (Unfortunately for all involved, bloomers were not in style that particular year!) I am sorry to say this tragic event only became worse when the gallant second baseman from my team decided to defend my honor and give the runner a black eye. But I am happy to say that even after having lived through such an awful event, both boys turned out fine. One is a doctor and the other is a lawyer. (I, on the other hand, have very serious emotional issues that involve bloomers!)

It is a very basic desire to want to be "picked." Little children learn early on to jump up and down and yell, "Pick me, pick me." Somehow, I don't think we grow out of this desire to be wanted and chosen. We just learn to control the actual jumping up and down and yelling, "Pick me."

Some weeks back, a friend of ours was teaching piano lessons to a family. The mother followed our friend out to the car and let her know that as a family they have been praying for Pastor and our church. She made a statement that sounded so strange (and a bit hard to swallow for all of us). The mother said something like this: "Your church and Pastor must be so special for God to have chosen them to go through this trial!" When our friend relayed this story to me, I was not feeling very special. Preacher was in the hospital and I was running back and forth trying to be a mom and a wife. (This is definitely more difficult when the kids and husband are in different places!) I was only barely making it from one day to the next. I looked a wreck and was very tired. I thanked our friend and told her to let the student's family know how much we appreciated their prayers (no mention of the "being special because God had chosen us" part!). The following evening after thinking we were going home the next day, Pastor needed an emergency chest tube in the middle of the night. It was 3:00 in the morning and I didn't want to call Preacher's parents and scare them, so I headed out of the room to wait by myself, praying that all would go well. I called my dad and asked him to pray. (No matter how old you get, it's always nice to talk to your daddy!) I suddenly remembered a group of cards that some of you had sent Preacher that was in my purse. (I admit, I read his mail before he did that time.) In the group of cards was a card from some dear, sweet friends who are such an encouragement. The verse they had written in their card from Isaiah 48 spoke directly to me in my time of need. In verse 10 it says, *"Behold, I have refined thee, but not with sil-*

ver; I have chosen thee in the furnace of affliction." God is refining us with cancer not silver. We are so blessed to be chosen to endure this "furnace of affliction." The piano student's mother is right. We should be very honored to be chosen by God to go through this valley. What has God chosen you for? What is He using instead of sliver to refine you? We need to change our perspective on trials and realize we are so special to be "chosen."

I admit that this is an ongoing struggle to embrace our affliction as an honor given to us by God. Many days I am weary and long for life as I used to know it. However, in 1 Chronicles 28:10, God tells us just like he chose Solomon to build the temple he has chosen Pastor and our family to walk through the valley of cancer. "*Take heed now; for the Lord hath chosen thee to build an house for the sanctuary: be strong, and do it.*"

I love the way scripture makes things so simple. It says, "be strong and do it." I don't need Greek or Hebrew training to understand exactly what God means. Some days it will be hard. Some days we will want to quit. Some days the devil will try to discourage us. But we need to just *be strong* and *do it!* What has God chosen us to do? Pastor and I believe that God wants us to "Choose Faith!" Day by day, moment by moment we ask for strength and do it. *We choose faith!*

Blessed to be chosen,
Mrs. Evona

P.S. Preacher says, "I'm pumped to be preaching today. Please pray for power!" (Notice all the "P's"? It is obvious he greatly misses the pulpit! Maybe after today he will quit afflicting us with all his "alliteration!")

JULY 31, 2006—
A Day of Giving and God's Grace at Fellowship Baptist

God gave us a wonderful Lord's Day yesterday (July 30)! He allowed me to preach for the first time in three weeks. It was exciting to stand behind the pulpit and deliver a message from God's Word. I preached a sermon titled, "Water from My Father's Well." The message focuses on how water meets the needs of our bodies but the Lord meets the needs of our souls.

The H.O.P.E. Children's Home was with us in the morning services. We support this great ministry located in the Citrus Park area that ministers to children in dysfunctional situations as well as completely "parentless." I have preached there many times and I love the staff, the children and the work they are doing. The purpose of their visit was to present our family with a love gift. Each year, the children have a yard sale to benefit the home and the needs of the kids. This year the children decided that their yard sale would benefit the Frink family. They have been praying for us but wanted to go a step further and do something for us. The children put items of their own, some that they had recently received, in the yard sale. They prayed for $5,000.00, an amount they had never exceeded before. The proceeds of the yard sale were $5,011.00. The H.O.P.E. Thrift Store added their proceeds for the weekend which brought the love gift to our family to $6,181.00! Our hearts were overwhelmed. We had been praying for a specific amount of money we needed as a family to be able to send our children to Land O' Lakes Christian School. Up until this year Evona has homeschooled our boys. She has done an amazing job, but we felt like with all the extra health issues and having a one-year-old to care for the kids and Evona would benefit from the boys attending a traditional school. God used children to meet this enormous need, and not just any children...children in need themselves. I could hardly thank them, my heart was so full. It never ceases to amaze me the means God uses to answer prayer. Of course God is right on time. The money is due on this coming Tuesday, and after the school bill is paid it will leave just enough money to buy school uniforms for the boys. "*Great is the Lord, and greatly to be praised…*" (Psalm 48:1).

We also received an anonymous gift to our church debt for $15,000.00 and a special gift of $24,000.00 towards a much needed travel bus for the different groups of our church. This bus will be used to take trips, such as camp, retreats, conferences and any activities which would necessitate a larger bus traveling a longer distance than locally. I praise the Lord for His goodness on Fellowship during this trial. The people have been faithful in giving and our attendance has been over 450 on a weekly basis. With the children's home present this morning, we had over 500! It blesses a pastor when the church thrives, even while he is absent. The church is built on Christ not the pastor, and the faithfulness of God's people bears that out.

We returned on Sunday night (July 30) prepared to preach again, but God had other plans. We enjoyed our "5th Sunday Sing" where we feature special singing in the music program. The music was exceptional and we enjoyed a great variety of music. Before I was to speak, I asked my dear friend, Humberto Gomez, a missionary to Mexico, to come and give a testimony and have his wife, Imelda, sing. Humberto told us about his son, Humberto Jr. who at 15 was stricken with "Non-Hodgkin's Lymphoma." The Gomez family fought this cancer for two long years and it looked as if Humberto Jr. was going to succumb to the disease and go home to be with the Lord. He could no longer take chemotherapy because his body was too weak. The family was called. Humberto Sr. felt "God was going to take his son to glory." After waiting and watching their son suffer, wondering if this would be the day he would be taken to glory, they saw Humberto Jr. lift his hand on his own. This was something he had not done in a very long time. The family rejoiced! Each day he gained more strength until finally he walked out of the hospital. Today Humberto Jr. is preaching and overseeing the ministry of his father in Mexico. The doctors said he would not have any children. He is married with three lovely niños. God is the one who decides our future. He is well able to take an impossible situation and turn it into a miracle, by which He can get glory.

After Humberto's testimony, Imelda began singing and I felt a special moving of God. I looked down at the altar and saw my wife, Evona, praying with my sons, Micah and Caleb. I joined her and we began praying. Soon my parents and my cousins from out of town were gathered with us and we continued praying. We thanked God for His goodness and His grace upon us. We praised God for never doing wrong and always doing right. We asked for strength through suffering and my eventual healing. It was a blessing to be surrounded by my family calling out to God. When I got up from the altar I realized that God had touched others' hearts as well. There were many people gathered at the front of our church praying everywhere. The Lord had moved through our church in an unusual way. I believe we are in the midst of revival! I did not preach my evening sermon. I stepped out of the way and let the Lord move as He saw fit. It was one of those services we will never forget. I'm so glad I was in the house of God to experience it.

At this point, I have had no side effects from the chemotherapy on Thursday (July 27). This is an answer to many people's prayers. I thank God for sparing me some of the things we've read could take place. The verse in 1 Corinthians 10:13 says it best: *"There hath no temptation taken you but such as is common to man: but God is faithful, who will not suffer you to be tempted above that ye are able; but will with the temptation also make a way to escape, that ye may be able to bear it."*

Finding Him faithful,
Preacher and Mrs. Evona

August 1, 2006—
Preparing for Battle

> *"The horse is prepared against the day of battle: but safety is of the LORD."*
>
> PROVERBS 21:31

So many times we confuse faith in God with sitting by idly waiting on Him to do it all. The Bible says in James 2 that *"faith without works is dead."* We have been reminded over and over of this truth as we battle cancer. After over a week in the hospital, I was feeling discouraged and a little sorry for myself. I was struggling with a loss of appetite, weakness from the chest tube and breathing limitations. Evona and my mom had tried everything they knew to motivate me, to no avail. While Evona was spending time with the boys, Aunt Cathy and Mom headed out on yet another excursion, trying to find something that would appeal to my taste buds. After they left, I began praying for God to raise me up. He plainly impressed upon my heart that He was doing His part, now it was time for me to do my part. Mom and Cathy returned to find me out of the bed and in the chair exercising. We have learned that this principle holds true in every area of our lives, especially dealing with this recent health crisis.

In Proverbs 21:31, Solomon so wisely teaches us that safety is ultimately up to the Lord, but we must actively prepare for the battle. There have been loving friends and family and many helpful professionals that have given us advice that has helped us prepare for our battle. We wanted to share a few tips with you, in hopes that having the information ahead of time might make your battle preparations easier. This card was recently sent to us and now ranks as my all-time favorite! We all know that insurance can be one of the biggest issues we have to deal with when illness strikes. If you are not sick before you start dealing with all the details, you will be after!

1. Review your insurance coverage and know ahead of time what your responsibilities are (referrals, co-pays, in and out of network providers, etc.).
2. Most insurance companies provide you with a person called the "patient advocate." This is a very valuable relationship to cultivate. This is the liaison between you and your insurance company. They can help you obtain medical supplies, sort out filing issues, even help when a claim has been denied.
3. "Manage your own healthcare!" A doctor friend gave us this advice and it has been invaluable. You must take the initiative and keep track of all of your medical needs. Doctors, hospitals, and all other healthcare providers are very overworked and understaffed. Help them by keeping track of what is going on!
4. Ask for a copy of all your medical records. You have a legal right to any medical information that concerns you. Make copies and keep them with you during office visits. Many times doctors won't have all your information. You can provide them with helpful copies that will enable them to make sound decisions.
5. If you have any procedures or tests done, you can fill out a medical release form and receive a copy of the findings as soon as the report is completed. You don't have to wait for your next visit with your doctor to find out the results. The down side is that trying to read a medical report without medical training can be very upsetting. Think about this before you make your decision to get you report ahead of time.
6. Be kind and friendly. Learn the names of all the staff and nurses you will be dealing with. It helps when they know who you are when you call. Value nurses highly. They can be a tremendous help in time of need. We bring snacks and goodies with our family picture taped to the box and a note thanking our caregivers for their kind help. This helps them remember that Pastor is not just a number but a person with a family and we appreciate their dedication.

7. Try to use the same pharmacy for all your medications. The computer system should alert the pharmacist when medicines might interact. When you have several doctors prescribing, this can become an issue.
8. Keep all medication information in one location. You may need to leave in a hurry and not be able to grab all your bottles. (Hurricane, last minute trip, etc.) Most pharmacies have little cards that are printed with the RX number and medication name that comes stapled to the bag of your prescription. I tear these off and file them so when I need to call in refills they are all together.
9. Type up a current list of all your medications, and the history of all your procedures. When you need to fill out all those endless forms, you can ask them to staple the typed copy to your form and not have to write it all out.
10. When you need to go to the hospital, if your doctor calls ahead, you usually don't have to wait in the ER to be seen. (Ask your doctor to call!)
11. Be proactive. Be early for appointments. Be prepared. Read up on your condition and have a list of questions ready. Don't be afraid to ask your doctor to explain something again when you don't understand. Write everything down as you speak with your doctor. Somehow things you thought you would remember disappear from your head as soon as you leave the office.
12. Preacher says, "Throw all hospital food out the window!" However, most hospitals have the ability to provide food not listed on the regular menu. You can write on the regular menu "cheeseburger and fries" or "hotdog and chips" and have a fairly good chance of getting what you ordered.
13. Learn the system. Every office, hospital or clinic has a system. Figure it out by asking a lot of questions, and then try and work within the system. Things work better this way.
14. Last but not least, always pack a nightgown or lounge pants when you are headed to the hospital. Trust me, those gowns they give you DO NOT offer enough coverage under any circumstances!

Proverbs 4:5: *"Get wisdom, Get understanding..."* You can count on God to do His part, but we must make the choice to actively pursue the knowledge that will help prepare us for battle.

Getting the horse ready for battle,
Preacher and Mrs. Evona

AUGUST 2, 2006—
Do the First Works

Do you ever find yourself lacking the motivation to do the things you ought to be doing? I think this is a common problem in all our lives. We know we need to get up early and spend time with God before we rush off into our day, but we push the snooze until our hands are numb and finally get up in time to throw our clothes on and run out the door. The scriptures will have to wait…we've got to go through Starbucks before we punch the clock.

We know we need to go to church faithfully and worship the Lord, yet we find excuses to miss the services and we let one week turn into a month. Then the devil uses guilt to keep us away even longer, telling us that everyone at our church will be disappointed with us for being out of church so long and look at us with a judgmental scowl.

We know we need to be good stewards with our finances. The Lord has blessed us with the financial resources we have to live on and our part is being responsible in spending and saving, yet we splurge and squander and fail to save. Then when the bills come due, we panic and begin the awful ritual of trying to juggle our funds to cover our obligations.

We know we should eat right and exercise to take care of our bodies, God's temple, yet we can't stop sneaking those Reese Cups and the extent of our daily fitness regimen is checking our emails.

In my situation, battling cancer, I know that I need to build my strength so that I can fight this disease. It has been emphasized over and over by everyone involved in my healthcare. All my doctors have told me how important this is in this battle. Yet there are days when I don't get out of my chair to go walking or do a light workout. In my mind I know that I should be actively building my strength. My family and my church need me, so I should be doing this for them…but I fail to do it.

Paul had this same problem in his life when it came to doing the things God wanted him to do. He writes in Romans 7:15: *"For that which I do I allow not: for what I would, that do I not; but what I hate, that I do."* What we probably don't want to hear is the reason Paul teaches that we fail to do the things we ought to do: Romans 7:17 and 20: *"Now then it is no more I that do it, but sin that dwelleth in me...Now if I do that I would not, it is no more I that do it, but sin that dwelleth in me."*

James 4:17 confirms Paul's conclusion when it says, *"Therefore to him that knoweth to do good, and doeth it not, to him it is sin."* It is important that we see our "lack of motivation" to do what is right as not merely a poor choice on our part, but sin. When we see something as sin, we realize our lives are in opposition to God's will and we must change. Sin is always against God. God is holy and He cannot accept sin. It was our sins that God's Son Jesus came to earth to pay for by dying on the cross and rising from the dead. Sin is very serious. It cost the sacrifice of Christ.

When you see your failure to do what is right as sin, you're ready to change. God is always ready to help you change. God used John to write the book of the Revelation. In chapters 2 and 3, John writes seven letters to seven churches. These letters teach us lessons about different types of Christians and churches. In Revelation 2, John writes to the church of Ephesus. Ephesus has a problem. Verse 4 reveals the problem: *"Nevertheless I have somewhat against thee, because thou hast left thy first love."* Ephesus was no longer putting Jesus Christ as the center of her affections. They had allowed other interests to crowd Christ from the throne of their hearts.

In the case of Ephesus, God gives us the formula for overcoming this sin of failing to do what we should. He says in verse 5 to *"Remember therefore from whence thou art fallen..."* Think back to the days when you did find the motivation to do what is right. It feels good to get up and do the things you know you should. You'll find that you're creating a desire to change. Next God says, *"...and repent..."* which means "turn around." We turn from our sin and we turn to our Savior. Turning from sin is confessing to God that you have sinned in your life and then asking His forgiveness. God always forgives sin when we confess it as sin (1 John 1:9). Now we are ready for true change, as the verse continues, *"...and do the first works..."* In other words, get out of bed early enough for your devotions; go to the house of God faithfully; be a good steward with those finances; take care of your body and build your strength to fight this cancer. It will amaze you how God blesses obedience. Now that we are doing what God wants us to do, we find that He is with us and giving us power to do what we know we should.

They say that tomorrow is a new day, but why wait until then? There's never a better time to change than now.

Working hard to do the first works,
Preacher

August 3, 2006—
Fear? Flight? Or Faith?
(From Mrs. Evona)

Boy, how much difference a year can make in your life. Really, how much difference a day or an hour can make. As a little girl, when I would make a mistake or misbehave, I would wish and wish I could just take back that one moment when I made the wrong decision. I can't count how many times I have wanted to turn back the clock these past few months. My human heart wants things back the way they were. I thought things were perfect. We had three little boys, a beautiful home, an awesome marriage, a great job and a wonderful church. Yet now after Preacher's diagnosis, all these things are the same, yet different. However, my spiritual heart realizes that our life is so much sweeter now that we have to trust the Lord for every second. We have such a close fellowship with God that I know we would have never had if things were not as they are. We pray and cry and talk to God every minute of the day. You frequently feel like you are about to lose it. But somehow God gives you the strength to face the next minute and you just trust Him and go on. People say, "How do you do it?" I almost want to scream and say, "What else can I do?" But I stop (mostly because they would take me to the funny farm if I start screaming at people!) and remember it is not me that is "doing it." It is God.

God has given so much grace to help us through this valley. Each day we face new challenges. We have to be even and calm, giving our boys the security they need during this time. We have to train and teach little Lucas, because he is at that stage of life where he is beginning to learn to obey, and if we miss it, life will not be pleasant. Our sweet baby got his sense of humor from Preacher, evidenced by his laughter when the stooges are playing! (I tried so hard to shield him from this poor quality entertainment, but I am vastly outnumbered!) But unfortunately, he got his bad attitude and tendency to stomp his feet when he doesn't get his way from me! My mom has been no help. She just laughs and laughs when I share with her about his behavior! (She mumbled something about this being the best part of becoming a grandparent!) There have been new challenges I have had to face causing me to spread my wings as a wife and mom. I have had to physically lift and move things, and do some of the 'daddy' stuff that Preacher wants to do but can't. We do have a lot of help, but it is not the same. Last night, the curtain rod fell off the wall, and I put it back on by hammering it with my nail polish bottle. Maybe that is just my being too lazy to go get the hammer. Before, however, my sweet husband would have taken care of it. I almost can't breathe when I watch him struggle to do something that only two months ago would have been a piece of cake. When he is in pain, I am so helpless. I don't know what to do. The 'mommy' person fixes things but I can't fix this. All I can do is cry out to God, "Please help me. I know You can, but I am scared. The devil keeps telling me that I am pretending everything is OK, but that it really isn't. I do have faith in You, God. And I know You are in charge. You have had this planned for so long. But it is really new for me and so uncomfortable to have absolutely no control."

When I read Psalm 55, it is like God is writing about me and my emotional journey—a journey I take over and over again. It begins with my broken heart in verse 4. *"My heart is sore pained within me."* Later in the same verse God writes about the reality of death that man has declared *upon us and the terror that tries to take hold. "The terrors of death are fallen upon me."* My human reaction is fear and anxiety, as in verse 5: *"Fearfulness and trembling are come upon me, and horror hath overwhelmed me."* Dealing with this fear and stress has made me want to hide and pretend that none of this is really happening. Verse 6 says it like this. *"And I said, Oh that I had wings like a dove! For then would I fly away, and be at rest."* But if I give into this temptation I will be running away from the purpose God has for this valley. This will only send me further away from God not closer. Verse 7: *"Lo, then would I wonder far off, and remain in the wilderness."* If I were in charge, now that the cancer has been found and documented, I would have a miracle happen and the next scan would show no more cancer and we could all go home. Verse 8: *"I would hasten my escape from the windy storm and tempest."* But I have to make a choice now that we are in the valley—a choice to trust God. This is not always my feeling. Many times I do not feel strong. There are many days, hours and minutes that I fear. I have to make a choice of my will to choose faith: Faith in God; faith that He has the plan, not me; faith that He is going to do right; faith that no matter what, God is still good; and faith that He will sustain us. Our sufficiency is not in ourselves our sufficiency is of God. In verse16 it says, *"As for me, I will call upon God: and the L*ORD *shall save me."* This is a daily, hourly, minute by minute decision. The only way to make this decision is through prayer. God already knows our hearts and minds. Why shouldn't we talk to him about how we feel and the fear that keeps trying to stomp out our flame of faith? Verse 17: *"Evening, and morning, and at noon, will I pray, and cry aloud: and he shall hear my voice."* After I choose to trust God, no matter what my human mind and feeble feelings are telling me, God sends His peace. This is a peace that I never understood or knew existed (*"passeth understanding"*). This is a peace to carry with us into battle. We are in a battle against Satan and against human doubt and limitations. Even good loving people still share doubt and fear with us instead of faith. We know God is able and we trust His will. Verse 18: *"He hath delivered my soul in peace from the battle that was against me."* Along the way God sends others to help hold up our hands of faith. Just like Moses during the battle with the Amalekites when his uplifted hand was needed to give Joshua and the army in the valley below victory, we get tired. We can't do it on our own. However, God sends others to help. Verse 18: *"...for there were many with me."* This is the only way we have been able to keep it all together. There have been hundreds of people there praying for us—many we don't even know. Our church people and family have shared our situation with others, asking them to pray for us. This has been so comforting. Verses 22 and 23 remind us that our only responsibility is to cast our burdens on the Lord. *"Cast thy burden upon the L*ORD,*...and he shall never suffer the righteous to be moved...I will trust in thee."*

Preacher is feeling better and improving more each week. We praise God and trust Him to sustain us. We are anxiously waiting and looking forward to the "We Choose Faith Rally" coming up this next week. If you are in the area, please don't miss this opportunity to be with us and experience revival.

Casting all our cares on the Lord,
Mrs. Evona

AUGUST 4, 2006—
In the Shadow of Thy Wings

Evona and I had devotions yesterday (August 3) from Psalm 57. This Psalm is rich from its beginning. Verse 1 says, *"Be merciful unto me, O God, be merciful unto me: for my soul trusteth in thee: yea, in the shadow of thy wings will I make my refuge, until these calamities be overpast."*

David is obviously troubled. He prays for mercy from God twice. This is the period in his life when he was on the run from King Saul. God had prophesied to King Saul through the prophet Samuel, that because of his disobedience, He had stripped the kingdom from him and given it to David. Samuel anointed David as the future king of Israel and so began the hunt. Saul was relentless in his pursuit of David, driving him into caves at times to hide for his life.

In the darkness of the cave, David finds something wonderful. He finds that the darkness the devil would seek to enclose him in with fear, is actually the shadow of the wings of God, who draws him in to show mercy, love and grace. God has enabled David to see the threatening darkness that surrounds him as the shadowy wings of God pulling him in to protect him.

There is something neat about a "shadow." To be in someone's shadow, you must be physically close to him/her. David discovered that in his calamities, God was with him. This is the realization that we are in the presence of God and there is nothing that can separate us from this. There is nothing as encouraging as the presence of God when you're surrounded by darkness. God knows the way ahead, and He will eventually deliver us to the light as we remain fixed under the shadow of His wings. We can pray, sing, praise and give Him glory as we draw close to Him in the dark.

It is also a blessing to consider the picture God gives us here of His "wings." We know that God does not have wings, yet He likens His love and care to a mother bird, who spreads her wings over her children, covering them from all that threatens to harm them. In the same way, God covers us with His spiritual wings *"until these calamities be overpast."* In other words, He will cover us as long as it takes for our troubles to come to an end. This is the realization that we are in God's protection and He never fails in His watching over us. When you hear the winds howl and the storm swirling around your life, imagine God closing in His wings even tighter around and above you.

What are you seeing as you face the darkness today? Has Satan got you focused on the calamities that threaten to destroy you? Or will you instead see the darkness as the shadow of God's wings? Will you realize His presence as you abide in His shadow? Will you feel His protection as His wings cover you? It's up to us. God invites us under the shadow of His wings, but He does not force us to come under. Jesus said of Jerusalem, "...*how often would I have gathered thy children together, even as a hen gathered her chickens under her wings, and ye would not!*" (Matthew 23:27). Let's receive our Lord's invitation to draw under the shadow of His wings.

We had an interview with Michelle Bearden of the Tampa Tribune. Michelle writes religious columns in the "Faith" section of our paper. Michelle carried my personal testimony in her column several years back. She is a sweet person and easy to talk to. One of our members had told Michelle about our upcoming "We Choose Faith Rally," and she wanted to report on it. She also interviewed me about the battle our family and church are facing with cancer and our decision to "Choose Faith" in God through it. I told Michelle that this is the reason we're having the rally that we might let everyone know the stand we're taking. The interview will appear in the "Faith" section of the Tampa Tribune this Saturday. God is good to give us this type of promotion for our rally.

Yesterday (August 2) was a good day. I felt pretty good all day. I have been concerned about my appetite. I know that to gain strength, I must eat. I find myself not hungry for a lot of food, which does not lend itself to becoming stronger. At Wednesday Night Prayer Meeting, I asked our people to pray for my appetite to increase. That night about 11:00 P.M., I got hungry. Evona fixed me a plate of what we'd had for supper and I ate the whole thing! I haven't done that since getting home, so needless to say, it was encouraging. God answers prayers and oftentimes; He answers them "speedily."

Tucked beneath His wings,
Preacher and Mrs. Evona

∽ ∽ ∽

AUGUST 5, 2005—
A Sport Not for the Faint of Heart
(From Mrs. Evona)

The two older "smelly monsters" (Micah and Caleb) finally talked me into the annual trip to the ice skating rink. Somehow, just going isn't as much fun if the "gang" isn't there. So off I head with a car full of very smelly monsters, many not even my own. Why do I have to smell other people's monsters? Oh well, at least they were a well behaved "monster gang." It is not my idea of fun to strap on shoes (that only come in full sizes and don't fit) that have a small metal blade that you are expected to balance on. To top it off, the object of this "so-called fun" is to slide around on wet, cold, ice while trying not to look like an uncoordinated monkey. (Most of the ones I am watching are not being very successful with the 'not looking like a monkey' part!) However, because all of the parents here paid to let their monsters do this, I keep hearing the same sentence over and over. "You will keep skating; we paid to do this and you are having fun!" And yet next year the same miserable wet smelly monsters will beg and plead to do it all over again. It had to have been a genius who came up with the idea of having us actually pay money to hear our kids whine.

Part of the problem with ice-skating and skating in general is the lack of scenery; round and round they skate, over and over, never really getting anywhere. There are those few who wear the cute little Olympic skate outfits, with the little skirts, that don't skate in circles. They have it figured out. They stay in the middle and do little twirls and jumps. But after three hours of watching, they don't seem to be getting anywhere either. How frustrating to work so hard to balance on such awful contraptions never gaining any ground. Only a child or really bored person could enjoy this pastime.

So many times during our recent trial we have felt this same frustration. We feel like we are trying to balance and someone changed our shoes. We were doing fine on the flat, nicely treaded tennis shoes. Our Christian faith was working fine. We were in full-time ministry and serving the Lord. Things were on a nice even keel. Now we are wobbling and teetering on new shoes that seem to have only a small blade to balance on. Cancer and sickness is all new and we are out of our comfort zone. Just walking from one place to another requires much effort. Because we trust the Lord, we lace on the skates and do our best. Things seem to be going OK for a minute or two, but then it is time to head out to the ice! Dealing with doctors and medicine, fatigue and complications, weakness and change has made life very slippery. Every day we seem to have to regain our balance and try again. Proverbs 16:11 tells us that the Lord will help with our balance. *"A just weight and balance are the Lord's:..."* Once we feel a small amount of security in our ability to balance, we are called to skate around in circles seemingly gaining no ground. But God's ways are higher than ours and His thoughts are not understood by man. We don't see our progress but God knows the outcome, and each lap brings us closer to His perfect will and our ultimate good.

There is a big machine called the Zamboni that periodically resurfaces the ice. This resurfacing requires a scraping of the ice to produce a smooth surface for the skaters to enjoy. Pastor and I feel like we are being run over by the Zamboni, and trust me, it is not fun. Job 23:10: *"But he knoweth the way that I take: when he hath tried me, I shall come forth as gold."* What a comfort to know that God is aware of all that is going on and that there is a purpose for our trial. The scraping that God is doing, will make us more like His precious Son and suitable for His use. Romans 8:28–29: *"And we know that all things work together for good to them that love God, to them who are the called according to his purpose. For whom he did foreknow, he also did predestinate TO BE CONFORMED TO THE IMAGE OF HIS SON..."*

We want to keep skating and let God work His beautiful and perfect will in our lives. Yet many times it is tempting to think we have it figured out and stay in the middle of the rink. There we can show off and do all our "spiritual twirls and jumps." This plan of action will not allow God the control He needs to lead us and bring us closer to Him.

While all the sweet smelly monsters were skating, I watched this very young little girl skate. Every so often she would take a break and head off the rink right into her mother's arms. The little girl would wait patiently while her mom pulled off the wet gloves and rub each cold little hand and warm her up again. Then off she went, ready to do twenty more laps. God is waiting on us to turn to Him and find the comfort we need to keep making those laps. Psalm 71:21: *"Thou shalt…comfort me on every side."* (You should read that entire Psalm. It is incredible. Oh no, I feel another update coming on!)

There are times that life does not seem to make sense. Just like my inability to see the purpose or fun in ice-skating, we can fail to understand the direction God has led us. But it is so nice to know that it is not our responsibility to understand it all. It is our job to trust. Psalm 71:5 says that God is our HOPE and TRUST. So take a seat, pull off those comfortable tennis shoes you have been wearing for years, and lace up those ice skates of faith. God has great things in store for those who love him enough to "Choose Faith."

If you are going through a valley or have a loved one who is in a trial, come to hear the speakers during our "Choose Faith Rally." God has worked miracles to make all four of these men able to be with us during this short time. This can only mean great things are going to happen. Satan will send many excuses and roadblocks to keep you from being blessed. Don't let this happen. Join us as we stand together as a family, as a church and as a community and "*Choose Faith*"

Making each lap count,
Mrs. Evona

August 6, 2006—
The Caregiver

"Her children arise up, and call her blessed; her husband also, and he praiseth her. Many daughters have done virtuously, but thou excellest them all."

Proverbs 31:28–29

I am writing this update in honor of my wife, Evona. She is my best friend. She is my one true love. She is my beauty queen. She is the one I bear my soul to. She is my confidant. She is my world.

And now she is my caregiver. This is not a role either of us could anticipate. Nor is it a role either of us was prepared for. Evona has always taken care of me throughout our married life. But the role of caregiver is different. Evona has the responsibility of our household; she has the role of wife and mother to fill; she has the responsibility of school; she has the responsibility of our finances; she has the responsibility of being the church pianist; she has the responsibility of her part-time job; she has the responsibility of home and car maintenance and now she has the responsibility of me.

"Me" is a big responsibility. I have a plethora of medications to keep track of, a blood-thinning shot I must take each evening, doctor's appointments I must be present for, four Boosts I must be encouraged to drink, pool-jogging I must be prodded into and on and on it goes. Evona has become my pharmacist. She keeps track of my medication and makes sure I take everything at the right time. Last week she gave me my handful of pills and one of the pills was unfamiliar. I looked closer and found that it wasn't really a pill but an un-popped kernel of popcorn! I am sure the popcorn kernel wouldn't have hurt me, but it is still a little scary.

Each day I discover something else Evona is doing for me. I don't think it's that she just started doing it, but probably that I finally noticed.

> "...but in lowliness of mind let each esteem other better than themselves."
>
> PHILIPPIANS 2:3

Caregivers are unselfish. They are also sacrificial. They put their needs second after the object of their care. If they relax, it's because time stopped as we know it. If they get to eat, it's because there's no more food anyone wants. Yet they unselfishly press on in their role as caregiver.

It is difficult to watch Evona taking care of everything and then taking care of me. My body strength is limited so there's much I can't help her with. She remains undaunted and fills her various roles almost automatically.

I think the essence of caregivers is their hearts. The things they do go beyond obligations and responsibilities, they are done through love. God's love is in our hearts, and that love becomes the fountain from which our actions flow. In the book of Ruth, we see that Ruth leaves her home country of Moab to be with her mother-in-law Naomi. Ruth becomes somewhat of a "caregiver" for Naomi. How could a young girl do these things? She loved Naomi and she loved Naomi's God.

Well, Evona, I hope my deep love for you as my caregiver shines through. I hope that my extreme gratitude for each act of care you give me is obvious. I love you and I thank God for you. There's no caregiver like you in the whole world!

Praising God for my caregiver,
Preacher

August 7, 2006—
"We Choose Faith Rally" Off to a Great Start

We had a great opening service of our "We Choose Faith Rally" on Sunday night (August 6). Dr. Johnny Pope, a pastor in Houston, Texas, was our speaker and preached a powerful message called "Stand Your Ground."

We had two saved and one baptized! What a thrill to watch God move over hearts as many life-changing decisions were made.

We look forward to the remaining two nights of the rally on August 8 and 9. There will be gospel concerts each night at 7:00 P.M. and services at 7:30 P.M. On Tuesday night, August 8, we will host Dr. Eric Capaci and Dr. John Bishop, both from Arkansas. On Wednesday night, August 9, we will host Dr. John Bishop and Dr. Steve Roberson, from Tennessee. All three men will make you laugh and cry. They will inspire and encourage you. They will challenge and convict you. This promises to be one of the greatest meetings we've ever had. Don't miss standing with our family and church while declaring "We Choose Faith!"

It was a blessing to preach the morning message. I was very weak in my legs as I prepared to go to church. I believe Satan was attacking me trying to *"pervert the right ways of the Lord"* (Acts 13:10). I also believe 1 John 4:4 which says, *"Ye are of God, little children, and have overcome them: because greater is he that is in you, than he that is in the world."* And so I prayed myself to church. By the time I got there, I was feeling fine and focused on preaching in the pulpit. My sermon title was "Let God Be Magnified."

Within this sermon was the point that God is magnified through our powerful commitment to the will of God. We went on to say that God's will is His specific plan for your life. The will of God must be discovered. There are nine guidelines to finding the will of God in your life:

(1) Walk with God in holiness
(2) Submit your body as a living sacrifice unto God (Romans 12:1 and 2)
(3) Daily be filled with the Spirit of God (Ephesians 5:18)
(4) Pray for wisdom to discern the will of God (James 1:5)
(5) Wait on the Lord to speak (He'll use His Word and His Spirit)
(6) Seek godly counsel
(7) More prayer, more waiting! (Try fasting as well)
(8) Get solid confirmation from the Lord
(9) Commit in public to do the will of God for your life (gives accountability and support).

Dr. George Truett said, "To know the will of God is the greatest knowledge. To do the will of God is the greatest achievement."[6]

There's not a more fulfilling, joy-giving and safer place to be than in the center of God's will. We feel that we are in His will as we battle cancer. God is going to get so much glory when I stand in Fellowship one day and declare that God has delivered me and I am "cancer free!"

Striving for the center,
Preacher

August 8, 2006—
Getting the Troops Ready for Battle
(From Mrs. Evona)

Darkness still covered the land in the wee hours of the morning as the troops began to stir. Emotions ran high. No one had gotten much sleep due to the anticipation of the upcoming battle. The weary general valiantly worked to rouse the men, hoping that soon the adrenaline would begin to flow. Years of planning and preparation had gone into these men, culminating in this one momentous event. Would all their training pay off? Only time would tell. Quietly they donned their armor. On went protective vests of green and leg coverings of blue. Proudly they wore their uniforms. Weapons were packed and food was secured for the journey. Soon the test of their training would come. Would they turn and run, or would they stand their ground? Finally the hour arrived. The men disembarked from the vehicle, backpacks in one hand and lunchboxes in the other. I, the "general," with tears running down my cheeks, strained to get one last glance or wave from the "troops." With my nose pressed out of shape into the car window, I saw what every "general" fears yet longs to see...my men oblivious to my misery, smiling and skipping toward their classrooms on

their first day of school!

Yes, it has finally come: the time for students to go back to school. This year, however, it has been a very different scene at our home. Our battle preparations included the boys getting ready to go to what they call "real school!" (After 12 years of school, 4 years of college and 8 years of teaching, you would think what I did with them as a homeschool mom was pretty real! Obviously not?!) I have homeschooled both boys from kindergarten until today. I am anxious yet excited for the boys. They are beyond excited. It took hours for them to go to sleep last night, due to the anticipation. God has miraculously worked out the situation so that they are able to attend a Christian school in our area for the first time in their young lives. They are handling this much better than the "general." I am having all those same feelings young mothers have as they leave their new babies in the nursery for the first time. Will they be OK without me? Who will tie their shoes and wipe their noses? (Oh yeah, they can do that for themselves now.) Who will make sure that they make perfect scores on all their papers and see that they perform to their "full potential?" (Oh yeah, that well-educated person they call the teacher.) Oh well, I am sure they need me for something. What will I do with myself? Well, to soften the blow, I am headed for Wal-Mart. It's not shopping—it's Retail Therapy! Whoever said you can't buy happiness just doesn't know where to shop! 🖐 After Wal-Mart I might get my nails done and then head home for a cup of tea. Wait a minute, I feel better already. What a wonderful idea, this school thing has turned out to be. Baby Lucas and I are gonna have a great time!!

The Bible talks about a mother named Jochebed that had to deal with much worse than sending her boys to school. She had to trust God as she gently placed her young infant in a homemade basket and allowed him to float down the Nile River. Many dangers lurked in the bulrushes and under the murky water, yet by FAITH she pushed him out into the deep. (Exodus 2:1–9) However, years later her sacrifice and faith paid off as her young son, now a grown man, made a choice of faith of his own. Hebrews 11:24–25: *"By faith Moses, when he was come to years, refused to be called the son of Pharaoh's daughter; choosing rather to suffer affliction with the people of God, than to enjoy the pleasures of sin for a season;..."* What an awesome act of faith Jochebed and Amram made, trusting God to protect their young infant in the crocodile infested waters of the Nile. I think I should be able to give my fears and anxiety over my boys going to school over to the Lord. Besides, there aren't even any wild animals at school that they are going to have to deal with (except World Geography and Algebra, but we have a few years until those animals appear!).

Every day, we all have to make an ongoing choice to give our fear and stress over to the Lord. First Peter 5:7 says, *"Casting all your care upon him;*

for he careth for you." Both of the words "casting and careth" are in the present ongoing tense. We can continuously cast our cares on Him and He in turn continuously cares for us. What a beautiful relationship we can have if we choose. We must make the choice to trust God. It doesn't matter if it is worry over finances, a sick loved one, a new situation, a wayward child, personal health issues or just watching your "sweet smelly monsters" go to school for the first time. God cares and wants us to trust Him enough to turn it all over to Him. We must "Choose Faith" in all areas of our lives.

Trusting God with the "Troops,"
Mrs. Evona

August 9, 2006—
600 Plus Come to "Choose Faith" at Rally

I admit my human flesh was concerned as we packed the kids into the car and headed to the "We Choose Faith Rally." I voiced my concern to Evona as we drove down Highway 301 toward the church. However, as we sat waiting on five or six cars to turn into the church campus, my heart began to beat faster. We made the turn and were so excited to see that at before 7:00 cars had overflowed the parking lots and were having to park up and down the streets of the church. I dropped the family off and had to drive to the back of the property to find a place to park. (We need a "reserved for Pastor" parking place! Who's in charge anyway?) After having to hike back to the building I came in the side door of the main auditorium and heard wonderful singing and saw a room filled to capacity! God is so good. There were over 600 people seated and they were bringing in more chairs to handle the continuous flood of people coming to join me, our family and our church "Choose Faith."

We were so blessed by the early concert from the Greens and the Turnmires. Our hearts were touched and ready for the service. Our church choir began with an exciting and inspiring song, "I Stand upon the Rock." This song led perfectly into the congregation's raising the roof with a medley of songs about our Lord's return. I am sure the neighbors could hear the faith and assurance in our voices as we sang straight to the Lord. Dr. John Bishop presented Evona and me with a beautiful bound copy of the devotional *Streams in the Desert,* and then he opened God's Word and preached 2 Corinthians 1:4: "*Who comforteth us in all our tribulation, that we may be able to comfort them which are in any trouble, by the comfort wherewith we ourselves are comforted of God.*"

We were reminded that not only does God care that we are going through trials, part of His very nature and name is the "Comforter." God is always right and God is always good. Dr. Bishop has had serious health issues of his own but came and allowed the Holy Spirit to work through him and his trials to turn around and comfort us as a church and community.

Dr. Capaci then brought a message about the three cries that Jesus heard: the maniac of Gadara, Jairus and the woman with the issue of blood. Each time a person cried out to Jesus in faith, He heard the cry and answered the need. Brother Capaci challenged us to cry out to God in faith and "touch Jesus" with our prayers. Not only does God reward our faith, we can inspire others to have faith. Jairus's daughter was near death, and Jesus stopped to heal a woman who had been ill for over 12 years. The woman had so much faith she knew all she needed to do was touch Jesus to be healed. This faith affected Jairus. When his servants came and told him his daughter had died, he brought Jesus back to his home anyway. There this man saw the impossible, but Jesus said, "*Weep not; she is not dead, but sleepeth*" (Luke 8:52). Jesus heard the cry and raised Jairus's daughter from the dead! What an awesome God! That is the same God we are privileged to take our burdens to and He takes the time to hear our cries.

We stand together as a family, and as Fellowship Baptist Church and as a community to cry unto God, the Comforter and "Choose Faith." I can't imagine how tonight can be any better, but it will! If you don't have a place to attend this evening, come see what God is doing as we come together and "*Choose Faith*"

We Choose Faith,
Preacher and Mrs. Evona

AUGUST 10, 2006—
Great Final Service of "We Choose Faith Rally"

Are you standing in need of a miracle today?
Even doctors don't know what to do.
God is able to make a way from no way,
He's still able to carry you through.
If we would just learn to trust and obey,
we'd find that our Savior turns darkness into day.
He alone can handle the challenges life brings.
GOD IS STILL DOING GREAT THINGS!
 (Verse 1 from "God is Still Doing Great Things")[7]

This song has been an encouragement to our church in recent days and has been so true during our "We Choose Faith Rally." What an awesome end to our rally we had last evening. Once again our building was full of people: friends, family and Christian brothers and sisters standing with us as we "Choose Faith."

Tremendous music prepared our hearts for two powerful sermons. Dr. Steve Roberson preached a sermon called "Right Thinking in Trials," followed by Dr. John Bishop's sermon challenging us to be prepared and have right priorities through our suffering. These messages met the key needs in our church as we daily face the challenge to "Choose Faith" through our trials.

We truly appreciate all the speakers and musical guests and their families. It was a sacrifice for each family to come and be a part of our "We Choose Faith Rally," and we thank God for all of them. Many pastors and friends from other churches came and joined with us and encouraged our hearts. We want to also thank our "church family" for their faithfulness to this rally. All of you touched us with your loving show of support. Our family was blessed beyond measure.

Each day we see new answers to prayer. My appetite is steadily improving. Once again I raided the kitchen for a midnight snack! Our next hurdle is the upcoming series of scans on Monday, August 14. This has been foremost in our minds as the date rapidly approaches. We are daily amazed at how God gives us the perfect verse to meet our needs from a book written thousands of years ago. Psalm 62:8 has helped us when our hearts have been overwhelmed: *"Trust in him at all times; ye people, pour out your heart before him: God is a refuge for us. Selah."* God knows that our feeble hearts can only handle so much, and He longs for us to turn and "pour out" our cares to Him. This verse tells us that we can trust God at ALL TIMES. Our trust is based on the character of God not our current circumstances. Praise the Lord, even in these modern times He is Still Doing Great Things.

> Trust Him when dark doubts assail thee,
> Trust Him when thy strength is small;
> Trust Him when to simply trust him
> Seems the hardest thing of all.
> (Unknown)

Trusting God no matter what,
Preacher and Mrs. Evona

AUGUST 11, 2006—
Why, Lord?
(From Mrs. Evona)

Several days ago, after dropping our children off for their first day of school, my friend Melody and I headed to Wal-Mart. We were energized and ready to shop until we dropped. However, upon entering the store we noticed something was amiss. It looked like someone had taken the store and turned it upside down and shook it around. Every single item was moved to a different place. They are remodeling the store and all the merchandise has been moved to temporary spots. Every department seems to be moving to another part of the store and they only moved half of the items when they relocated. We found hemming tape in the automotive department among the spark plugs and other boring items. Needless to say, this is very, very, very annoying when you are trying to find many items on a list. After searching fruitlessly for a long while for a container to help keep the backpacks organized we decided to ask an associate for help. Unfortunately, we chose poorly. The poor, tired, unhelpful clerk had no idea where the organizer items had been moved and no desire to help us locate someone who did have the answer to our question. Because of the disastrous state of the store, we never found the container we were searching for.

Almost ten years ago, after much anticipation Preacher and I brought home the cutest little bundle of joy. Unfortunately for him, we had no idea what we were doing. We mistakenly thought that being pet owners had prepared us for parenthood. Obviously not…Micah cried from the time we brought him home until he turned one. Strangers would come up to us and ask us what was wrong with him. Had we fed him? Was he hurt? All we could say was that we were not sure what the problem was; he had just come out that way. Even our family avoided inviting us places, due to the loud volume of his cries. Of course, during this same time my brother and his wife had birthed the "angel baby" named Kayla. While Micah screamed and everyone cringed, Kayla cooed and played with her toes while sitting contentedly in her baby carrier. I am sure that her sweet behavior only made Micah look that much worse. (I think my brother did this on purpose!) However, one clear sunny day in September, almost a year after he was born, we took Micah with us as we dropped my younger brother off for a youth activity. The activity was at the home of a couple who had a farm. Micah looked out the window of the car and said, "I want a goat!" We all turned around with our mouths hanging open and wondered when the "baby" had learned to talk. (Of course the answer to his goat question was NOOOOOOO!) That day was the turning point in Micah's young life. No longer did we have a screaming baby; we had a very articulate young man. The best that we can figure is that all the crying was because he was very frustrated at not being able to communicate (and he also had a lot of gas). This was all very exciting until the 7,000 questions. Once he began to talk, we have not had a quiet moment since. From the time he wakes up until he goes to sleep, Micah's mind is full of questions. How do cell phones work? Why would you bury someone if they are really in heaven? Is that lady going to have a baby or is she just fat? Why do ants bite me when I haven't hurt them yet? Do all old ladies have gray hair? How can that large man fit in that small car? Why doesn't make-up make all ladies look better? Can you stick a bean into your ear and blow it out your nose…and on and on and on. He is such a joy. We are very glad he is older and wiser. We have much fewer embarrassing situations now! At some point, Micah quit asking me questions. He still talked a blue streak, but didn't continuously ask me questions. One day curiosity got the best of me and I asked him why he didn't ask me very many questions anymore. His honest childlike answer was a large piece of humble pie. He sweetly replied, "I didn't want to bother you anymore, and besides, I wanted to ask someone who actually knows the answers to my questions, so I ask Papa!" To this day, we will find Micah and Papa sitting together in the leather recliner chair discussing how things work and many other complex life questions.

We are going through a very difficult time in our lives and many times I find the circumstances hard to understand. Some preachers teach that it is wrong to question God and that we should quietly submit to His will and never ask God "Why?" Strangely enough, after looking into this issue myself, I found over 275 times the word "why" is found in scripture. I believe that asking God "why" is not wrong. In Judges 6, Gideon is called a *"mighty man of valour."* And then in verse 13 he asks God a question that has been on my heart a lot lately. *"And Gideon said unto him, Oh my Lord, if the LORD be with us, why then is all this befallen us? And where be all his miracles which our fathers told us of…"* God hears Gideon's question and lovingly answers his cry. In verses 14-16 God says, *"Go…have I not sent thee?…And the LORD said unto him, Surely I will be with thee…"* God knows that Gideon was not asking why because he was angry. God knew Gideon was asking why because he knew he was asking the ONE who did have the answer. We spent a lot of wasted time in Wal-Mart trying to figure things out on our own, and then we asked the wrong person to help us. Many times we do this during a trial. We waste precious time being angry and bitter and then seek help from friends or others who do not have the answers we need. Just like Micah recognized the need to ask his questions to someone who would have the answers, we must head straight to God and pour our hearts out to Him. This is not questioning God's sovereignty; it is putting our trust in the character of God and realizing He is the only One who can answer our troubled cries. He alone sees the entire picture and knows how this small piece of the puzzle will fit to make us more like His Son.

Every few months, I have to take Baby Lucas to the doctor and voluntarily allow them to hurt him. Why would I do this? Because I can see that allowing the doctors to give him his shots may hurt for the moment, but they prevent potentially life threatening illness later on. When I look into his sad tear-filled eyes, I hurt knowing he is in pain. However, I am allowing the pain for his good. I can tell that he doesn't understand and this prompts me to comfort him even more. The big boys hate to go to these office visits, because they don't want to see Lucas cry. There are others who love us and are watching as we as Christians go through trials. It may be family, or friends, coworkers or neighbors. They only see the hurt and sadness in the trial. And just like the big boys, they may not want to see us having to go through such heartache. However, the One who knows best is holding us close, comforting us much like I would the baby after he gets a shot. I put my arms around Lucas and wrap his blue 'blankie' around his stiff body and love on him until the hurt goes away. This is what God does for us during our suffering. First Peter 5:7: *"Casting all your care upon him; for he careth for you."* We can turn to God and confidently ask "why" knowing that He has all the answers and that it is all for our good. First Peter 1:6:

> *Wherein ye greatly rejoice, though now for a season, if need be, ye are in heaviness through manifold temptations: That the trial of your faith, being much more precious than of gold that perisheth, though it be tried with fire, might be found unto praise and honour and glory at the appearing of Jesus Christ:...*

Turning in faith to the One who has all the answers,
Mrs. Evona

∞ ∞ ∞

August 12, 2006—
We're not Alone

We receive many emails from our "Pastor Health Update" page on our church web site, all of which are a blessing. We attempt to return emails but the number coming in grows faster than we can return them. One day we will catch up. We received a very special email we want to share with you in this update. It is from Mrs. Iola Cox. We were amazed at the parallels between our lives:

> *Pastor and Mrs. Evona,*
> *Thank you for documenting your story on the web. You have a lot of words of encouragement. I am writing from Winter Park, Florida, where my husband was diagnosed with a Glioblastoma Grade IV. We have three sons; ages 10 (Christopher), 8 (Caleb) and 7 months (Joshua). We also drive a red Ford Expedition. Surgery in April left Michael paralyzed on the left side of his body, unable to swallow, fighting pneumonia and unable to speak. Hospice gave him two weeks to one month.*
>
> *Through much prayer and rehab, Michael can eat and speak. It was such a treasure to have our first meal together as a family. It is such a treasure when he is able to communicate. (I didn't always value Michael's ability to talk throughout our thirteen years of marriage!) We continue to thank the Lord for each day that He has made and allowed us to be together in fellowship.*
>
> *We will remember you in our prayers.*
> *Iola Cox*

Evona and I were burdened by the trial the Cox's are facing. But at the same time, we were blessed by their thankfulness to God for things He had done through this tragic road. Notice the word, "treasure." Things that we once took for granted become treasures when we lose them and then get them back.

"*Giving thanks always for all things unto God and the Father in the name of the Lord Jesus Christ*" (Ephesians 5:20). There's something about thankfulness amidst trials. It shows faith in God's righteousness and goodness. Please pray for the Cox family as they walk with God through this valley.

We have received so many other messages of hope and stories of trials from many of you. A reoccurring theme for us has been needing to recognize the blessing it is to have such a large and caring support system. Many others going through trials have not been able to have this. It has been such a help and comfort to have our family, our wonderful church and all our friends and fellow Christians praying, sending cards and emails, helping with food and financial needs. We do not take you all for granted. We are truly blessed beyond measure.

Remembering others in the same boat,
Preacher & Mrs. Evona

August 13, 2006—
For Such a Time as This

When we face trials and tribulation, we search and search to find meaning in all our suffering. Many times it is not readily evident and we feel abandoned by God. It is so difficult to reconcile with our small minds that God has such wisdom and knowledge that we are not always going to be able to understand His purpose. However, in every situation, whether visible or not, there is a specific purpose scripture has given us for our trial. Romans 9:17: *"Even for this same purpose have I raised thee up, that I might shew my power in thee, and that my name might be declared throughout all the earth."* Strangely enough this verse was in reference to an unsaved, ungodly Pharaoh of Egypt. How much more can God use us and show His power through us as Christians if we are submitted to His will. We can be tools to show the unsaved God's power. God wants us to be available and willing tools. We find it such a comfort and privilege to be tools in God's hands used to declare His wonderful name throughout the earth and bring Him glory.

We don't understand nor would we have necessarily raised our hands and volunteered for our current situation, but God is in control. Each one of us has been uniquely chosen and placed in our own set of circumstances by a loving God. Mordecai told Esther in verse 14 of Esther chapter 4: "…*for who knoweth whether thou art come to the kingdom for SUCH A TIME AS THIS?*" God knows that we are here for "such a time as this" and that we all can bring glory to Him if we are willing.

Today is Sunday and I praise God for the growing strength He has given me this week, enabling me (God willing) to stand in the pulpit and declare the Almighty's name to all who will hear. "Who knoweth" if today is the day a lost soul will come to Jesus? "Who knoweth" if family will be in need of a loving church to join? "Who knoweth" if a young person will hear the call to serve the Lord? I want to be a willing tool in the all-knowing Father's hands "…*for such a time as this.*"

Tools in His hands,
Preacher and Mrs. Evona

August 14, 2006—
You Want to, Now Will You?

What a privilege it is to serve at such a faithful and loving church. Once again we had wonderful Spirit-filled services. It is such a blessing to know that no matter what condition I am in that our people will be there serving the Lord and ready to support me and my family.

I brought a message titled, "You Want to, Now Will You?" We as a congregation were very moved during our "We Choose Faith Rally" and are excited about serving the Lord. However, after the emotions fade and the memories are all we have left, we are still called to serve. We must take the burden God has laid on our hearts and continue steadfastly in the work of the Lord. Moses gave God a list of excuses, not unlike many of ours, yet God responded by saying, *"Certainly, I will be with thee"* (Exodus 3:12a). It doesn't matter what situation you find yourself in, God wants to mold you and make you usable. Evona closed the sermon out with a song by Jon Mohr called, "You Want to…Now Will You."[8]

> You've heard the words and know they're true, for now they ring inside of you.
> They're calling you to come away, now will you come or stay?
> You want to, now will you?
> The truth that burns within you like a bed of fiery coals,
> Contains the power to liberate a thousand captive souls.
> But if the truth will ever set you free depends on you.
> You want to, now will you?

Today we need to "Choose Faith" together. We are headed to Moffitt to take the first set of scans since the original diagnosis in May. The CT scan is at 8:30 A.M. and the brain and spinal MRI will be around 2:00 P.M. We are praying for a miracle. What a blessing it would be to confound and confuse the doctors with a significant change in the results. (I plan on drinking a gallon of "spot remover" before my tests—you never know!)

God is the Great Physician and He has everything under control. We know we can trust His loving mercy and depend on his grace to get us through. We will not know the results of the tests until Thursday afternoon. Keep us in your prayers, especially Evona; waiting is not her strong suit. (She stands at the microwave and hollers hurry!)

Trusting God for good results,
Preacher and Mrs. Evona

∽ ∽ ∽

August 15, 2006—
Holding Hands in the Dark
(From Mrs. Evona)

One morning after not sleeping well, I got up early. I love to head upstairs and work for a while before my family gets going in the mornings. I hate to disturb the preacher so I usually leave all the lights off and just feel around until I find my way out of the room. This particular morning, I was very tired and disoriented. I got out of bed and headed toward what I thought was the door leading out into the kitchen. (Remember, I have lived in this house for over 5 years and we have not moved the door or the kitchen during this entire time!) I spent a good 5 minutes groping and feeling, stumbling and searching, trying to find my way out of the darkness in a room I knew very well. Finally, Preacher asked what I was doing and I had to admit I was trying to find the door. I would love to tell you that he lovingly took my hand and led me out into the kitchen. However, those who know him wouldn't believe me anyway. I heard snickering and laughing from my sweet husband's side of the bed as he got up to help me out of the room. (Of course, he did kiss me and thank me for making life interesting for him.)

So many times in our lives we are traveling a road we think we have been down a thousand times, and then all of the sudden the lights are off and things seem different. This is when we are required to walk by faith and not by sight. We know the bed is there, and the dresser is there and somewhere is a door, but we can't seem to find our way alone in the dark. This is when we must hold out our hands with total trust and allow God to lead us (just like Preacher lead me, minus the giggling!).

Hebrews 11:1 says, "*Now faith is the substance of things hoped for, the evidence of things not seen.*" This verse means that we have absolute confidence and belief in something unseen, and that belief becomes our proof. We meet so many people that know about our circumstances and look at us with such pity in their eyes. They are sad for us, thinking that we are simple and naive, ignoring reality by "Choosing Faith" in God. Our choice is not one of ignorance. It is a choice to trust that God is good, even when the situation is not. It is a choice to trust that God is right, even when the circumstances we are in cause pain. It is a choice to trust that no matter what the outcome God is working ALL things for our good and His glory. "Choosing Faith" means that we run to our loving Father and place our hands in His, pouring our hearts out to Him in prayer and then trusting Him enough to know He will do right.

People have expressed their concern and worry over the boys and the effect Preacher's illness is having on them. We have had to learn to give them to God. It has been a struggle to know exactly what to say. We finally decided that we would together as a family "Choose Faith." Teaching them to "Choose Faith" does not mean we are telling them when they talk to God that He will answer exactly how they pray. That would not call for faith. Telling God what should happen doesn't require faith. Crying out to God and sharing your fears and hurts and then trusting Him to do what is right for us is what "Choosing Faith" is all about.

Yesterday we spent the day taking tests that can bring very good or very bad news. I would love to lift my handy dandy cell phone and call God, telling Him the specific outcome we would like. However, that is walking by sight not by faith. When we walk by faith, we acknowledge that God can and will do a miracle on His time table and in His own way. Just like Baby Lucas raises his chubby little hands in the air, knowing I will grab his sweet baby hand and lead him, we must raise our hands to a loving Father who will lead us through the darkness.

> "When I said, my foot slippeth: thy mercy, O Lord, held me up. In the multitude of my thoughts within me thy comforts delight my soul."
> PSALM 94:18-19

Thanking God for leading me in the dark,
Mrs. Evona

August 16, 2006—
Mirror, Mirror

You may have noticed the link labeled "Pastor Look-A-Like Contest." It will take you to a page where you may vote on who I most resemble in the world of famous baldies. Take your time now; there are some pretty good baldies. We'll tally the votes and announce the baldy that the majority chooses in a month.

They say that everyone has a look-alike; someone in the world who could pass for your double. Are you nervous yet? Your double could be on a crime spree and they'll be flashing your picture (your double's picture actually) on "America's Most Wanted," and boy, you will find out who loves you when you recognize your mother calling in, disguising her voice but ratting you out. Or your double could be lying in the street in front of your local pet store with other activists protesting the Poor Treatment of Poodles and by tonight, you'll have 25 messages on your machine making dog jokes, barking and panting and general dog humor.

There is someone you and I must strive to look like and that is Jesus Christ. Romans 8:29 teaches, *"For whom he did foreknow, he also did predestinate to be conformed to the image of his Son…"* This refers to every believer in Christ. It is our destiny to become like Jesus. The ultimate transformation will take place when Jesus raptures us from this world and we receive our new bodies (1 John 3:2: *"Beloved, now we are the sons of God, and it doth not yet appear what we shall be: but we know that, when he shall appear, we shall be like him; for we shall see him as he is."*). However, there is a responsibility today to be conformed to the image of Christ. (Philippians 2:5: says, *"Let this mind be in you, which was also in Christ Jesus."*) We cannot wait to become "Christlike," we must begin today!

One way to be more Christlike is to be filled with the Holy Spirit and allow Him to produce the fruit of the Spirit in your life (Galatians 5:22 and 23.) These are the character qualities of Christ that He exhibited in His time on this earth. As we yield to the Spirit and ask Him to produce the fruit, we will demonstrate Christ's character in our daily lives. This will affect how we treat the checkout girl and the bank teller. It will affect how we act at our children's games toward the opposing team, coach and referee.

Another way to be more like Jesus is to focus on others. In the passage from Philippians Chapter 2 teaching us to *"put on the mind of Christ,"* the two verses before this one focus on serving "others." This is the essence of Christ's mindset. He loved others enough to leave heaven and take on flesh. He loved others enough to die for our sins on the cross. He loved others enough to rise from the dead, providing salvation for all. The bottom line is…Jesus loved others! When we shift our focus from ourselves to others…Jesus is visible in our lives. Focusing on others involves listening. (James 1:19 says, *"…let every man be swift to hear…"*) People have heartaches and you and I can be like Jesus as we take the time to hear their hearts. We can also look for opportunities to do good to others. This is how Jesus lived His life.

Let's make it a goal to look in the mirror each day and see less and less of us, and more and more of Jesus.

Conforming to His image,
Preacher and Mrs. Evona

P.S. Don't forget to vote!!!!

August 17, 2006—
I'll Take the Good News First...
Actually, with God...It's All Good News!

I began having some tightness in my chest, sharp pains on my right side and shortness of breath over the weekend, which increased in the beginning of the week. We called the doctor because we were concerned I might have some fluid on my lungs. It was the same type of symptoms as before when I had fluid drawn off my left lung. We had taken the CT scan and the MRI on Monday and asked that the doctor take a look early to see if there was an immediate problem due to the pain. Tuesday evening we were called and asked to come in early Wednesday morning instead of Thursday. They were concerned with what the radiologist called a pneumothorax. (This is air leaking outside the lung.) I was so discouraged and upset at the prospect of yet another chest tube. We cried and prayed together and then gave it over to the Lord. It was so difficult to understand how this was for our good. But we must "Choose Faith" no matter what. Psalm 62:7–8 once again spoke to our hearts. *"In God is my salvation, and my glory: the rock of my strength, and my refuge, is in God. Trust in him at all times; ye people, pour out your heart before him. God is a refuge for us. Selah"* Trust in God even when you are headed towards the hospital knowing a chest tube is waiting. Trust in God even when you are worried that another hospital stay will be more difficult on your family now that the kids are in school. Trust in God even when you know you will not be able to preach the Word to your people. Trust in Him at all times.

We met with the doctor who had reviewed all of our scans. He did see a small increase in the air outside my lung but felt it was not an issue to be dealt with at this time! PRAISE THE LORD! NO THIRD CHEST TUBE! We were so overwhelmed that we almost missed the rest of the results. The chest CT showed that the mass in my lung had shrunk and the brain MRI showed that no new tumors had grown. The spinal MRI, however, showed that the cancer had grown some on my bones. Dr. Simon decided that it was time for what he called the second line treatment. It is a treatment that will be taken at home in pill form daily. This new medicine has had great success with patients with lung cancer that have never smoked. The doctor said he was very optimistic that this medicine would help fight my cancer. We are very excited that we will have 2 months on this medicine. This will give me time to regain my strength and not have the fatigue and other side effects from standard chemotherapy.

Each day brings new challenges for all of us. We may not know what the day may bring, but we know who can help us through. Psalm 28:7: *"The LORD is my strength and my shield; my heart trusted in him, and I am helped: therefore my heart greatly rejoiceth and with my song will I praise him."*

Praising Him with our song,
Preacher and Mrs. Evona

◯◯ ◯◯ ◯◯

August 18, 2006—
The Heavenly Taste Test
(From Mrs. Evona)

We often discuss among ourselves how sorry we are for the poor unknowing ones who blindly married the "Boyette" kids (my maiden name). It has been especially hard on Pastor because of my two brothers. From the time we began dating, we always had one or the other hanging around. They have enjoyed giving each other grief from early on. Several months ago we had a family get-together at my mom and dad's house. As usual, my mom went all out. We had enough food to feed all of you and then take home leftovers. (Somehow we seem to eat it all though!) This particular time my mom was trying out a new recipe, and the boys couldn't wait until their "sweet" brother-in-law Cliff would arrive. As usual, Preacher headed straight for the kitchen and started munching. Ever so quietly they brought out the new recipe. It looked beautiful. She had made a lovely meat dip with crackers arranged all around. It only took about 2 seconds for Preacher to spy the new dish and dive in. He made yummy noises so loud Micah, Caleb and I were embarrassed. I figured something was up, due to the whispering and pointing going on in the kitchen. (My dad and mom did not seem to be involved, but you never know!) After about three or four crackers had been wolfed down, my brothers could not contain themselves any more. Loud laughter burst forth and everyone came in to see what was going on. Kevin took great delight in announcing to Preacher that the "yummy meat dip" was really a dip made from salmon (the fish!). I have never seen the preacher move so fast as he headed down the hall to swish and spit and try to get the fish taste out of his mouth! Over the years, Preacher's aversion to seafood has given my family much entertainment!

Unfortunately, the reluctance to try new foods has been passed down to our children. I have had much "fun" trying to get the boys to branch out and try new things. The older two were much more willing to try things when they were little. Now, they pretty much want everything to be separate and green beans are the vegetable of choice. However, something happened when we brought Lucas home from the hospital. I think while I was sleeping that first day, all the boys (Daddy included) went in and told Lucas that I would try to make him eat weird things before he was big enough to protest. He evidently remembered this "talk" and has developed food opinions at a very early age. He loves to eat; if you are eating, he is highly offended if he is not included. Now, I know I don't want to eat the same dish three meals in a row, but babies are different. They are not supposed to care. Not so with our little Lucas. He will absolutely eat more food than I do for dinner, and then refuse to even taste the same dish the next day for lunch. He will bang on his tray with his spoon, announcing to everyone that he is ready for dinner. I put his dinner on the table and begin to feed him. He takes one "look" at what is on the spoon and passes instant judgment on the meal. If it doesn't look exactly like what he wants, he screws his little face up and will not even open his mouth. I thought babies would at least wait until it hits their taste buds to spit it out. No such luck with our little one. He can tell by just looking at the food if it is what he wants or not. I got the bright idea to squeeze his fat little cheeks

together and shove the spoonful right on in. I mean, he ate it last night, right? It is not that he doesn't like it; it is that he just doesn't realize what it is. This plan was not my best and resulted in a very happy dog and a very messy floor. We have had to compromise. I will vary his meals and he will eat what we give him. (I am not sure who is winning this game!)

God has made us a beautiful banquet of promises. He has lovingly prepared them just for us. Yet we walk by the table and make the ugly face Lucas makes and refuse to even try out a sample. How many times have we said to our children (or husbands?) "Just taste it! It's good! You'll love it if you will just try it!" Psalm 34:8: "*O taste and see that the Lord is good: blessed is the man that trusteth in him.*" God is asking us to do the same thing we want from our children. Just try it. It may look strange, smell different or be something that is new, but just try it. It is good! God doesn't ask us to eat the entire table full of promises. He just wants us to taste a little bit and see. The end of the verse says that we WILL be blessed if we trust in him! How many blessings are we missing? How many answers to prayer are we not hearing? How many trials do we have to handle on our own because we refuse to even "taste" just a little bit of what the Lord has prepared for us?

From experience, the table He has laid out does have some wonderful sweet desserts. There are also many dishes filled with vegetables and other foods that are not so easy to acquire a taste for. But they all are laid out for our good, providing us with a balanced meal that will produce a strong, healthy faith in God. We can trust God to give us just what we need to eat, if we will only "taste and see."

> *I will bless the Lord at all times…O magnify the Lord with me…I sought the Lord, and he heard me…This poor man (or lady) cried, and the Lord heard him…O taste and see that the Lord is good…for there is no want to them that fear him…Come, ye children…I will teach you the fear of the Lord…The Lord is nigh unto them that are of a broken heart…and none of them that trust in him shall be desolate.*
>
> PSALM 34

Branch out and "taste" the goodness of the Lord. You don't have to eat it all; just give it a try and "taste and see." I know you will find, just like we have, that "the Lord is good."

Feasting on the goodness of the Lord,
Mrs. Evona

∞ ∞ ∞

August 19, 2006—
Seeing through Satan's Lies and Surrendering to Christ's Truth

So far eighty-three votes have been cast, with Curly in the lead, but not by a long-stretch; breathing down his 27-inch neck is Uncle Fester (still a delight in any race), followed closely by Mr. Clean and King Yul. If you don't know what I'm talking about, go back several pages to the page titled "Pastor Look-A-Like Contest." We thought we'd have some fun amidst this challenge we've been facing. Now, it's no less a challenge when you learn to laugh as you suffer, but it sure does make the experience a lot less painful. So…check out the page and vote if you haven't already.

Now, let's get spiritual. That's what we say in church when we've told all our jokes and used up all our filler material. Evona has started leaving me little sticky notes to find when I get up after she has left to take the kids to school. This is something we did years ago when we were first married and she'd have to leave early to teach school. We called it, "Sticky Note Devotions" and I still have a lot of the ones we left each other back then. She leaves them in places she knows I will go in the morning…the mirror (I have to check my part), the fridge (I have to drink my lovely morning Boost) and my wallet (I have to check my secret compartments to see if the cash is there.) Funny…she never leaves one on the dishwasher or the washing machine!

This morning, one of her sticky note verses was 2 Corinthians 10:5, which says: *"Casting down imaginations, and every high thing that exalteth itself against the knowledge of God, and bringing into captivity every thought to the obedience of Christ;…"* The context of this verse is the spiritual war we are fighting with Satan in our daily lives. Satan uses imaginations and high things that exalt themselves against the knowledge of God. To the Apostle Paul, these were various attacks on the Word of God as he endeavored to preach. Satan would seek to draw Paul away through "imaginations," things with no substance. He would seek to hinder Paul by using false teachers to exalt high things against the Scriptures. Paul would have none of it! He worked through God's power to bring his every thought into the captivity and obedience of Christ.

We, too, are being attacked by Satan in this subtle way. In our situation, the devil will whisper in our ears, "If God cares about you and your family, why is He letting you go through this?" or "No one in the medical profession believes you will beat this cancer. Why don't you just quit fighting and accept the inevitable?" If we can see Satan's attacks and arguments, and a host of others, for what they are, "imaginations"—things with no substance, and "high things"—things that seek to exalt themselves above God's Word, we can bring all our thoughts into Christ's captivity and obedience. In other words, we can see through Satan's lies and surrender to Christ's truth. We still believe God cares about our family in all the trials of life and we have met many medical professionals who are praying for my healing! It's all about who you're going to listen to.

I found another sticky note that I'll leave with you. It said, "Fear is a feeling, faith is a choice."

Fighting the fight with faith,
Preacher

AUGUST 20, 2006—
In Acceptance Lieth Peace
(From Mrs. Evona)

After years of testing, I have found that stomping my feet when things don't go my way does not eliminate or fix the problem. One evening I was frantically getting ready for a date with the wonderful, handsome, dashing, young youth pastor of our church at the time, Preacher Cliff. He was patiently waiting on me to "beautify myself" for our date. I was trying with little success to make my hair cooperate. (Now remember, it was the end of the '80s and big hair was in!) While waiting, Preacher needed to wash his hands and so he headed down the hall towards our back restroom. This path led him right past my room where I was vainly trying to finish getting ready. I had taken my curling iron (the old kind with plastic teeth like a brush) and wound my hair around too many times. Those of you who have used this terrible contraption will immediately know the result of my haste. My lovely, long, permed, frizzy hair was now hopelessly caught in the awful curling iron. I responded in my normal grown-up way by fussing loudly at the curling iron and stomping my feet. That is the exact moment I made eye contact with "my date." Fortunately for me, I already had him "hooked" and he overlooked my small outburst and married me anyway. He was also a very good sport about having to take me out on our date with a very large "rat's nest" in the back of my hair. I have learned to control these episodes; however, our youngest inherited the "stomping of the feet" gene. Pray for us! We are in for a long battle.

I have recently started reading a new book by Denise Siino called: In Her Steps, Women of Courage and Valor.[9] One of my favorite contemporary examples of faith, Elisabeth Elliot, was one of the women chosen for the book. Elisabeth Elliot grew up in a missionary's home. Her outlook on practical Christian living was dramatically shaped by true, dedicated, everyday men and women who loved the Lord. Even as a child, she recognized the principal of being a true disciple of Jesus Christ. Luke 9:23–24: "*And he said to them all, If any man will come after me, let him deny himself, and take up his cross daily, and follow me. For whosoever will save his life shall lose it: but whosoever will lose his life for my sake, the same shall save it."* She didn't know the extent or the size of the cross she would be given to carry, but she was willing. After having been married less than 3 years to Jim Elliot, they, along with four other couples, felt burdened to evangelize the Auca Indians. These five men and their families bravely traveled far into Ecuador reaching out to a lost and needy people. On January 8, 1956, five days after the men had set up a field base on a stretch of beach along the Curaray River, the families lost contact with the missionary men. Two days later the wives were told that all five men had been murdered by the same Indians they had longed to reach for Christ. Elisabeth held her 10-month-old baby girl in her arms and remembered the words of the nineteenth-century missionary, Amy Carmichael: "In acceptance lieth peace." With a broken heart she turned toward God and accepted His sovereign decision. Her response to others who asked about her sense of peace was this: "What else can you do except turn to Christ and say, 'Lord, you are in charge, I accept this.' Following means one step at a time, one day at a time."

What a woman of faith! However, her story does not end there. She and her daughter eventually returned to the Auca Indians and lived there for over two years. She evangelized this lost tribe, showing Christ's love and forgiveness through her own life. She has taught countless others through the years that serving Christ requires denying self and being willing to carry your cross.

In acceptance lieth peace. What a profound truth. When we are faced with trials, we can stomp our feet and argue with God, or we can trust His sovereignty. Psalm 63:7: *"Because thou hast been my help, therefore in the shadow of thy wings will I rejoice."* We can turn around and survey our lives and see the sovereign hand of God. Based on His past faithfulness we can safely rest in the shadow of his wings. I don't understand why we have been chosen to travel this path, but I do know that God is in control.

Every time I think we are making progress, we seem to face new challenges. Preacher was not feeling well at the beginning of the week. Knowing the scans were coming also added additional stress. After hearing good news about the scans, we headed home with a bag of new medicines. One of these new medicines caused a severe reaction and we were knocked down once again. During that night, the baby woke up with croup. I sat holding a miserable baby, asking God to just get me through the night. His sweet peace came down and covered me in the shadow of his wings. The circumstances had not changed, but my perspective had. Morning came and Preacher's allergic reaction was improving and the baby was feeling better. Elisabeth Elliot said, "Following means one step at a time, one day at a time." We can confidently turn to God and trust Him. Following Him one step at a time, one day at a time.

"He is no fool who gives what he cannot keep to gain that which he cannot lose." Jim Elliot (Elisabeth's martyred husband)

Accepting God's plan and receiving God's peace,
Mrs. Evona

August 21, 2006—
Tarceva Begins!

We had a great day at Fellowship yesterday, August 20, with a tremendous crowd, wonderful music and the empowerment to preach both morning and evening services. I began a three-part series called "Forming a Friendship with Christ."

The series will focus on three different ways from John 15 that we can form a friendship with the Lord Jesus. This message focused on the principle of "intimacy." Christ compares our relationship with Him to the relationship of the vine to the branches.

John 15:5: "*I am the vine, ye are the branches…*" As the branches draw their life from the vine, so we draw our life from Christ. To enjoy an intimate relationship with Christ, we have to "abide" in Him. To "abide" in Christ, we must spend time in His Word and in prayer. John 15:7: "*If ye abide in me, and my words abide in you, ye shall ask what ye will, and it shall be done unto you.*" These two elements, prayer and time in the Word of God, deepen our friendship with Christ as we commune with Him in prayer and He reveals Himself to us through His Word. There is no way we can make it through our daily trials and challenges without an intimate relationship with Christ. His is a friendship we cannot afford to live without.

We began the new treatment called Tarceva last evening. Tarceva is a pill that I will take every day for two months which fights lung cancer in patients who have never smoked. It has a 25 percent response rate, which is a much higher response rate than traditional chemotherapy. Our oncologist, Dr. Simon, is very optimistic about the prospects of this treatment. Please pray that as I begin this treatment, I will be spared the side effects that sometimes accompany it.

My appetite is getting better every day. Night before last (August 19), after we'd settled in for bed, I got hungry. I got up and made myself a plate of lasagna (from supper) and enjoyed it so much, I made another one. On Sunday afternoon, I wanted a snack before church and then ate dinner after we returned home. Praise God for answering your prayers and touching my appetite.

Throughout this entire process, we have found Christ to be a faithful friend. Whether we were facing whole brain radiation, chemotherapy or weeks in the hospital with a chest tube, He was always there to comfort and guide us through. We long for each one of you to find the peace that comes from an intimate friendship with Christ.

Abiding in Christ,
Preacher and Mrs. Evona

August 22, 2006—
When No One's Looking

> *"For I rejoiced greatly, when the brethren came and testified of the truth that is in thee, even as thou walkest in the truth. I have no greater joy than to hear that my children walk in truth."*
>
> 3 John 3–4

The Apostle John writes this to a young pastor named Gaius and his church. John calls himself "the elder," which implies he is older and he looks upon this congregation as a father does his children. John has intended to come and visit Gaius and his people but has been prevented by a prideful man in the church named Diotrephes. John commends the church, "my children," for walking in truth in his absence. He is filled with joy that some of his "children" in the faith were doing right whether he was with them or not.

I have 3 John 4 hanging in my office at church. It is a reminder to pray that our boys will do right when they are away from us. This year the verse has been put to the test. We have homeschooled the boys up until this year and the bulk of their time has been spent with us. This past year, with the new baby arriving, Evona and I prayerfully decided to send the boys to Christian school—" Real School" as Micah calls it. (His mother loves it when he says that!) We were nervous about many things, such as finances, finances and finances. This turned out to be the least of our worries as the Lord provided the funds for their entire year within a month. We were also concerned about the boys doing right while they were away from us. Would they respect authority? Would they treat other kids like Christ would? Would they make the right friends and talk right? Would they belch out loud? (This one particularly worried me, as I knew that I would receive the blame if they should commit this transgression.) It has not been a month since starting school, and we have already received notes from both of the boys' teachers commending their behavior and their attitudes. Just today, Caleb noticed at lunch that one of the boys at his table didn't have a drink, so he gave him his drink. The teacher noticed and gave him a "move up," which is a reward for doing good. At the pep rally last week, the principal was throwing candy to everyone and Micah caught a piece. He noticed a little girl on the front row did not get any candy, so he gave her his. It makes us proud that the boys are doing right when we are not with them and many times when they think no one is looking.

Our church, Fellowship Baptist Church, has been a real example of this truth. When I was diagnosed with cancer, I turned over pastoral care to our associate pastor and began to work from home. I also have limited my time at church on Sundays and Wednesdays to strictly preaching or attending the services. This is due to fatigue and insulating myself from germs and infections. I don't like it but it is a necessary evil right now. In my absence, our church has stepped up to the plate! People are faithfully attending and serving in their ministries! Our offerings are outstanding as our folks are giving extra! People are volunteering to do things around the church to help! It is a blessing to see the church is not built on the pastor but the Lord, and whether I am there or not, the great people of Fellowship do what's right.

My father-in-law would always say to his kids, "Do right, because it is right to do right!" Let this be our goal as believers—to do what is right no matter who is looking or if we think no one is looking. The fact is we are under the watchful eye of the Lord at all times. He is the One we must live for each moment of every day.

So far I've had no side effects from my first Tarceva treatment. We'll keep praying this treatment treats my body well and works to destroy this disease. We would ask you to pray with us in this.

Doing right when no one's watching,
Preacher

∞ ∞ ∞

August 23, 2006—
We Do Not Well

> "Then they said one to another, We do not well: this day is a day of good tidings, and we hold our peace: if we tarry till the morning light, some mischief will come upon us: now therefore come, that we may go and tell the king's household."
>
> 2 Kings 7:9

This verse is from an event that took place in the days of the prophet Elisha, when the kingdom of Israel's capital, Samaria, was being besieged by the Syrians and were facing the worst famine they had ever known. God miraculously delivered Israel by causing the Syrians to hear chariots in the night. The Syrians fled leaving behind a camp filled with food and drink, as well as gold, silver and expensive clothing. That same night, four hungry lepers decided to throw themselves at the mercy of the Syrians, only to find the empty camp and the unbelievable spoil left behind. They began to partake when one of the lepers said to the other four, "We do not well..." referring to keeping the blessings God had given them from their starving countrymen. They traveled to the king of Israel and let him know the good news and everyone enjoyed God's blessings!

God's blessings are made to be shared, not stockpiled. The Lord blesses His people for their good. All of us can give testimony to God's blessings and could go on for hours of His goodness upon our lives. Yet we fail in an important area if we stop with ourselves. "We do not well" if we keep the blessings of God to ourselves. God gives so that we can be a channel of blessing to others in need. When God blesses us financially, we can find someone we can bless that is in financial need. When God blesses us with something new for our houses, we can find someone to bless with the item being replaced. (We don't have to put everything in the "Flyer"). When God blesses us with children, we can find someone who cannot have children and bless them with encouragement. When God blesses us with success in our jobs, we can find someone who has not succeeded and bless them with an anonymous gift. There is always a way to let God's blessings flow through us to others if we look for it. We can either be like the Dead Sea, a sea with no outlets that flows nowhere and stockpiles all of its precious minerals; or we can be like the Jordan that flows to countless inlets and feeds them with its bubbly water. "We do not well" if we keep God's blessings to ourselves when they were meant to be shared.

I'm still doing great after two treatments of Tarceva and rejoicing in no side effects so far. Of course, these side effects can come later, as well, so keep praying. My appetite gets better and better every day and I believe I'm getting stronger. My cough is almost gone (What a blessing—that cough irritated everyone, especially me). My voice is also getting stronger. I notice the improvement in the pulpit when I preach and the volume comes out loud and strong. (I hope I'm correct about this because I do have hearing loss! Evona accuses me of having selective hearing loss, but I don't know what she is talking about!) The Lord has been unbelievably great to our family! We cannot thank Him enough and all of you for your loving support. I look forward to the day when God heals me and we can stand together at a rally someday called "We Choose Glory" and give God all the glory for delivering me!

Flowing like the Jordan,
Preacher

AUGUST 24, 2006—
Packing for the Journey
(From Mrs. Evona)

Over the past few months I have learned that to take a journey of faith you have to do a lot of leaving. I know that sounds odd; if you are going to go somewhere, first you have to leave where you are, right? This concept has totally eluded me until this past week. In Genesis, Noah must follow God by faith and build an ark. (That was the easy part.) Then he has to talk his wife and family into leaving their home and getting on the ark with a lot of smelly animals. Ruth must leave her homeland and follow her mother-in-law, of all people, (now I have a wonderful mother-in-law, I am referring to those of you not so fortunate!) and head to an unknown land! Things aren't so great when they arrive and Ruth ends up gathering the grain that the workers dropped. David is actually anointed KING of Israel, but must leave his home and his family and head to the palace to serve the man who he is going to replace! When God called Elisha, he has to kill his oxen (his source of income) and eat them and then leave his home. (Preacher thinks fish is hard to swallow…try oxen!) Joseph is taken away from his home and sold into slavery, by his brothers no less! Daniel and the three Hebrew boys are relocated from their home away from their families and then have to only eat vegetables and drink water! Deborah the Judge has to leave her comfortable position under the palm tree to head into war with Barak. Jonah is called to an ungodly city to preach, decides he is not going and ends up being swallowed and then thrown up by a whale. (Talk about a rough start to a journey!) The disciples are told to put down their nets and follow Jesus and then they end up being followed everywhere by sick and crazy people wanting to be healed. And on and on it goes. I could fill the page with biblical examples showing that the first step in our journey of faith is the call to leave.

 We must leave behind our "perfect" plans for our own future. We must leave our comfort zone and head into uncharted waters. We must surrender our own dreams and allow God to lead us and replace those dreams with something bigger and better. I was very comfortable with being married to a wonderful man, homeschooling my boys and working hard in our ministry. I loved just being a MOM! However, God has called us to leave behind these things as we know them and set out on a journey! The great part about this journey is that Preacher and the boys are right there with me. (I could have left the dog and hamster behind, but strangely enough God called them too! Side Note: The hamster's days are numbered!)

My favorite journey of faith is the Exodus of the children of Israel from Egypt. God does amazing miracles, showing that He is ready for them to begin their journey of faith to the Promised Land. Off they head, singing and dancing, all excited about the trip until the reality sets in of what they left behind. God really has a wonderful sense of humor. He dealt with the men through their stomachs. They have to eat the same things day after day until they learn to trust God. He dealt with the women by making them wear the same pair of shoes for the entire 40 years! After a year or two I bet a lot of the ladies were wishing they had worn their walking shoes, not their cute stylish sandals!

When it is time to leave on your journey of faith, what are you going to pack? What shoes will you take? The year after Preacher and I were married, we took a wonderful mission trip to the Philippines. I was very concerned with my wardrobe. It was important to me that I had 3 weeks of different clothes and matching shoes for each outfit. When we arrived in California, we had to pick up our luggage and carry it across the very large airport and check it in with the international airlines. I had to carry all four of my personal suitcases by myself the entire way! Preacher was helping the older ladies in our group with their luggage and carrying his own. I was not a happy little newlywed! But I kept telling myself that it would be worth it when we arrived and I had matching shoes for every outfit. No one bothered to tell me that we would be hiking, riding in a motorcycle sidecar while holding on to my flannel graph board and squishing down dirt roads after it had rained the entire time we were there! I wore the same ugly pair of tennis shoes with every outfit for all three weeks. However, we still had to carry the very heavy suitcases, filled with my "cute stylish sandals." There were many things I wished I had left behind on that journey.

Jeremiah 1:7–8: *"But the* LORD *said unto me, Say not, I am a child: for thou shalt go to all that I shall send thee, and whatsoever I command thee thou shalt speak. Be not afraid of their faces: for I am with thee to deliver thee, saith the* LORD." God gives Jeremiah the call to leave in these verses. He then promises that even though Jeremiah must leave behind many things, one thing is certain…God is going on the trip with him! What a comfort to know that no matter where we are called to go and what we have to leave behind, God will be there every step of the way!

Where is God calling you to go? What is God asking you to leave? Make sure you pack wisely for your wonderful journey of faith. Leave the heavy, bulky hindrances that will cause you to slow down. Make sure you pack your running shoes not the little flip flops that are hard to walk in and fall off every time you turn around. You never know, you might have to wear whatever shoes you pack for the entire 40 years! Focus on the wonderful reward waiting for you if you "Choose Faith." Isaiah 61:3 tells us just where our journey of faith will lead. *"To appoint unto them that mourn in Zion, to give unto them beauty for ashes, the oil of joy for mourning, the garment of praise for the spirit of heaviness; that they might be called trees of righteousness, the planting of the Lord, that HE MIGHT BE GLORIFIED."* Our trials and heartaches will be worth it all one day when we see Jesus. Until then, we will pack our bags and head out, leaving behind our human dreams allowing God to lead us so that He might be glorified through us.

Packed and ready to go,
Mrs. Evona

August 25, 2006—
Comfort from the Comforter

"I, even I, am he that comforteth you..."

ISAIAH 51:12a

"Blessed be God, even the Father of our Lord Jesus Christ, the Father of mercies, and the God of all comfort."

2 CORINTHIANS 1:3

"And God shall wipe away all tears from their eyes..."

REVELATION 21:4a

What wonderful verses from God's Word promising us comfort when our souls are in anguish. The most beautiful thing in these verses is the source of our comfort...the Lord Himself. God promises Isaiah who faced numerous burdens that He would comfort him. God used Paul to encourage the Corinthians, who had their share of heartache and trial, that He was the God of *all* comfort. There was nothing that He could not comfort them regarding. God promises us through John's Revelation that we will ultimately be comforted in eternity and have all our tears wiped dry forever. There is no way around it—God purposes to comfort us in our sorrows, trials and burdens.

It is God's nature to comfort His children. A mother cannot hear her child crying and leave him/her to suffer alone. She will rush to the child to take him/her up in her arms and kiss the hurts away. It is her nature to comfort her own. How much more does God hear our cries and rush to us with needed comfort? God's nature is love (1 John 4:8b: "...*God is love.*") and He acts consistently with His nature. When His children need comfort, He comes to comfort them.

You may wonder—how does God comfort me when He is invisible and dwells in heaven? God provides His Holy Spirit to live with every believer. The Holy Spirit never leaves the believer and is called in John

14:26, "the Comforter." The Holy Spirit comforts us with an inward peace that we do not quite understand (Philippians 4:6–7). The Bible says that God's Spirit bears witness with our spirit (Romans 8:16) and He even intercedes with us in prayer when we are unsure how to pray (Romans 8:26). You may not recognize this as the Holy Spirit comforting you when it happens but He is actively coming alongside of you when you're hurting and He is helping you by comforting your soul.

God also provides His promises as a source of comfort when we're in need. The Word of God is called the "balm of Gilead" in the book of Jeremiah. It is a medicine that soothes our deepest hurts. When you need comfort, turn to the Psalms and allow God to pour in His healing Word into your heart. Psalms like:

3:3–"But thou, O LORD, art a shield for me; my glory, and the lifter up of my head."
6:2–"Have mercy upon me, O LORD; for I am weak: O LORD, heal me; for my bones are vexed."
9:9–"The LORD also will be a refuge for the oppressed, a refuge in times of trouble."
23:1–"The LORD is my shepherd, I shall not want."
91:1-2–"He that dwelleth in the secret place of the most high shall abide under the shadow of the Almighty. I will say of the LORD, He is my refuge and my fortress: My God; in him will I trust."

You can also find God's comfort in Lamentations 3:21–23: *"This I recall to my mind, therefore have I hope. It is of the Lord's mercies that we are not consumed, because his compassions fail not. They are new every morning: great is thy faithfulness."* Comfort is available in the New Testament in the book of Matthew chapter 28, verse 20 where Jesus promises, "...*and, lo, I am with you alway, even until the end of the world. Amen.*" or Hebrews 13:5: where Jesus assures us, "...*I will never leave thee, nor forsake thee.*" Some of the greatest comfort I have ever received from God has been from my Bible. It is indispensable when you need comfort.

One last way God comforts us is through His people. Just as a runner in a marathon is refreshed by people providing water along the way, God sends His people who have been through trials themselves to offer comfort to us. Second Corinthians 1:4: "*...that we may be able to comfort them which are in any trouble, by the comfort wherewith we ourselves are comforted of God.*" There is nothing that comforts a widow or someone who has lost a child like the embrace of another who has walked the same path.

If you are hurting today, there is no reason to remain without comfort when the Lord has provided such abundant resources to comfort your broken heart.

Enjoying the comfort of God each day,
Preacher

August 26, 2006—
The Taste Can Be Deceiving

It never ceases to amaze me how much change a few months can bring. If you had told me that at some point in my life I would need to worry about consuming MORE calories, I would have fallen out of my chair laughing. Food has always been one of my dearest friends. I would plan what I was going to have for lunch while eating my breakfast of pop tarts and diet Coke! Simply stated…*I love food!* As a Baptist preacher I am not allowed many vices, but I am allowed to eat.

Since the first round of chemotherapy, I have battled with a loss of appetite. I know, I know, many of you girls would love to have my problem, but the doctors seem to think I need to maintain my current weight. I never thought I would sit down to a plate full of fettuccini alfredo and feel sick just thinking about putting it in my mouth. People have been so kind bringing me all of my favorite foods, but nothing has even tempted me. The only way I have been able to keep my weight at a reasonable level is by drinking the "pond water" Boost supplements.

On our last visit to the doctor, he prescribed a new medicine designed to increase my appetite. We were so excited, praying the results would be good. The first morning Evona rushed to the cabinet and measured out a teaspoon of the "wonder syrup." I confidently called all three boys in to witness the pending miracle. With great drama I took the medicine dropper and downed it like a thirsty man marooned on a deserted island. The only way I can describe the taste of this "wonder syrup" is a cross between milk of magnesia and the bottom of a mud puddle. The disgusted, grossed-out face I made was so scary that it sent the baby crying from the room and left the big boys lying on the floor holding their sides from laughter. The amazing thing was that at lunch time I ate two helpings of lasagna and a large bowl of fruit!

How can something so awful produce such good results? The writer of Hebrews addresses this same issue in chapter 12 when he teaches about the blessing of chastisement. Hebrews 12:11: *"Now no chastening for the present seemeth to be joyous, but grievous: nevertheless afterward it yieldeth the peaceable fruit of righteousness unto them which are exercised thereby.*" We have given up buying real toys for our Baby Lucas because he has developed an obsession with kitchen utensils. His favorite pastime is emptying out any kitchen drawer low enough for him to reach and running all over the house with the contents of the drawer. Evona found a spatula in her purse and I found an egg beater in my shoe. This was very cute until he began running with forks. We knew it was time to make a change. Lucas, however, didn't appreciate being "de-forked" and let us know loudly at the top of his lungs of his displeasure. Our decision to correct and chasten him was not pleasant for him at the time, but ultimately it was for his safety and well-being.

God sends many things in our lives that at first taste as awful as my appetite enhancer but yield tremendous fruit in the future. If we could embrace this truth we would experience the good results much sooner. Even Christ had to drink the "bitter cup" of the cross so that we might taste the sweet grace of God. Hebrews 12:2: "*Looking unto Jesus the author and finisher of our faith; who for the joy that was set before him endured the cross, despising the shame, and is set down at the right hand of the throne of God.*" Thank God He was willing to face the cross to purchase our salvation.

We are taking a little time off together this weekend, thanks to Evona's mom and dad offering us the use of their vacation place. Melody and David Spencer are keeping our boys. What a complete joy and blessing it is to feel well enough to take my wife off for a weekend. And by the way, I ate a very large steak for dinner!

Getting fat and sassy,
Preacher (Evona says SHE is NOT getting fat and sassy!
Well, at least not fat!)

AUGUST 27, 2006—
Choosing Faith One Step at a Time

> *These all died in faith, not having received the promises, but having seen them afar off, and were persuaded of them and embraced them and confessed that they were strangers and pilgrims on the earth. For they that say such things declare plainly that they seek a country. And truly, if they had been mindful of that country from whence they came out, they might have had opportunity to have returned. But now they desire a better country, that is, an heavenly: wherefore God is not ashamed to be called their God: for he hath prepared for them a city.*
>
> HEBREWS 11:13–16

In this passage we see a clear pattern revealed to us by the many heroes of faith—a pattern that was given to us by God, to help us recognize where we are in our walk of faith. Knowing that all of these wonderful saints died before they saw the evidence of the promises they were given, it is confusing to see the phrase *"but having seen them afar off"* in these verses. If we only rely on our human sight, it will blind us to God's best. There are many blessings we blindly step over because we are not using our "eyes of faith."

Step number one in our journey as we walk by faith and not by sight is being persuaded. It is difficult to learn to lean and depend on God until fear and trouble makes us shaky and weak in our own strength. These great heroes of faith all went through trials that "persuaded" them that they needed to depend on God. Noah was laughed at; Abraham was required to forsake his homeland; Sarah was barren for most of her marriage; Moses was separated from his parents; Abel endured conflict with his brother for doing right; Joseph was forced to adapt to a new culture and then be treated unfairly. Their secret is given in Hebrews 11:34:"...*out of weakness were made strong*..." When we learn to depend on God through our weakness, we are persuaded that He is able.

Step number two is embracing the promises faith has allowed us to see and be persuaded of. We must passionately embrace the path God has laid on our hearts. This stage can be very scary. It may require sacrifice and heading out into unknown territory, but it is a necessary step on our journey. We need to continue to walk by faith and not by sight and embrace God's wonderful design for our lives.

The third and last step of faith listed is confessing our faith to others. Our attitude will help or hurt us as we strive to walk by faith. Confessing a positive attitude and spirit not only encourages others, it strengthens your own faith. Strengthening your faith is like building muscles—the more you exercise them the bigger they get! If you want to grow a strong and healthy faith, you have to have a positive attitude and confess this faith to others.

During your walk of faith it is easy to become discouraged and bitter. Even the great heroes of faith in Hebrew battled bitterness. Hebrew 12:15: *"Looking diligently lest any man fail of the grace of God; lest any root of bitterness springing up trouble you, and thereby many be defiled."* Bitterness can be very deadly to our faith. Confessing the goodness of the Lord to ourselves and others will help keep our faith strong.

Identify where you are in your walk of faith and strive to continue to grow. You will encounter opportunities to turn back and head where you came from. Hebrews 11:15: *"And truly, if they had been mindful of that country from whence they came out, they might have had opportunity to have returned."* However, if we keep in mind the awesome place God wants to take us if we will just trust him, we won't turn back. The heroes of faith "desired a better country" and knew God would give them the strength to walk by faith.

Taking it one step at a time,
Preacher and Mrs. Evona

August 28, 2006—
The Best Pain Medicine

Cancer can be so unpredictable. I have not had any pain to speak of for quite a while. The Tarceva treatments are going well and I get stronger physically and have a better appetite each passing day. This is why I wasn't expecting the sharp pain that hit me in the side this past Friday. It was so intense I had to sit down and hold a pillow tightly against my ribs to get it to ease off just a little. I took a pain pill and the pain subsided in about half an hour, leaving a lasting tenderness. There was no more pain until the next day when the same sharp pain hit me again in my side and this time also in my shoulder. We know that these pains are the cancer on my ribs and clavicle. A certain amount of pain is to be expected when you have a disease like this, but we also have medication designed to alleviate the pain. I am not one to hurt when I don't have to. If there is a medication available to help me that my doctor approves of, I will take it. I want to do my part to keep the pharmaceutical business thriving.

The problem we discovered was that my pain was stronger than my dosage of pain medicine. The medication would only take the edge off. I suffered through the night on Saturday, sleeping only short periods of time due to the pain waking me up often. The Lord and I did a lot of talking through the night. Sunday morning finally arrived and I was still experiencing the pains in my side and shoulder. It broke my heart that I was unable to attend church on Sunday morning and preach the sermon the Lord laid on my heart.

Pain is an unfortunate part of life. Everyone has some sort of pain they are dealing with. It may be physical, it may be emotional, and it may involve your family, your job or your church. Whatever the source of your pain, there are several things for certain…it is real and it hurts. One of the worst things that can happen to us when we're in pain is to have someone minimize our pain or even dismiss it. It happens many times because we have not experienced the pain of the other person and it doesn't seem real to us. The great news is we always have an understanding ear with our

Lord Jesus Christ. Hebrews emphasizes the priesthood of Christ and His ministry to us as our Great High Priest. It says in Hebrews 4:14–16:

> *Seeing then we have a great high priest, that is passed into the heavens, Jesus the Son of God, let us hold fast our profession. For we have not an high priest which cannot be touched with the feeling of our infirmities; but was in all points tempted like as we are, yet without sin. Let us therefore come boldly unto the throne of grace, that we may obtain mercy, and find grace to help in time of need.*

Jesus is the one person we can go to who ALWAYS knows how we feel. He not only has felt our pain, He is touched by the "feeling" of our infirmity. We do not have to explain our feelings to Him, He already knows. We hear a lot about "feelings" today, and rightly so, they are too often used to excuse wrong behavior. Jesus won't cater to our selfish feelings, but He will embrace our feelings of pain. With Christ, you can wear your feelings on your shoulder. Jesus cares and He waits to give us the mercy and grace to help us in our time of need. Mary and Martha were heartbroken at the death of their brother, Lazarus. Their tears moved Jesus to weep (John 11:35). He was touched by their pain...and He is by yours and mine. Pain medicine is valuable but Christ, our great High Priest is invaluable when we're hurting.

I was able to go to church Sunday night and preach! I preached from a stool because I was still a little short of breath. Praise God, though, I had no pain at the services whatsoever. The church was praying for me all day and I took my pain to the One who gave me the mercy and grace I needed.

Pain-free through Christ,
Preacher

August 29, 2006—
Who Is Like unto Thee?

"Thy righteousness also, O God, is very high, who hast done great things: O God, who is like unto thee"

Psalm 71:19?

This was the verse we used for our church staff devotion this morning. I asked the staff to meditate on the phrase, *"Who is like unto thee?"* throughout the day. Let's consider the phrase now and look at some of the verses that come after this one.

Verse 20 says, *"Thou, which has shewed me great and sore troubles, shalt quicken me again, and shalt bring me up again from the depths of the earth."* Who is like unto thee when we face troubles in life? Over and over again, our updates talk about life's troubles. We have learned through this struggle with cancer that we are not an island. Most people are facing some sort of trouble. Job 14:1 says, *"Man that is born of a woman is of few days, and full of trouble."* Life is both brief and burdensome. When we face troubles, it is time to ask ourselves, "Who is like unto thee?" God is always aware of our plight. We are never out of His watchful eye and His merciful care. Someone once said, "When God allows His children to go through the fires of affliction, He keeps one eye on you and the other eye on the thermostat." God promises to come to our rescue in times of trouble. Isaiah 33:2 says, *"O Lord, be gracious unto us; we have waited for thee: be thou their arm every morning, our salvation also in the time of trouble."* I don't know what your trouble is but God knows and there is no one like Him to deliver you in your time of need.

Verse 21 says, *"Thou shalt increase my greatness, and comfort me on every side."* Who is like unto thee when we experience great success? Life is not only filled with trouble, it also includes triumph. Amidst our valleys, there are many victories. Along with the sorrows God permits in our lives, He blesses us with successes. Oftentimes we let pride creep into our hearts and begin to think that our successes are of our own making. The Bible tells us in James 1:17, "*Every good gift and every perfect gift is from above, and cometh down from the Father of lights…*" Every success we experience is God-given. Who is like unto Him when it comes to our increasing greatness? We must give Him all the glory for all things.

Verse 23 says, "*My lips shall greatly rejoice when I sing unto thee; and my soul, which thou hast redeemed.*" Who is like unto thee when I needed redemption? All of us are born sinners. We can trace it back to Adam, who fell into sin and took the rest of mankind with him. Romans 5:12 says, "*Wherefore, as by one man [Adam] sin entered into the world, and death by sin; and so death passed upon all men, for that all have sinned.*" We received our sin nature through Adam but all of us are also sinners by choice. We are sinners by birth and sinners by choice. The penalty for our sins is eternal death in hell. A holy God must judge sin to remain holy and His judgment is death. This is where Jesus comes in! God's Son came to die in our place on the cross and pay our penalty. He was buried and He rose from the dead the third day in victory over death! All who will place their faith in Jesus Christ as their personal Savior receive eternal life in heaven. We call this salvation or redemption. Salvation means "deliverance" while redemption means "to make good use of." We have only One to look to for our redemption. Who is like unto Jesus in saving our souls? If you have never trusted Christ as your personal Savior, why don't you do so now? There is absolutely no reason to wait. Pray and confess your sins to the Lord. Confess that you believe Jesus died, was buried and rose from the dead to pay for your sins. Ask Jesus to forgive your sins and be your Savior. Salvation is by God's grace and through faith. This is a prayer God always answers "yes" to. Who is like unto thee? The answer is: NO ONE!

If you realized your need for redemption and prayed this prayer, we would love to hear from you. Having just one person accept Christ as their Savior would make any amount of suffering we have endured worth it all. Don't delay. You can never know what tomorrow may bring. For some of you it may be a mountain, but for others it may be the beginning of a valley.

Rejoicing in our redemption,
Preacher and Mrs. Evona

August 30, 2006—
How Does Your Garden Grow?
(From Mrs. Evona)

Whither is thy beloved gone, O thou fairest among women? Whither is thy beloved turned aside that we may seek him with thee. My beloved is gone down into his garden, to the beds of spices, to feed in the gardens, and to gather lilies. I am my beloved's, and my beloved is mine: he feedeth among the lilies.

Song of Solomon 6:1–3

In some households there are very distinct lines of responsibility drawn. Ours happens to be this kind of home. I always, always, always cook! Preacher won the "worst cookies ever baked" award at the men's bake-off several years back. His idea of cooking includes a George Forman counter top grill and hotdogs! Preacher always, always, always gives the dog a bath. I keep leaving the door open "on accident" and the dog runs outside. (I'm really trying to get the dog to run away but he is not smart enough to leave the yard and someone always brings him back!) Because of this bad habit of not being careful with the dog, Preacher doesn't trust me to not "accidentally" drown the dog while bathing him. I do the washing of our clothes, so that we don't have pink socks. He keeps the pool nice and blue, because the only color I can make our pool is green. I keep track of our schedule and Preacher tells me if the boy's pants are blue or black. (I can never tell the difference between blue and black.) And finally, he makes the money and I spend it! (I learned this from my mom!)

In the verses above, the question is asked, "Whither is thy beloved gone?" The answer is the same answer I give quite frequently at our house. "My beloved is gone down into his garden." Now, I don't really say those exact words. If I did, the boys would fall out of their chairs laughing. I do say that "Daddy is in his garden." Preacher spends a lot of time reading his Bible and praying in his garden. This is his place of peace (except for the mosquitoes! They are the size of birds here in Plant City! He says they have taken more of his blood than the nurses at the hospital).

For some reason, I was not asked to help with the planting or with the maintaining of "my beloved's" garden. This really hurt my feelings! Everyone who visits our home comments on the "beautiful" garden in the front and I would love to say (with great humility of course) "Oh, thank you. I just threw it together. Have I showed you my prizewinning roses on the other side of the house?" But NO! I am forbidden to help with the gardening around our house! How hard can watering and stuff like that be? I am quickly reminded by "my beloved" of the many, many, many house plants that have been handed the death sentence when they were given to me. I usually have one great week with them and then they head out to the back porch to die. Preacher says I have a "black thumb." A couple of weeks ago when I heard during the Sunday morning church service they were going to let the Preacher out of the hospital unexpectedly, most of you thought I darted out the side door to go directly to the hospital and be with the preacher. In reality, I rushed home to water all his "special" plants that I had neglected over the previous two weeks. Unfortunately, most of them were past the point of no return. I, however, did the noble thing and blamed the children!

Even those of us vegetationally challenged are still expected to "grow" good flowers in our garden of life. God expects us to plant, water and feed the tiny seeds that are in our lives and show a beautiful flower garden to all those who are watching us. Can you see a big open yellow sunflower of salvation in your garden? Ephesians 2:8–9: *"For by grace are ye saved through faith; and that not of yourselves: it is the gift of God: Not of works, lest any many should boast."* Are we growing beautiful lilies of love? I Peter 1:22: *"...see that ye love one another with a pure heart fervently."* Are there vibrant, colorful tulips of tenderness showing forth in your life? Ephesians 4:32 *"And be ye kind one to another, tenderhearted..."* Do the daisies of diligence spring up all over your lawn? Proverbs 21:5: *"The thoughts of the diligent tend only to plenteousness..."* Is the exquisite orchid of obedience flourishing for you? Deuteronomy 11:27: *"A blessing, if ye obey the commandments of the Lord your God..."* And finally, can you see a multitude of the marigolds of ministry showing others of your desire to serve your Lord and Savior? First Corinthians 4:1–2: *"Let a man account of us, as of the min-*

isters of Christ, and stewards of the mysteries of God. It is required in stewards that a man be found faithful."

It is a sad thing to drive by a home and see a dead withered yard and a neglected landscape. My back porch is a graveyard for poor unsuspecting plant life. Don't let your life be a dried up barren patch of ground. Grow beautiful vibrant flowers, showing others of your love and commitment to the One who gave himself for you on Calvary.

A gardener at heart,
Mrs. Evona

August 31, 2006—
I'm Sick of Cancer!

"I'm sick of cancer!" I said to Evona as we prepared to go to Wednesday Night Prayer Meeting. I had already been saying this to the Lord several times throughout the day. The Lord was gracious to listen to my list of complaints...I'm sick of being limited in what I can do physically...I'm sick of getting tired in the afternoons (I sleep through all my favorite soap operas, not really)...I'm sick of drinking Boost (I can't believe people actually make money on that old pond water!)...I'm sick of getting a shot each night (especially when my wife smiles while thrusting in the needle)...I'm sick of pills...I'm sick of not being able to hear clearly (although it comes in handy when someone hits a flat note in the choir behind me)...I'm sick of not being able to eat sweets and only wanting water to drink...I'm sick of itching because one of my meds doesn't like one of my other meds (why can't they get along?)...I'm sick of shortness of breath (if I have to be short in height, I shouldn't have to be short in breath)...I'm sick of controlling pain with a patch...I'm sick of my feet and hands being numb and getting cold then hot in a matter of seconds...I'm sick of sleeping in a chair because my chest tube incision scars hurt when I lie flat...I'm sick of having the driest mouth in Plant City (I wake up at night and think I've been sucking on cotton balls and sand)...I'm sick of having no hair and getting stared at in public (if they're gonna stare, they should compensate me)...I'm sick of not being able to stay after church and fellowship (except when it comes to the people I hate and don't want to talk to—I AM KIDDING, there is no one like that in our church; I ran them off years ago)...I am sick of not being able to pastor like I want to and like I used to...I am sick of doctor's appointments and treatments...I am sick of IV's, blood transfusions and that rubber belt they tie around your arm for labs...I'm just sick of the whole mess!

The Lord listened to me patiently today during the times I came to Him with my complaints and He seemed to be telling me that He had something to show me later that would help me with my feelings of frustration. After I voiced my feelings to my wife, we went to Prayer Meeting and just being in the house of God changed my attitude. The singing was good and Brother David Spencer brought a great message about preparing and dealing with the storms of suffering we all face. I came home and the Lord decided to show me what He had been saving for the right moment.

First, the Lord took me to the cross where Jesus suffered and died just for me. No one has ever suffered more than this. I hung my head, thinking of all Christ had done for me in saving my soul and how it cost Him His very life. The Lord spoke to my heart and said, "Isn't your life verse Philippians 3:10?" Of course I answered yes and then the words of the verse rang out, "*That I may know him, and the power of his resurrection, and the fellowship of his sufferings, being made conformable to his death.*" "Your own life verse says you want to know Me in the fellowship of My suffering. This is your chance, Cliff. You can join me in a deeper fellowship that many know nothing of. As you suffer, I will be right there with you. This is a fellowship."

Then, Christ took me to Moffitt Cancer Center, where the rooms are filled with cancer patients suffering terribly. Some are confined to the hospital for months as they get bone marrow transplants. Some are having chemotherapy that lasts for hours and is administered five days a week. Some are having surgeries to remove large tumors at great risk. I already knew what God was trying to tell me. There are so many who are suffering much worse things than I have. Instead of complaining, I can pray for them and minister to them. In fact, God has been very merciful to me through this entire process. He has worked miracles to get us where we are today—under the care of a tremendous oncologist and at one of America's top cancer treatment facilities. God did that! He has guided my doctors through treatment plans that have yielded good success. God did that! He has spared me of so many side effects and carried me through so many complications. God did that too! All the while, my suffering has been minimal. What a precious Lord we serve.

Finally, God showed me some of the faces of people who have been blessed and changed because of His allowing our family to face this trial: people in our church, people in other churches, people across the world that we've met through the website, people at Moffitt and people in our own family. If I had my way, these people would have remained unblessed and unchanged. How can I cheat others out of a blessing because I am sick of cancer? Well, I can't, and I won't. I'll stop complaining, accept the position God has placed me in, start praising and praying more and rejoicing in the opportunities God has given us through this battle.

At this point, I have had no side effects from the Tarceva treatments. My biggest problem is remembering that you have to take the pill 2 hours after you've eaten and you cannot eat one hour after you've taken it. For some reason, I get hungry as soon as I take that pill and have to wait an hour, which seems like an eternity when you have warmed up steak and rice on your mind. My snacks are not sweets, they are mini-meals. We praise God for giving me my appetite back!

I am also using a pain patch to control my pain from the cancer on the ribs and shoulder. We were controlling it with medication before this but this required a regimen of every four hours. The patch controls the pain for three days at a time! I have not had any side effects from the patch. Again, I see God's mercy on me. I am going in to the church office several half days a week now and I am planning on preaching in the midweek services as God allows me. Little by little, we're moving forward. Getting sick of cancer doesn't accomplish anything, but letting God use my cancer can accomplish a lot.

Learning to look at life through God's perspective,
Preacher

∽ ∽ ∽

SEPTEMBER 1, 2006—

Why Doesn't the Toilet Paper Fairy Come to My House?
(From Mrs. Evona, Obviously)

My understanding was that miraculously at the exact moment you said, "I do," you suddenly became responsible, mature and organized! However, I was given erroneous information (mostly from TV and true love novels). My wedding day came and went and the honeymoon was over. (The actual trip I mean! Because, of course, we are still newlyweds at heart!) We actually had to get up and go to work every morning. At that time I thought that if you had checks left in the checkbook, it meant you still had money in the bank. Obviously that mean man at the mortgage company didn't realize how important the three new outfits and the shoes to match were, or he would not have even asked why I spent the house payment money on them! One area I was very secure in was my cooking. I was a very good cook, as long as the base of the recipe had spaghetti sauce! After only 6 months of marriage, Preacher asked if maybe one night we could have something that didn't have noodles and require parmesan cheese. How ungrateful! During our first year of marriage I was very shocked to find a serious problem with our new home. Immediately I called my mom, knowing she would have the solution to my dilemma. After only thirty-four rings, my mom picked up the phone (she even has caller ID; I don't know why it took her so long to answer!) and I blurted out "Why doesn't the toilet paper fairy come to my house? He visits you every week and even puts the new rolls on the holders, but he hasn't shown up once at my new house!" For some reason it took her several minutes to regain her composure before she broke the terrible news that the toilet paper fairy was not real! I spent all my life taking for granted the fact that when the last little square of paper was gone, "someone" having already bought the toilet paper would rush right in and replace the empty roll with a nice, new, very soft roll of paper! Come to find out, it was my mother all along. Becoming an adult can be very painful at times!

Even with a new home, if things are not maintained, they fall apart. If you don't change the air filters, the air conditioner doesn't work very well.

If you don't put salt in the water softener, your water leaves spots all over everything. If you don't pull the weeds in the flower bed, you will not be able to see the beautiful landscaping Preacher spent so much time planting. If you don't empty the refrigerator once in a while, your son's science teacher asks if he can bring the class over to do experiments on the leftovers! Life requires a constant stream of maintenance. The pantry gets empty (especially trying to keep three boys fed), and if you don't go to the store and replace the food, there won't be anything to eat. The clothes do not jump out of the laundry basket (that is assuming they were even put in the basket) and run to the washer and wash themselves. (I knew those Tide commercials were too good to be true.)

Why do we think our spiritual lives will be any different? We seem to think that once we get saved, we are miraculously mature and sin free! This is a lie from the devil to keep us out of fellowship with God. We are given a new nature, but our old nature is still alive and well. We must do constant maintenance on our hearts to stay right with God. Colossians 3:8–10: *"But now ye also put off all these; anger, wrath, malice, blasphemy, filthy communication out of your mouth. Lie not one to another, seeing that ye have put off the old man with his deeds; and have put on the new man, which is renewed in knowledge after the image of him that created him:"*

Being homeowners has taught us many things. The most important thing we have learned is that it is very, very important to make sure your remember trash day! Trash that has sweltered in the hot garage for a week is not any fun! We have decided that our family is the "trashiest" family on our block! (Now, there are only two other houses on our block, but we always have at least one more full can of trash than either one of our neighbors!) In Colossians the verses talk about the type of "life maintenance" that requires "putting off" certain things. Just like trash from your home, you must discard sin that accumulates in your life. Anger, wrath, malice, blasphemy, filthy communication and lying are only a few of the sins we need to toss out to the curb. Getting rid of the trash and sin in our lives brings us closer to God and helps us maintain a wonderful open relationship with Him. Home maintenance is not only about making sure you get rid of things in a timely manner, it requires replacing and fixing items that need some work. We must "put on the new man, which is renewed in knowledge after the image of him that created him." We are to always strive to be more like Christ. We must "put on" the fruit of the Spirit." Galatians 5:22–23: *"But the fruit of the Spirit is love, joy, peace, longsuffering, gentleness, goodness, faith, meekness, temperance: against such there is not law."* These are not things that come naturally to us. We have to allow the Holy Spirit to work in us and give us knowledge that is only from heaven. Loving someone who has hurt us is not easy. Having joy during a trial is very difficult. Feeling peace in the midst of a storm that has destroyed our security is not natural. Being patient and gentle with those who have caused us pain and doing good for evil is impossible without God's help. "Choosing Faith" when circumstances seem to be insurmountable and responding to others with meekness and temperance when you are stressed and upset is overwhelming. But the good news is just like home maintenance, if you take it one little project at a time and go to the expert, you can keep things in good running order! God is patiently waiting for us to run to Him for his "expert" help. When we built our home, we didn't know how to lay tile or replace the "flusher thing" on the toilet, but we learned. We are given God's Word, the manual for "life maintenance." All we have to do is follow the instructions and things will stay well maintained.

Finding out that the toilet paper fairy was not a real person, and that I was responsible for making sure things were bought and replaced was eye-opening as a new bride. We are the bride of Christ and He wants us to grow and mature, making sure we keep our lives clean and pure through constant maintenance. First John 1:9: *"If we confess our sins, he is faithful and just to forgive us our sins, and to cleanse us from all unrighteousness."* God loves us and wants to help us clean up our lives and teach us to maintain a right relationship with Him.

Preacher was feeling great, and then I drug him shopping all over Brandon! I am sure this is just natural "guy" fatigue from shopping. For some reason, guy stamina is very limited when the words, "a few stores" or "mall" are mentioned! He is doing very well with his new medicine and has been able to resume some of his normal activities. Thank you for all your love and prayers.

Gone to buy Charmin,
Mrs. Evona

SEPTEMBER 2, 2006—
Delay Is Not Denial

This week our son, Micah, tried out for a chance to sing in the All-State Choir. If you make it in your local school auditions, you can send in a CD of your singing to the All-State committee, who will then decide if you get to sing in the actual choir. He tied with another student in the auditions for the final slot and the teacher said that she would call the house of the one who won that evening. All afternoon, Micah thought about the All-State competition. I could tell by the things he was saying that he did not think he had won. The more he had to wait, the more he seemed to decide that he had definitely not won. Then that evening, the call came...Both Micah and the other student won a slot and would be able to try out for All-State! He was thrilled! The waiting almost killed him though.

Most of the time in our lives we view waiting as negative. Now, don't get me wrong...I hate waiting! I stand in front of our microwave and yell "hurry!" I detest waiting for an appointment at the doctor's office. I think if you have an appointment at 1:00, you should see the doctor by 1:05. But that's not how it works. You wait in the big waiting room for an hour with magazines from the '60s and people with hacking coughs. Then you go to the small room and wait another hour. Of course, they send a nurse in to take your vitals and break up the wait time and she always says the same thing, "The doctor will be with you in a moment." This is an absolute lie. You should take a pillow because you will be there another 45 minutes sitting on that high table with the paper lining. I also hate waiting at theme parks in those lines that fool you. They look like you're almost at the ride, and then you turn a corner only to discover you're heading away from the ride. And there's always that person who is looking at the cracks on the sidewalk and holds up the line until someone thumps them. I don't like waiting! I don't like waiting in the bank line. I don't like waiting in the check-out line. I don't like waiting on hold to order a pizza. I don't like waiting in traffic. I don't like waiting on something to come in the mail. I don't like waiting at a restaurant for a table. I don't like waiting for the family to get ready so we can get out the door. *I just don't like waiting!*

Unfortunately, for me and many of you, waiting is a part of life. When I was much younger, I used to daydream about new inventions I could create to make my life better. One of these was a "No Waiting Club." I would be the president, of course, and admit members based on their level of intolerance for waiting. This club would have membership cards that permitted them to go in front of everyone else in the line and be waited on, while smiling and saying, "Sorry, but I cannot wait or I will grow depressed and winsome." This card would allow its bearer to march into the doctor's office and bypass the sign-in sheet and go straight back to wherever the doctor is and say, "Forget about him, I'm in room 3…NOW!" This card would permit you to put a police light on the top of your car and sound a siren so that you could move ahead of all other traffic as you passed by announcing in a loud speaker, "So long, slow pokes." This card would entitle you to never be put on hold through a device in your phone that would shock the apron off any pizza boy or girl who tried to push the hold button. Being a member of this club allows you to walk in front of the drive-up crowd at the bank, snatch the tube from the person in front, send your deposit through and say, "Waiting is for the pathetically average." It wasn't a nice club, but then again, I wasn't a nice person at the time. It's a good thing the Lord got a hold of me, isn't it?

Waiting. This is something we experience with God as well in many areas of life. God is sovereign and has His own timetable. We pray and we are ready for our answer. God always hears but He does not always answer us immediately. Sometimes, we're tempted to think God did not hear our prayers. There are too many scriptures that teach the opposite.

> Psalm 34:17 says, *"The righteous cry, and the Lord heareth…"*
> Psalm 65:2: *"O thou that hearest prayer . . ."*
> Proverbs 15:29: *"The Lord is far from the wicked: but he heareth the prayer of the righteous."*
> 1 John 5:14: *"And this is the confidence that we have in him, that, if we ask anything according to his will, he heareth us."*

God always hears our prayers and He always answers our prayers. God answers prayers in one of four ways, "Yes," "No," "Wait" and "I have something better than what you're praying for." We love "Yes" and "Something better." We hate "No" and "Wait." Yet God always has a purpose when He makes us wait. His timing is never wrong. He is omniscient (all-knowing) and He sees our entire lives. As a popular Christian song says about the story of Jesus raising Lazarus, "He was four days late, but He was right on time."

Often God wants to teach us patience through waiting. He plans to answer our prayer but He is using the experience to cultivate this fruit of the Spirit in our lives. Delay is not denial but it may be for development of our faith. Other times, God is testing our resolve in prayer. Will we give up if we don't get our answer right away? Will we take our bat and go home? Joshua had to march around Jericho 7 days for victory. Elijah's servant had to look at the skies seven times for rain. Naaman the Syrian had to dip in the Jordan seven times for healing. If they had given up on the sixth time, God would not have honored their resolve. Don't stop praying when the answer is not forthcoming. Show the Lord your resolve in prayer. Again, there are times when God is waiting on us to purge some sin from our lives. He is not going to answer a prayer of blessing on our lives if we are not walking in fellowship with Him. Confession and repentance many times brings the answer to prayer we have long been waiting on.

Waiting on God builds character and brings divine strength: Isaiah 40:31: *"But they that wait upon the LORD, shall renew their strength; they shall mount up with wings as eagles; they shall run, and not be weary; and they shall walk, and not faint."* Our family is waiting on God's healing of my body. We don't know how long it will be, but we plan to wait on the day when I can cut this purple "We Choose Faith" band off my wrist at church and declare by God's glory, I'm "cancer-free!" We're finding as we wait, He is fulfilling this verse and renewing our strength. Waiting isn't so bad when it's the Lord you're waiting on.

I am feeling great. Still no side effects from the Tarceva pill or the pain patch. Praise the Lord! I picked up a cold so we'll have to deal with that. Pray that it moves through my system quickly. I'm looking forward to being in church with my family this Sunday and preaching God's Word. I am even going to teach a Sunday School class for a month, and I am planning to be in the pulpit on the first Wednesday night of September. This will be my first time in the pulpit on Wednesday for months. I want to do all I can do while I feel so good. Keep our family in prayer as often as you can. Please don't be offended by my humor. I have always been like this and cancer is not going to change that about me! I love to laugh, to joke and to tease. It makes life better! If you don't care for the funny stuff, just eat the fish and spit out the bones (who wants bones anyway?)

In God's waiting room,
Preacher

∞ ∞ ∞

SEPTEMBER 3, 2006—
The Key Is to Start on Saturday

A few years ago, I was visiting with a deacon in our church. We went to see a young couple with four children. The couple had visited our church but had not been back in several months. We began talking with them about their children and their family when suddenly my deacon asked, "So why haven't you come back to visit with us?" The couple was shocked and to tell you the truth, so was I. After a brief pause, the wife began giving reasons why they had not returned, which included difficulty getting the family's clothes picked out and ironed, trouble getting the kids out of bed, bathed, fed, dressed and ready to head out the door and the trouble with finding Bibles, offerings and car keys. Without a moment's hesitation, my deacon replied, "If you're going to be in church on Sunday, you have to start on Saturday." I have never forgotten that statement. It speaks of preparation.

Preparation is one of the keys to succeeding in life. I have heard since I was a freshman in college the phrase, "Plan your work and work your plan." When we fail to prepare, we doom ourselves to either failure or mediocrity. Preparation is the foundation upon which we build. We prepare for presentations at work; we prepare for taking our children to school each day; we prepare for our vacations; we prepare for our financial futures and so much more. But do we prepare when it comes to the things of God? God is a God of preparation. Proverbs 8:27 speaks of when God prepared the heavens. Psalm 147:8 says that God prepares rain for the earth. First Corinthians 2:9 tells us we have never seen nor heard of all the things God has prepared for us.

Amos 4:12 says, "*...prepare to meet thy God...*" There is a judgment day coming for every man. For those who have rejected Jesus Christ as their personal Savior and His work on the cross, there is the Great White Throne Judgment where all the lost will be judged and cast into the lake of fire (Revelation 20:11–15). For those that have received Jesus Christ as their personal Savior and His work on the cross, there is the judgment seat of Christ where all the saved will be judged on their Christian service (1 Corinthians 3:11–15; 2 Corinthians 5:10). The question is: "Are you prepared to meet God?" Romans assures us we will ALL stand before God without exception (Romans 14:11–12). The ONLY way to prepare to meet God if you are unsaved is to receive His Son as your personal Savior. The way to prepare to meet Christ if you are saved is to serve Him faithfully for His glory and not your own.

First Samuel 7:3 says, *"And Samuel spake unto all the house of Israel, saying, If ye do return unto the LORD with all your hearts…and prepare your hearts unto the LORD, and serve him only: and he will deliver you out of the hands of the Philistines."* The prophet Samuel is calling Israel to turn from idols, prepare their hearts and serve God only. The promise God gives if Israel will do this is deliverance from their enemies.

Here in Florida we are constantly reminded to "prepare for the hurricane." We learned last year that after the storm hits, it is too late to prepare. Not only is it not safe to drive, there will be no water, batteries, flashlights and most importantly, diet Coke in the stores. During one of the hurricanes last year we were "preparing" ourselves to possibly go without electricity for a few days. Because we live in the country, this means no electricity for the regular house stuff but also no water or septic. We fill all the sinks and tubs with water so that we can have water to wash with and water to make the toilets flush. We were so busy patting ourselves on the back for planning and preparing ahead of time that we forgot to turn off the water in the laundry room and flooded our house even before the hurricane hit. Of course, right when we needed the shop vac to suck up all the water the electricity did go off! However, we had plenty of water!

Just as we need to prepare ahead of time for the physical storms we face in life, we must prepare for the spiritual storms as well. Samuel begged Israel to turn away from other things that came before God and prepare their hearts to serve Him. We must put God first in our lives before the storms come so that we are prepared to make it through the rough weather. When the trials and testing come, we don't want to have to take the time to confess and get right with God before we can fall on our face and cry out to Him. We should have such a close and right relationship with Him that we can immediately find comfort. We must prepare our foundation of faith so that we are ready when the trials come.

I am feeling so much better and am excited and ready to preach today, Lord willing. Remember, part of the preparation God expects is for us to be faithful to the house of the Lord.

Prepared to hit the pulpit preaching,
Preacher

◎ ◎ ◎

September 4, 2006—
Taking It Easy on Labor Day

We had a wonderful crowd at church yesterday. We began our Sunday school campaign called "Stand Fast in Liberty" taken from Galatians 5:1: *"Stand fast in the liberty wherewith Christ hath made us free."* Our goal for the month is for us to have fifty first time visitors in our Sunday school. We were so excited to receive the total at the end of the morning service and be able to announce that we had seventeen first time visitors just today! What a blessing for our church to "Stand Fast" telling others of the liberty we have been given in Christ. We also received our "Marathon Offering" to help reduce our debt so that we are ready to take the next step of faith and build our new auditorium. I challenged our people to try to sacrifice and give, praying to receive about $5,000 toward our debt reduction. At the end of the service last evening, our treasurer handed me a note with the Marathon Offering total and I was astounded to announce that we had given $12,469.16! Ephesians 3:20: *"Now unto him that is able to do exceeding abundantly above all that we ask or think, according to the power that worketh in us."*

God was so good to allow me to feel well enough to teach Sunday school and preach both services. My sermon this morning was titled, "Forming a Friendship with Christ through Obedience." We must be obedient to God's Word and live a holy life so that we can maintain fellowship with God. In our evening service we studied Lot in Genesis and learned from the "Downward Fall of a Righteous Man." We must all avoid sin and the steps that lead to "vexing our righteous souls." Sin is very rampant in our society and it is easy to become hardened to wrongdoing. It is our responsibility to love sinners but take a stand against the sin.

Today is Labor Day. This is a day that allows us to take time off from our busy schedules and rest from our "labor." My favorite part of Labor Day is the food, of course! Why food and Labor Day go together I am not sure, but praise God they do! We are thanking God that He has enabled me to feel well enough to work. Many people (I sometimes) are too ill to do the work they want to do. We are blessed just to have the physical strength to work for God. Each day we find new reasons to thank the Lord. Our many blessings outweigh the trials. My least favorite part of my illness now is the nightly shot. However, taking the shot is much better than the alternative and getting another blood clot! Every time we find ourselves discouraged or upset about our situation, Evona or I will say, "In acceptance lieth peace." (A quote from Amy Carmichael the missionary) The peace God gives defies understanding. It gives comfort when nothing else can.

We hope you are able to take some time off and enjoy some rest and relaxation with your family. We are planning on spending time with the kids, lying around, eating and then taking a nap! (Not necessarily in that order!)

"Chilling" in Plant City,
Preacher and Mrs. Evona

SEPTEMBER 5, 2006—

Lucy and Ethel
(From Mrs. Evona)

Have you ever had a friend who is always willing to jump on board with whatever crazy idea you have? Years ago when I was in 6th grade, I took piano lessons from a very interesting little old lady named Mrs. Akin. She would have us all dress up and perform long, excruciating recitals. However, there was one family who had several girls who took lessons and the youngest girl always stole the show. It was not fun, let me tell you! On to the stage she would walk. She was a cute, blond, little five-year-old who could play better than all the rest of us who were twice her age. The year I graduated from high school I ran into one of her older sisters. I immediately asked about the "darling child" piano player and was very surprised to find out that she was only a year or two younger than us! All those recitals, everyone thought that she was a child protégée, and come to find out, she was just SHORT! I expressed the unfairness of this entire situation and her sister replied, "If you think having to be compared to her one time a year in a recital was hard, try living with her your entire life!" This common injustice we had both experienced knit our hearts together as nothing else could have! (We both obviously had very sheltered childhoods if this is the worst that happened to us!) We have been friends ever since. A few years later I was in her wedding and then she was in mine. (A fun superfluous side note to our saga is that my mother-in-law was in my friend's mom's wedding over forty-five years ago! You never know.) We are now next door neighbors and making our own children perform in excruciating piano recitals (minus the short child protégée). We have been getting in trouble together for over 15 years now. (The cute, blond sister turned out to be a petite, blond, incredibly nice grownup!)

Last year, my friend and I decided to start yet another project. We were going to do ALL the tile-work in her new home. We both have steak tastes on hotdog budgets and couldn't afford to hire out the amount of tile-work we wanted done. We decided it didn't look too difficult slapping some glue stuff on the back of a few tiles and sticking them to the wall, so off we went! This was the exact moment Preacher dubbed us "Lucy and Ethel." I am not sure who is whom, but I have a pretty good idea! We were knee deep in tile work for weeks (while trying to keep Lucas from eating construction trash and pulling up all those little spacer things you have to put down to keep the tiles straight!). During this time many other subcontractors were working on my friend's house. Without exception, each male worker noticed that we were doing our own tile work and proceeded to instruct us on the "right way" to do the job! We decided that if they had spent more time doing their own job the "right way" and less time instructing us, she would have been in her new home 2 months earlier! Each worker had a different technique and different advice. After listening to the first two or three workers, we decided that they didn't know what they were doing either and we would just do it our own way! Many, many weeks later we finished our project and had become "tile experts" in the process!

In life there will be many "self appointed experts" telling you the "right way" to live. I have not met one expert yet who understands or agrees with our choice of faith. "Choosing Faith" defies reason. It goes against common sense and requires trust in an unknown. Our faith is based on the firm foundation of the character of God Almighty. It has been said that "your faith is only as good as the object or person you choose to trust." It is very difficult to know the "right way" to go. There are so many decisions we must make in life and we can not make them on our own. In John 14:5, Thomas, one of Jesus' disciples, asked the same question that plagues us today. *"Lord, we know not whither thou goest: and how can we know the way?"* How can we know the way? Jesus answered so clearly and directly that there is no room for any misunderstanding. *"Jesus saith unto him, I am the WAY, the truth, and the life: no man cometh unto the Father, but by me"* (John 14:6). This is true in salvation and in our everyday walk with Christ. He is the WAY. If you are facing a situation that seems like there is NO WAY, remember Jesus said, "I am the way!" He can give us direction when the path seems unclear. Jesus said, "I am...the truth!" He gives us promises to live by in His Word. Jesus said, "I am...the life!" He can enable us to receive eternal life and live a life of purpose for Him on this earth.

Jennifer Rothschild lost her sight as a fifteen-year-old girl and had to make the choice to become bitter or trust the Lord. She "Chose Faith" and now ministers to people all over the world with her music, speaking and books. She said she realized that, "Believing is seeing!" That is the confidence it will take to trust God and set out on your own journey of faith. You will not know where He is taking you, or what He wants to accomplish in you, but "believing is truly seeing!"

Every time we go to Moffitt, Preacher shares our choice of faith with others. Many people shake their heads and don't "see" how this can work out for us. No matter what happens, we are not looking at our trial through human eyes, we are seeing through the eyes of faith. On the days that Preacher suffers with pain, as well as the days like yesterday when he is feeling great, we know that we must follow the path that has been given to us. We will be able to know the "right way" to go by walking by faith and not by sight!

Looking through the eyes of faith,
Mrs. Evona

September 6, 2006—
A Heart to Heart Talk

During the first few years of our marriage, it required many words to achieve true communication. Being a man, this was a lesson that took me a while to learn. I figured when cabinets were being closed very hard and I asked, "What is wrong?" and she answered, "Nothing!" that she really meant nothing was wrong! However, in "wifeeze" that meant, "Boy, are you in trouble!" How was I to know? If she asked, "Do I look fat in this dress?" The answer should *always* be, "Of course not!" (even if she does look a little wide!). When she asks, "Have you seen my keys?" you are not supposed to answer "yes" or "no," you are to immediately get up and help look for the missing keys. Who makes these rules? One of the most delicate communication issues was her cooking. Even if the biscuits were as hard as hockey pucks, you had to eat at least three in spite of the risk of breaking your teeth.

As the years passed, our communication became easier. I learned to speak "wifeeze" and she worked on her biscuit recipe. Issues that seemed so difficult to talk about a few years earlier were now much more comfortable to share. It only took a few words to convey our thoughts and feelings.

Now, after being married 13 years, I have developed my own language called "husbandeeze" and she has discovered biscuits in the frozen food section! There are many times we communicate volumes without a single word being said. A smile or raised eyebrow can speak clearer than the hour's worth of words spoken during those first few years. Our hearts have learned to speak one to another. This is such a wonderful place to be in a relationship.

In John 11, a family is going through one of the worst valleys a family can face: the death of a loved one. Lazarus had been dead for four days and Jesus was finally able to come and minister to his sisters. They heard that Jesus was on his way and Martha immediately jumps up to meet him while Mary "sat still in the house." Martha begins at once to talk and tell Jesus how he had let them down and how hurt they were over the situation. Jesus is kind and patient with Martha and tries to share with her that He alone is in charge of the situation. Once again she is too busy talking to truly understand what Christ is trying to communicate to her. As Jesus neared their home, Mary "went to where Jesus was" and fell at his feet. She did not try to run ahead and intercept Christ earlier like her sister; she sat still and waited and then when he came near, she went to where he was. Her first reaction was not to tell Christ what should have been done it was to fall at his feet and pour out her heart to Him. In very few words she shared her heart and Jesus responded with deep compassion and cried. What an obvious difference in levels of their relationship with Christ. Mary had a wonderful deep relationship that needed very few words and evoked a personal response from Christ. Martha's relationship was still on the level that required many words and was full of misunderstanding on her part. Oh that we can mature to the intimate level in our relationship with Christ that requires few words and deep compassion. Hebrews 4:15: *"For we have not an high priest which cannot be touched with the feeling of our infirmities…"* Our communication with Christ can be so personal that he can even be "touched" with our feelings. We don't have to work at communicating with Christ. We can turn toward the cross and run to Him and fall at his feet. Our heart can communicate our needs and hurts and trust that He will do what is right.

It has taken years of trial and error trying to learn to communicate with Evona on a deep and personal level. God offers us the chance to come boldly before the throne of grace and know He cares and is touched by our trials. All He asks is for us to "sit still" and have faith in Him.

I am feeling better each day and look forward to being in the pulpit tonight. It will be the first time I have been able to preach at Wednesday Evening Prayer Meeting in months. I can't wait to see what tomorrow brings. Each day gets better and better!

Grace and peace,
Preacher

SEPTEMBER 7, 2006—
Our Time

Since the boys started Christian school, our schedule has changed drastically. Evona is up most mornings by 5:00 A.M. to have devotions and work on her latest writing project. I am not up at 5:00 A.M. to do anything. She gets the boys ready for school and takes them, along with our neighbor's two children, to school. One morning a week she gets up at 5:00 A.M. and goes to work at her part-time job cleaning our church. Oftentimes, she and "Ethel" become immersed in special projects and spend the afternoons working tirelessly. On afternoons she's not on a mission she straightens the house, or balances the checkbook or works on her personal writing projects. She still gets dinner together each night, works with the boys on their homework, gets them ready for school the next day and handles any problems the boys are having in school. And did I mention, she has our one-year old, Lucas dogging her every step from about 9:00 A.M. to 8:00 P.M.? This is the life of mothers, the unsung heroes of our homes.

I, on the other hand, get up about 7:00 A.M. and drink my first Boost. There'll be three more of those pond water cocktails before day's end. Sometimes I'll snooze in my chair for a while or get up and go pray in my garden until Evona gets home from taking the kids to school. We have our devotions from the Psalms, and the baby usually wakes up at that time and her day with Lucas begins. I have started going in to the office several days a week and on the off days I work on my sermons and administrative things involving the church. Often I do exercises in our pool or outside activities to strengthen my body. I am generally home for lunch with Evona and always home for dinner. We enjoy our family dinners (many times because some wonderful person has cooked for us) and we read a Bible verse and someone's name from the stack of Christmas cards we saved to specially pray for with the dinner blessing. The boys have time to play after dinner and I will work on the update or check emails. Then at 8:00 P.M., Evona puts Lucas and the big boys to bed. Once they're in bed, we let them read or play their Gameboys for a few minutes then we pray with them and kiss them goodnight.

NOW it's "our time." This is the time Evona and I have for each other. We get the unpleasant task of my shot out of the way first. It's a shot to prevent blood clots and we all know what they say… "A shot a day keeps the clots away." Evona has learned to give these shots with very little pain to herself. I, of course, bear the pain and suffering of having a 1.2 centimeter long needle thrust in my abdomen or thigh. It's a tough life but someone has to live it. After the injection, we turn to kinder, gentler activities. We are able to talk and spend quiet time together. We pray together just before we go to sleep. If the boys come in after they've been put to bed, they had better be sick, and even then they're required to cough up a lung to prove it. If the phone rings, we let it go to voice mail. *This is "our time!"* We cherish it and guard it fervently.

I wonder…do we have time with God like "our time?" Time we focus on Him? Time we take our minds off everything and everyone else and give attention solely to Him? Time we cherish and guard? Time we look forward to all day long? When I first got the news I had cancer, I ran to His feet and I didn't let go. Each day was punctuated with meetings with the Lord and tears and comfort. The further I get from the diagnosis, the less "our time" I spend with Christ and the less cherished it can become.

"O GOD, thou art my God; early will I seek thee: my soul thirsteth for thee, my flesh longeth for thee in a dry and thirsty land, where no water is; …" Psalm 63:1

The psalmist is longing after God. He is thirsty for God's presence. The key is to remain thirsty for God. Thirsty to enter His sweet fellowship which no one can take from you; thirsty to commune with him in prayer and pour out your heart to the Lord; thirsty to open His Word and let it soothe your soul and provide just what you need for that hour. If we'll thirst for "our time" with Jesus, we'll find ourselves running to the well and cherishing every moment of it. "Our time" becomes non-negotiable and part of our daily lives. Even when life pulls you in every direction and time is a luxury you have very little of…you'll be sure you spend "our time" with Jesus so you can face the rest of your life.

Striving to spend "our time" with the Lord every day,
Preacher

SEPTEMBER 8, 2006—
The Man Chair

You have heard the phrase "good copper/bad copper," but have you heard of "good shopper/bad shopper?" This is the term I have coined for Evona and me when she drags me...I mean, when I gladly take her shopping. I'm a "grab and go" shopper. Evona is a "browse and possibly buy" shopper. After about 20 minutes, I'm ready to pack it in and she is just getting started. This is why I began a tradition when we enter a store—"The quest for the man chair." The "man chair" is usually one single chair hidden somewhere in the store for the first man who can find it and park until forty-seven outfits later he hears the delightful words, "You ready, dear?" It is a wonderful feeling to find the "man chair" empty. If there is already a man in the "man chair," your heart sinks and you can't help giving the guy a look of disgust. You then begin looking for a display table you can use as a "man chair." It's a desperate thing to make your own "man chair" because there is often a mannequin on the table where you want to sit. The other day I sat under a mannequin's large leopard purse, the purse nearly resting on my head. I got some chuckles from passing shoppers but I didn't care—I'd made my own "man chair" and if it meant wearing a purse as a hat I was willing. One day the Lord richly blessed me in about the fourth clothing store we went in. After my search, I discovered a "man couch." This was grounds for a nap and I took the "man couch" up on it. I have found that it is easier to endure the rigors of an endless shopping spree if you find refuge in the "man chair."

In Psalm 57, David is fleeing for his life from a very jealous King Saul. Saul knows David has been anointed king and has determined to take his life. David is tired and discouraged from constantly being on the run. "*My soul is among lions: and I lie even among them that are set on fire, even the sons of men, whose teeth are as spears and arrows and their tongue a sharp sword*" (v. 4). David is filled with fear and desperation and realizes he is in a battle for his life. We are in the same struggle daily against the devil. As David likens his enemy to lions, we see in 1 Peter 5:8 that our enemy is also like a roaring lion. *"Be sober, be vigilant; because your adversary the devil, as a roaring lion, walketh about, seeking whom he may devour:..."* Satan is constantly seeking to devour and destroy our faith in God. We are on a long journey and there are going to be many times that we need to find a seat of refuge. On our shopping trips, I become tired and weary and find refuge in the "man chair." David found refuge in the light of God's presence even in the darkness of a cave. Psalm 57:1–2: *"Be merciful unto me, O God, be merciful unto me: for my soul trusteth in thee: yea, in the shadow of thy wings will I make my refuge, until these calamities be overpast. I will cry unto God most high; unto God that performeth all things for me."*

As we face our struggles, we can find a seat of refuge by sharing our burdens in prayer with other believers. Matthew 18:19: *"Again I say unto you, That if two of you shall agree on earth as touching anything that they shall ask, it shall be done for them of my father which is in heaven."* A seat of refuge is also found when we meet together in the house of God and worship the Lord with other believers. Matthew 18:20: *"For where two or three are gathered together in my name, there am I in the midst of them."* The Holy Spirit provides a wonderful seat of refuge for us when He wraps His loving arms of comfort around our hearts in our time of need. Romans 8:26: *"Likewise the Spirit also helpeth our infirmities..."*

Many times while shopping I am ready to give up and head home only to find Evona has just gotten her second wind. These are the times that the "man chair" becomes invaluable. So it is with the seat of refuge God lovingly provides. It can be the means that enables you to make it through your present trial.

Today we are in Jacksonville, Florida where I will preach at Trinity Baptist College Chapel. Please pray that the Lord will use the message to challenge the young people to "*Choose Faith*" and live every day for the Lord.

Enjoying God's seat of refuge,
Preacher and Mrs. Evona

SEPTEMBER 9, 2006—

Songs in the Night

(From Mrs. Evona)

Thursday, Preacher and I drove up to Jacksonville where he was scheduled to preach in the college chapel of Trinity Baptist Bible College on Friday. Preacher preached a sermon entitled, "That I May Know Him," after his life verse, Philippians 3:10. He used each phrase of the verse to represent a part of his life testimony from his salvation to the cancer trial we are facing. We had lunch with Brother Larry Appleby and Brother Mike Grover, two of the men on staff at the college. When lunch was almost done, Brother Larry handed us one of his business cards with a verse written on the back. The verse was Psalm 42:8, which says, *"Yet the LORD will command his lovingkindness in the daytime, and in the night his song shall be with me, and my prayer unto the God of my life."* Brother Larry shared with us that the Lord had given him this verse when he and his wife went through a deep valley.

My thoughts went to Lester Roloff, a preacher in Corpus Christi, Texas who God used to start a girls' and boys' home. Brother Roloff had many battles with the state of Texas over issues involving his homes. The state was relentless in its pursuit to shut the homes down and Brother Roloff was just as determined to stand against their efforts. Brother Roloff traveled the country recruiting preachers to stand with him for the children. He built an army of spiritual warriors who fought the state of Texas with him and in spite of going to jail, he remained faithful to the fight until the Lord took him home in a plane accident. Brother Roloff never stopped singing no matter what the circumstances were. He traveled with a trio named the "Honey Bees" and they sang backup to him as he would throw his head back and sing songs like "Zion's Hill" and "A Soul-saving Meeting." Brother Roloff would often break into song when he was preaching, bringing delight to everyone who had come for worship. He had a saying throughout his life that went like this: "Don't come around me singing songs in the light if you aren't singing songs in the night." Brother Roloff was tough in trials and he wanted those around him to be the same. He knew the power of songs in the night.

When you face the night of trial, do you give up singing? Is your singing replaced with complaining or silent sorrow? Just as God shows His lovingkindness in the daytime, He desires to give you a song in the night. Singing when days are dark delights the Lord. He sees that our faith is not only manifested on the mountains but also in the valleys. The Bible tells us in Psalm 22:3: *"But thou art holy, O thou that inhabitest the praises of Israel."* God dwells in our praise and His presence brings brightness to our nights.

Songs in the night are an inspiration to others who are also facing the darkness of trials. When a fellow-sufferer hears the songs God is giving you as you face the night season, there is a comfort that God gives through you to their hearts. You can be used amidst your night as you sing to your Savior.

A beautiful song that God has given Preacher and me in the night to sing is, "I Still Trust You, Lord."[1]

> I've seen the righteous man suffer, and it seemed like the wicked would go free.
> And in my confusion it just didn't seem right to me.
> I ask God for sunshine, but he sent rain. I asked for healing, but I only got pain.
> But I know your love will see me through, O Lord, I still trust you.
> I still trust you, Lord, I still trust you, Lord.
> I know you are able to see me through this dry barren land.
> And when I don't know which way to turn or go,
> I still trust you, Lord, so let me hold to your hand.
> I trust you for you've been so faithful to me.
> And I read in your Word that you would never leave or forsake me.
> "Lo I'll go with until the end"
> For his blood has cleansed me from all my guilt and sin.
> But I know your love will see me through, O Lord, I love trusting you.

Thanking God for songs in the night,
Mrs. Evona

September 10, 2006—
Where to Go with Your Problems

And Jabez was more honourable than his brethren: and his mother called his name Jabez, saying, Because I bare him with sorrow. And Jabez called on the God of Israel, saying, Oh that thou wouldest bless me indeed, and enlarge my coast, and that thine hand might be with me, and that thou wouldest keep from evil, that it may not grieve me! And God granted him that which he requested.

1 Chronicles 4:9–10

This chapter is one of those "names" chapters in the Bible—entire chapters that records genealogies. In the middle of this long list of names, God stops to focus on a man who He says is "more honourable than his brethren." His name was Jabez and in just two verses, we learn something very important about him: Jabez knew where to go with his problems.

Jabez had problems from the start of his life. Names to the Hebrews were very significant. Often men were named particular names based on the circumstances they were born in. Apparently, there was some sorrow involved in Jabez's birth and his mother named him accordingly.

Jabez could have lived with his problem and his name would have been mentioned without fanfare like the rest of the men in this chapter, yet he proved himself more honorable than his brethren by bringing his problem to the Lord. Jabez knew the Old Testament and he knew the story of Jacob. Jacob had a bad name as well. Jacob's name meant "supplanter, deceiver." Jacob, like Jabez, had no power of his own to change his name or his situation, yet God changed it Himself to "Israel" which means "prince with God." Jabez let his problem drive him to his knees in prayer.

When Jabez brought his problem to God, he prayed for God's provision: "...*bless me indeed....*" Our extremities are God's opportunities. God delights in meeting us in prayer over our problems. Just as God met Elijah at the brook by feeding him through ravens as he faced the problem of being a "wanted man" by King Ahab, God met Jabez as he bowed before the Lord and laid his problem at His feet. Jabez prayed for God's powerful change: "...*enlarge my coast...*" This was a prayer for more than land; it was a prayer for a larger life. Jabez wanted to have a greater impact in spite of his problems. He desired to stand, through God's empowerment, as a man who was larger than life's problems. Others would be blessed indeed as a result of Jabez's enlargement. Jabez prayed for God's presence in his life to lead him: "...*that thine hand might be with me....*" Jabez was asking God to hold his hand through life's problems. In order to hold hands with the one you love, there must be nothing between you. Jabez's heart was fixed on the God of Israel. Jabez prayed for God's protection: "...*that thou wouldest keep me from evil that it may not grieve me!*" Jabez desired God protect him from ever taking his problems anywhere but the Lord. He prayed God would protect him from Satan's attacks as he waited in prayer on God's answers.

The Lord answered Jabez's prayer: "And God granted him that which he requested." This should encourage you and me to do as Jabez and go to the God of heaven with our problems, no matter how big or small. A daughter asked her daddy, "How big is God?" The father answered, "God is always a little bigger than your need." We can take our problems to the psychiatrist; we can take them to the political arena; we can take them to the bottle...but the only place to go with our problems and KNOW they will be taken care of completely is the Lord.

Along this journey fighting cancer, we have faced so many different problems, some physical, some emotional. God has met us in each one with sufficient grace and mercy in our time of need. Let us never take our problems anywhere but to Him.

Going to God each day,
Preacher and Mrs. Evona

∞ ∞ ∞

SEPTEMBER 11, 2006—
Our Forever Friend

We enjoyed a wonderful Sunday at Fellowship Baptist yesterday! We are having a Sunday School campaign to bring first-time visitors to our Sunday School. In two weeks we have had thirty first-time visitors join us as guests for this campaign! I love Sunday School. It is the teaching arm of our ministry and it allows everyone to get involved in a group their age for fellowship and prayer. We have some of the greatest teachers in town and I want to invite you to visit with us one Sunday at 10:00 A.M. and be a part of the class that best suits you.

In the 11:00 A.M. Morning Worship we rejoiced to have a young single man walk the aisle and trust Christ as his Savior. This is one of the primary purposes of the church—evangelism. When we see people come forward and place their faith in Jesus Christ, we are seeing the church fulfill one of its primary purposes. The young man came back Sunday night and even came forward to pray about the message.

I was able to teach Sunday School at 10:00 A.M., preach in the Morning Worship at 11:00 A.M. and be back to preach in the Sunday Evening service at 6:30 P.M. Satan tried his best to stop me with pain but God enabled me to come to God's house and experience His power as He alleviated my pain long enough for me to preach. God is so very good. Please pray for these pains to subside. They are in my lower back and shoulder, both of which have tumors in them. The pain patch worked wonderfully until Saturday (September 9). Evona and I believe the new patch possibly never attached so the medicine could be administered, but we plan to address the issue with our doctor at our appointment this Wednesday. At any rate, the pain is not debilitating, only mildly irritating.

On Sunday morning, I preached the third message in a series about "Friendship with Christ" from John 15. The first sermon was entitled "Forming Our Friendship with Christ through Intimacy ("abiding in Christ"); the second sermon was entitled "Maintaining Our Friendship with Christ through Obedience" and today's sermon was entitled, "Deepening Our Friendship with Christ through Holiness." It is amazing to think that Jesus wants to enter into a friendship with you and me. John 15:13–15 says,

> *Greater love hath no man than this, that a man lay down his life for his friends. Ye are my friends, if ye do whatsoever I command you. Henceforth I call you not servants; for the servant knoweth not what his lord doeth; but I have called you friends; for all things that I have heard of my Father I have made known unto you.*

Intimacy is that daily abiding or dwelling in Christ (*"Abide in me, and I in you…* John 15:4). We should put all other relationships secondary to our friendship with Him. This intimate friendship He calls us into begins with salvation. Before we can know Christ as an intimate friend, we MUST know Him as our personal Savior. This takes place when we realize the Bible teaches that we are all sinners in need of salvation. We then must believe Jesus died for us on the cross, was buried in a grave and three days later arose from the dead to pay for our sins. Finally, we must receive Jesus Christ personally as our Savior. This begins our wonderful friendship with Christ.

Obedience to Christ is the key to daily maintaining our friendship with Jesus. (*"Ye are my friends, if ye do whatsoever I command you."* John 15:14.) The principles of His Word are to guide our steps that we might walk in His will. Christ cannot fellowship with us when we are disobedient to the Truth and go our own way. He gives us His Word to obey and walk in close friendship with Him.

Holiness in our daily walk (that is, yielding to the Holy Spirit and being like Jesus) is essential to deepen this friendship we've entered with the Lord. (*"If ye were of the world, the world would love his own: but because ye are not of the world, but I have chosen you out of the world, therefore the world hateth you"* John 15:19.) Christ cannot fellowship with unholiness; He is perfectly and eternally holy. He desires that even though we live in the world, we not be of the world. Rather, He calls us to be holy as He is holy so that we may walk with Him in close and sweet friendship.

Entering a friendship with the Lord Jesus Christ is the greatest privilege afforded us in life. It is available to ALL God's children. Don't miss it!

Finding a friend in Jesus,
Preacher

SEPTEMBER 12, 2006—
Attitude Determines Altitude

There once was a woman who woke up one morning, looked in the mirror, and noticed she had only three hairs on her head. "Well," she said, "I think I'll braid my hair today." So she did and had a wonderful day. The next day she woke up, looked in the mirror and saw that she had only two hairs on her head. "H-m-m," she said, "I think I'll part my hair down the middle today." So she did, and had herself a grand day. The next day she woke up, looked in the mirror to find only one hair on her head. "Well," she said, "Today I'm going to wear my hair in a pony tail." So she did, and had a fine day. The next day she woke up, looked in the mirror to discover there wasn't a single hair on her head. "YEAH!" she exclaimed, "I don't have to fix my hair today!"

Now, that's a good attitude! Unlike the man who always sees the negative in everything. His motto is: "If it rained soup, I'd have a fork."

Our attitudes are crucial in life. With a poor one, you'll endure life; with a good one, you'll enjoy life. So many successes and defeats can be linked to our attitudes. With a poor attitude, you can miss out on potential friendships because most people do not want to be around someone who is negative, critical and complaining. A poor attitude can also cause loss of opportunities in both the secular and the spiritual realm. A CEO is not looking for someone who cannot work well with others and is constantly complaining. A pastor is not going to draft someone with a sour spirit to greet first-time visitors. Our attitude affects our chances to be chosen for certain responsibilities and jobs. A lady said to me one time that she knew her attitude was bad when she stopped at a red light behind a pickup truck with a bumper sticker that said, "I Love My Truck." Under her breath she said, "I hate your truck!" On the other hand, a good attitude draws people to you and opens doors before you. There are multitudes of opportunities for advancement for the man with the good attitude in most every company. Churches rejoice when someone with a great attitude joins the work and ministry doors fly open in their path.

"*Then this Daniel was preferred above the presidents and princes, because an excellent spirit was in him: and the king thought to set him over the whole realm*" (Daniel 6:3). Here is a man with an "excellent spirit" or what we would call a good attitude. Remember who he is, now. Daniel is one of the Hebrews carried off by Babylon into captivity. Daniel took a powerful stand for God in chapter 1 which set him and his three friends apart. In chapter 6, Daniel has been serving in the government and King Darius notices his attitude. The way he leads in important tasks; the way he deals with people; the way he makes a favorable impression wherever he goes in the kingdom. A good attitude *always* attracts attention. Daniel's attitude would later be invaluable when he faced death in the lion's den. He displayed faith, courage, peace and fervency in prayer. Even though a good attitude could not keep Daniel from trials, it did see him through them. The opposite is true of some of Daniel's fellow dignitaries as Daniels 6:4 tells us, "*Then the presidents and princes sought to find occasion against Daniel concerning the kingdom; but they could find none occasion nor fault; forasmuch as he was faithful, neither was there any error or fault found in him.*" Daniel had enemies. The Babylonian princes resented a Hebrew being promoted above them and they went on a crusade to bring Daniel down. What a pitiful attitude. You don't get promoted and you're upset at those who do! This was nothing more than jealousy. Bad attitudes fester and grow and are even contagious. In verse 6 all the presidents meet to determine how they can destroy Daniel. It is a meeting of the "Bad Attitude Babylonians Club." They determine that Daniel faithfully prays each day at his window to the God of the Hebrews and convince the king to unwittingly sign a decree that no one can pray to anyone but King Darius. The punishment for violating this law was to be thrown in the lion's den. Daniel, of course, kept his time of prayer, and reluctantly King Darius had to keep the law and cast Daniel into the den with fierce, hungry lions. And how does God reward this Daniel with the "excellent spirit?" He sends an angel to shut the mouths of the lions through the night and Daniel is spared death. The "Bad Attitude Babylonians Club," on the other hand, became a feast for the same lions before the day's end.

    We have discovered in this battle with the disease of cancer that maintaining a good attitude is crucial to handling the different trials that have come along the way. First and foremost, we desire a godly attitude that we may view these trials as God's way of purifying our faith. Then we pray for a kind attitude that we may treat others with kindness no matter how we feel or what news we've received. Then we pray for a humble attitude to remember all the blessings God has given us are from Him and not self-made. Finally, we pray for a good attitude all around to bless others who are looking to us to "Choose Faith" and remain strong and steadfast in Christ. I even pray that I will keep making people laugh as I preach and minister. Our attitudes are a daily choice. Each day we can yield to the Holy Spirit or our sinful flesh. Whenever we realize that our attitudes have drifted from that "excellent spirit" of Daniel, we must immediately confess it and get back to the place God has chosen we abide "in Christ with a good attitude."

My motto is: "Cancer won't get me! God and I will get cancer!" I am still having some pain but it is not much and my medication has helped tremendously. In times like this our attitude can make the difference between giving up in the valley or going on to the victory. We choose to go on to the victory. How about you?

Desiring an excellent spirit in Christ,
Preacher

September 13, 2006—
A Blessing in Disguise!
(From Mrs. Evona)

Being the "new mom" in our car pool, I drew the unwanted slot—morning drop-off! I am daily amazed at how talkative children are in the mornings. Having homeschooled my "smelly monsters" until this year allowed me to ease into the day. I would sleep until about an hour before the "monsters" woke up. They would eat and get ready for the day alone and finally we would be ready to do school. Not this year! We are all up at the crack of dawn and they are full of energy. I didn't realize how long 30 minutes could be until the "smelly monsters" and their "monster friends" climbed into my car! One morning this week, one of the "monsters" began a very long, detailed story about his visit to the neighbor's house across the street. He waxed eloquent when the topic of the coveted "zip line" came up. The "smelly monster friend" explained that a zip line is a contraption with a cable strung on an angle from a very high point in a tree to the ground. He very enthusiastically described how you climb up the tree house and sit on the zip line's seat and push off, flying "hundreds of miles an hour" towards the ground! "How wonderful," we all exclaimed! In unison we asked, "Was it fun?" The sweet innocent "smelly monster" answered, "Oh, I don't know. I was too scared to try it! But I am going to try it next time." His next words were priceless. "The zip line is really scary when you're standing in front of it, but when you leave, you wished you had tried it!"

What a perfect description of our walk of faith. So many times God sends us up the tree house ladder and asks us to push off on the zip line of faith and we are too scared to try. We stand back, waiting on others to go ahead of us. We watch to see if they make it safely to the ground. Tentatively we step forward only to turn in fear and retrace our steps. Some of us even make it to the zip line seat and balk at the last minute. We scan the faces of those who have flown "hundreds of miles an hour" on the zip line and only see peace and a joy we can't understand.

In Acts 13 a wonderful journey is beginning. The church at Antioch sent a team of missionaries out to Cyprus: "*And when they had fasted and prayed, and laid their hands on them, they sent them away*" (Acts 13:3). This was an exciting time and John Mark was so honored to be chosen to accompany the great team of "Paul and Barnabas." He had worked and prepared all his life for an opportunity like this. John Mark was sent to minister to Paul and Barnabas. He was excited and ready to climb up the ladder to the top of the tree house. Without hesitation he headed up only to find things a little different than he expected when he reached the top. The missionary team encountered a sorcerer who was being used by the devil to try and keep a man from hearing the Word of God. The encounter with the sorcerer must have been very scary. Paul rebuked the devil and the Lord allowed Paul to strike the sorcerer with blindness. This is not what John Mark had signed up for in his "ministry to the missionaries" application! Just about the time it was John Mark's turn to take the ride of his life on the zip line, he bailed out. "*Now when Paul and his company loosed from Paphos...John departing from them returned to Jerusalem*" (Acts 13:13). This was a disappointing and hurtful event for all involved. John Mark's lack of faith affected himself and many others. Paul and Barnabas didn't allow the fear that defeated John Mark to discourage them from riding the zip line. They followed God's leading and "flew" to new heights of faith. However, the story has a great ending. Years later John Mark is given a second chance to climb the ladder to the top of the tree house. There he stood looking at the zip line, memories of past defeat clouding his vision, but the burning desire not to miss his chance again driving him forward. With the same fear tugging at his heart, he bends low, takes a seat and pushes off. As the wind whips through his hair, he shouts with joy. What a ride. John Mark recovered from his lack of faith and God honored his repentance. John Mark was one of four men chosen by God to write the life of Christ in the gospel of Mark. He was also a companion of Peter. "*The church that is at Babylon, elected together with you, saluteth you; and so doth Marcus my son*" (1 Peter 5:13). (Marcus is another name for John Mark.) Toward the end of the ride of his life, he is able to redeem himself and become a faithful coworker with Paul. "*Only Luke is with me. Take Mark, and bring him with thee: for he is profitable to me for the ministry*" (2 Timothy 4:11).

Praise God He allows us a second chance to ride the zip line of faith.

Don't wallow in regret. Climb the ladder to the tree house once again and step out on faith and get ready for the ride of your life. You never know what God has waiting for you. Just like John Mark was one of the four men chosen to record the Son of God's life on earth, you might be chosen for a special honor. You may never find out unless you let go of regret, embrace God's forgiveness and grace and push off. Hold on! "Flying hundreds of miles an hour" feels GREAT!

We are headed to the doctor's office today. This is just for routine blood work and a follow-up visit with Dr. Simon. Pray that all goes well and Preacher is able to continue taking the new medicine for another month. Keep the upcoming scans in your prayers. After one more month of the new medicine, they will do all the scans again and decide on a new course of action.

Learning lessons from the little ones,
Mrs. Evona

September 14, 2006—
Strength for My Soul

I will praise thee with my whole heart: before the gods will I sing praise unto thee. I will worship toward thy holy temple, and praise thy name for thy lovingkindness and for thy truth: for thou hast magnified thy word above all thy name. In the day when I cried thou answeredst me, and strengthenedst me with strength in my soul.

Psalm 138:1–3

It is strange dealing with the pain that I have due to cancer. Some days I have no pain, other days I have much pain. It also moves around from one spot to the next, never very consistent. During the night on Tuesday, I experienced much pain and was not able to get relief from my medication. I tried different positions, heating pads, cold compresses and nothing helped. I remembered that in Psalm 40 it reminds us to praise God in every circumstance. I began praising God and thanking him for my many blessings. It took a while to feel well enough to thank him for my pain, but eventually I even praised Him for my cancer. The next morning I shared with Evona how praising God brought me relief from my pain and we thanked God together for His goodness.

I then dressed and headed to Moffitt for my follow-up with Dr. Simon. After blood work we were able to see the doctor and be evaluated. He was very encouraged with the increase in my activity level and the improvement in my general overall health. We are going to be able to stay on the Tarceva pill that is taken at home and return in one month for repeat scans to evaluate the medicine's effectiveness. This is such an answer to prayer! I can't tell you how much better I feel being able to be at home with my family. God has strengthened my body so much in the past few weeks that I am able to preach and teach and minister at church more than any of us expected.

Psalm 138 is the prayer we have prayed over and over. It is a prayer that asks God to not only strengthen my body but my soul. As many of you know it can be very discouraging to deal with limitations and pain on an ongoing basis, but *"In the day when I cried thou answeredst me, and strengthenedst me with strength in my soul"* (Psalm 138:3). Praise God! Strength to make it through each day begins with praise and worship to our holy and magnificent Creator. We should praise Him for His lovingkindness, because *"...while we were yet sinners, Christ died for us"* (Romans 5:8). He loved us even when we were unlovely. We should praise God for his wonderful Truth he has given us in his perfect Word. He has written us an entire book of love letters and every word is truth! When I write Evona a "love letter" it would break my heart if she discarded it and would not read my words. God feels the same and wants to hear our praise for His Word. The type of praise that will help us make it through trials, comfort our hearts, ease our pain and strengthen our souls is praise from the *whole heart!* God deserves our complete attention and praise. Take time to stop and spend quality concentrated time praising God and give Him your whole heart. His response to our loving praise is to hear our cries and strengthen our souls.

Praising God with my whole heart,
Preacher

SEPTEMBER 15, 2006—
It's All in Who You Know

This statement has been used in the secular world for years to mean that if you want to advance in the world, you have to know the right people. This is very true. The people you know can open doors for you.

A preacher said years ago, "In the valleys, it's not what you know but Who you know that counts." Life's valleys are abundant and oftentimes unpredictable. We may be on the mountain top one day and by day's end we find ourselves in a valley.

What valley are you walking through? Is it a valley of death? Someone you love has died and you are not sure you can live without them. Is it a valley of a broken relationship? Your marriage dissolved before your eyes or a friendship fell apart and there was nothing you could do to stop it. Is it a valley of career loss or financial crisis? You thought you had job security but in one meeting everything changed. You have more going out than is coming in and you don't know how you'll survive. Is it a valley of depression or anxiety? You don't want to live this way; you want to enjoy life but you continuously slide back into these emotional states that hold you hostage. Is it a valley of sin? You want to walk with God but the temptation is unbearable and you fall over and over again to this life-dominating sin. Whatever your valley, God is the One who can help.

> *"Yea, though I walk through the valley of the shadow of death, I will fear no evil: for thou art with me; thy rod and thy staff they comfort me"*
>
> PSALM 23:4

What a wonderful promise from the "Shepherd's Psalm." The psalmist is walking through his lowest and darkest valley—the valley of the shadow of death. Yet he finds great comfort in the God of the valley. The shepherd had an instrument which was pointed on one side and curved on the other. With the pointed side (the "rod") he could prod the sheep in the right direction. There are some valleys of our own making and the Lord knows exactly how to chasten us back into the fold. With the curved side (the "staff") the shepherd could wrap the staff around a particular sheep and pull him gently to himself. Many valleys are not brought on by us but are part of God's plan to purify our faith and impact others. His gentle embrace makes the valley we're facing more like a walk with the shepherd.

Knowing Christ in the valley is essential if we would make it through to the mountain on the other side. If you know Christ, it doesn't matter who else you know, or what you know, you are personal friends with the "victor of the valleys." In Song of Solomon 2:1, the Lord calls Himself *"the lily of the valleys."* Lilies are known for their whiteness, which is a symbol of purity and holiness. It's good to know we have a holy God walking with us through our valleys who will protect us. Lilies are known for their beauty. Christ said in the gospels that all of Solomon's glory could not compare to the beautiful clothing of the lily. Jesus turns the ugliness of the valley into beauty as He uses our trials and tests to be a witness to others. Lilies are known for their sweet fragrance. What a blessing to see how the Lord uses our victory in the valleys to attract the attention of others like a pleasant aroma. When you're walking through your valley, look close and you will find growing there the "Lily of the valley." Don't be afraid to pick it; it's the Lord and He has been waiting for you in your valley all along.

Yesterday we had the opportunity to preach at Clearwater Christian College to a group of 600 students. It was a great blessing and Evona was thrilled to go back to her alma mater.

Enjoying the lily of the valley,
Preacher and Mrs. Evona

September 16, 2006—
The Thief of Time and the Grave of Opportunity

For years as a young single guy, my slogan was, "Never put off today what you can put off tomorrow." I was the president of the United Procrastinators of America and I was proud of it. I would brag that I work best under pressure when there's a deadline hanging over my head; all this being said while others are sick to their stomachs with worry, we'll get finished. It's one thing to procrastinate; it's another to take pride in it. Procrastination is nothing to be proud of. It is being irresponsible with our responsibilities. It wastes God-given time. Often procrastination brings a loss of opportunity. Always, procrastination affects others negatively. It is a tool of Satan that he uses successfully to thwart the leading of God in our lives.

In the latter portion of the book of Acts, Paul is taken prisoner. He, being a Roman citizen, was able to appeal to Caesar, the ruler of the highest court in Rome. The journey to Rome involved giving his testimony before several dignitaries, one of which was Felix (not the cat but a Roman governor of Judea.) Paul boldly gave testimony before Felix of how Jesus had saved him through putting his faith in Him. Upon hearing Paul's powerful gospel witness, Felix (not one of the "Odd Couple" but a Roman governor of Judea) *"reasoned of righteousness, temperance and judgment to come"* (Acts 24:25). I believe he was convicted by Paul's words. Yet Felix let the devil convince him to put off making a decision about the matter. Acts 24:25: *"…Felix trembled, and answered, Go thy way for this time; when I have a convenient season, I will call for thee."* We do not read where Felix ever trusted Christ. He procrastinated himself right into hell. You might point out in Acts 24:26 that Felix did call for Paul to commune with him more often after this event and that he possibly got saved during one of those visits. Verse 26 makes it clear that Felix's motives for seeing Paul were his own hopes of receiving a bribe to release him. Felix should have responded to the gospel while he was under the Holy Spirit's conviction instead of putting it off. Conviction wanes the further you get from the day it comes over you. It is one of the most dangerous things you can do to put off your salvation. Conviction may not come again. You may die prematurely or Christ may return and rapture all the saved from the earth, leaving behind those who were waiting for the perfect time to come to Christ. Just as a side note: Felix was replaced by Festus (not the deputy on "Gunsmoke" but Felix's replacement as governor of Judea).

In my own life, I almost let the devil talk me into putting off getting saved as a young boy. I thank God for using my mother to prod me to listen to the Holy Spirit as He drew me to Christ that night. I wish I could say that was the last time I was guilty of procrastination, but as you read in the opening paragraph, it took me many years to learn that putting off the leading of God and our personal responsibilities was a sin that I needed to forsake. There are so many areas of life in which we let Satan talk us into procrastinating. We put off dealing with problems; we put off sending that note of encouragement we felt led to send; we put off telling those we love how much we truly love them; we put off going to the doctor (that one is for me); we put off volunteering for that ministry at church; we put off getting the oil changed in the car; we put off making things right with others…the list goes on and on. Some would say, "My procrastination is not sin; it is simply a packed schedule that forces me to put some things off until later." It sounds like your schedule is controlling your life rather than the Holy Spirit. Schedules can be all-consuming and many times we must step back and reprioritize our lives so that we can follow God's leading. Be careful not to confuse procrastination with waiting on God. You will know the difference between these two.

When we were first told I had cancer, we immediately began praying about what the Lord would have us do. We received peace about treatment at Moffitt and began pressing to begin treatments as soon as possible. There was no problem with procrastination in this situation. I wonder if we approached our whole lives with that same urgency, how many things we would do today that we may have been tempted to put off until tomorrow?

Making the most of "today,"
Preacher

∽ ∽ ∽

September 17, 2006—
Who's 'We', Kemo Sabe?
(From Mrs. Evona)

God has abundantly blessed Preacher and me with such a wonderful family. We were so excited when we found out we were expecting our first child. We took all the classes and became "overnight experts." Suddenly, even though we didn't have any children **we** were the authority on parenting. Our parents, especially our mothers, were very gracious and loving. I assume they did their laughing at us in private. Finally after 42 weeks (I was 2 weeks late!) of waiting and 79 pounds later, the BIG day arrived. We were ushered into a beautiful room designed to make us feel at home. Preacher was very excited to find a TV and VCR (it was 10 years ago) in the room. However, we were here on business and he took his job as "labor coach" very seriously. We had practiced all the wonderful breathing techniques and were ready to go. Suddenly, the mild pains became more intense and I became less excited about our "wonderful" breathing techniques. Patiently, Preacher encouraged and helped me through the awful labor pains. In the hospital they have the little smiley faces on the wall that help you describe the level of pain you are experiencing at that moment. Somewhere between the mildly irritated looking face and the downright mean looking face I decided that the "wonderful" breathing techniques were for the birds and *I wanted my epidural, now!* This change in plans turned the "labor coach" into the official gofer. Preacher had to spoon my ice chips and wave the paper and fan me when needed. He was a wonderful fanner. He kept the right pace and never complained. We were so blessed to bring home a beautiful baby boy named Micah Daniel. Of course Preacher was so proud and bragged to every one he saw that *we* had given birth to an 8lb 10oz baby. I want to know, "Who's *we*, Kemo Sabe?" All he did was fan and give me ice chips. I did all the work!

Almost three years later, we were getting ready to head to the hospital to deliver our second baby. This time we were more prepared and knowledgeable. I had already called ahead and requested the anesthesiologist be waiting for me at the hospital door ready to give me the epidural. The big day arrived for the second time. We were getting our suitcase ready, waiting on my parents to come over to watch Micah. While we were waiting, I double checked the suitcase to make sure we had everything. I could tell from the look of guilt in Preacher's eyes that he was hiding something. Under all the important necessary stuff for the hospital, I found *two videos and a handheld battery powered fan!* I turned and pinned him with my "evil eye" and raised my eyebrows in disbelief. "Do you think we are going on vacation?" I enquired "sweetly." (Yeah, right! If you believe that, I have nice swamp property to sell you!) Out of the entire birthing process, all I asked was for a little ice and some fanning and this is what I get. He, being a man, didn't understand the problem. If all I wanted was air, he reasoned, the battery fan would do a much better job than a piece of paper. The final straw in our "discussion" came when he said that it took me so long to have our other baby that he needed something to fill the time, and so he packed videos. Needless to say, no videos or battery fans accompanied us to the hospital that night! The outcome was just as wonderful and we brought home our second boy, Caleb Nathaniel. He took credit for this 9-lb bundle of joy too! By our third trip to the hospital, we were both seasoned veterans. We BOTH packed DVDs and battery fans and enjoyed the peace and quiet of the hospital! This made for a much smoother delivery and we brought home our "finale," Lucas Samuel.

    In Ephesians 2:8–9 we read: "*For by grace are ye saved through faith: and that not of yourselves: it is the gift of God: Not of works, lest any man should boast.*" I wonder how many times God looks down and shakes His head at our arrogance and pride as we take credit for "our own" accomplishments and achievements? We are privileged to partake in the grace God offers. He did all the work and we are only here because of grace. I love the song, "Were it Not for Grace." It conveys the heart of the matter, that were it not for the grace of God, none of us know where we would be! Our own achievements are a mere reflection of the finished work of Christ at Calvary. We are so programmed to take pride in ourselves that it hinders our work for the Lord. Hebrews 9:14 says, "*How much more shall the blood of Christ, who through the eternal Spirit offered himself without spot to God, purge your conscience from dead works to serve the living God?*" We are saved from *dead* works to serve the living God. The blood of Christ as He offered himself willingly is the *real* work that was done. We are to serve Him because of His work of shedding His precious blood to make a way for us to go to heaven. If we could have done the work, there would have been no reason for Christ to die. Because we are sinners and God required a perfect holy sacrifice, we could not do the work ourselves. As much as Preacher wanted to help during the delivery of our babies, we all know that was impossible. We are not able to save ourselves no matter how hard we try. Thank the Lord He offers Himself willingly in our place and did the work that day on the cross. We must accept His free gift of love and trust Him as our Savior. We then can be purged from "dead works" to serve Him because of the wonderful work He did for us.

Leaving the work to Him,
Mrs. Evona

September 18, 2006—
Picking Priceless Pearls

Yesterday was fantastic! I felt the best I have felt in months. I spoke all day Sunday and had a great time preaching. The Lord blessed us with 450 in attendance and four more first-time visitors to our Sunday School for the campaign we're having, which gives us a total of thirty-four first-timers to Sunday School in 3 weeks. Our goal is to have fifty, so we have to work hard this final week to have at least sixteen! I believe the Lord will allow us to reach this goal and I'm looking forward to announcing it next Sunday.

The message for the morning worship service was entitled "Picking Priceless Pearls" from the parable of the "Pearl of Great Price" that Jesus gave in Matthew 13:45–46: *"Again, the kingdom of heaven is like unto a merchant man, seeking goodly pearls: who, when he had found one pearl of great price, went and sold all that he had, and bought it."* Parables are earthly stories with heavenly meanings that Christ used to illustrate doctrine. In this parable, the "merchant man seeking goodly pearls" is Jesus, the "pearl of great price" is the sinner He will redeem and the "price paid for the pearl" is the precious, sinless blood of Christ. This parable illustrates the doctrine of salvation well.

There are some interesting parallels between the pearl and the salvation of the sinner. First, the pearl is the product of a living organism. No other precious stone is such. The sinner saved by grace is the product of a living Savior! Jesus died for us on the cross, was buried and the third day arose in power. His sacrifice for our sins makes it possible for us to be saved through faith in Him as our Savior. Secondly, the pearl is the result of an injury. A pearl is formed when a grain of sand enters an oyster. The oyster begins wrapping it in a secretion called "nacre" or "mother of pearl" to protect itself, and then a pearl is formed. Sin is the one problem the sinner cannot conquer. It invades our lives from birth. Jesus wraps our sins with His righteousness as we place our trust on Christ until a sinner saved by grace is produced. As the pearl is the oyster's response to an injury, so the cross and the empty tomb are God's response to sin. Thirdly, the pearl is formed within the oyster where it cannot be seen. Salvation is an inward event. Faith is in the heart. If you're looking for a feeling or an experience to feel saved, you would do better to trust the facts of God's Word that you are saved if you have followed God's way of salvation. Fourthly, the pearl is not cut to make it valuable. Diamonds, rubies, emeralds, etc. have to be cut to bring out their value, but not the pearl. Nothing has to be done. Salvation is not of works. There is nothing you must or can do to be saved. You only need trust the finished work of Christ on Calvary. Finally, there are no two pearls alike. Just like your fingerprints and your DNA, each pearl is unique to itself. I rejoice that Jesus saves all men of all races and nationalities. He saves the White, Black, Oriental, Indian and Hispanic. He saves the rich, the poor, the middle-class, the brilliant, the average, the feeble-minded. He saves the male, the female, the young and the old. Jesus died for all men and He saves all who will place their faith in Him. To Jesus, we are the "pearl of great price" for whom He gave all that He had (Himself) to purchase and redeem.

Please remember me in prayer as I prepare to preach this Wednesday night in our mid-week service. I am asking God to continue to give me strength and stamina and improved overall general health.

Pleased to be one of His "Pearls of Great Price,"
Preacher

∽ ∽ ∽

September 19, 2006—
"We Press On"
(From Mrs. Evona)

When the valley is deep, when the mountain is steep,
When the body is weary, when we stumble and fall.
When the choices are hard, when we're battered and scarred,
When we've spent our resources, when we've given our all.

In Jesus' name we press on, in Jesus' name we press on.
Dear Lord, with the prize clear before our eyes,
We find the strength to press on.
Press On. – Words and Music by Dan Burgess[10]

Preacher's life verse is Philippians 3:10: *"That I may know him, and the power of his resurrection, and the fellowship of his sufferings, being made conformable unto his death."* Boy, I wish we had known that we were going to have to live out his life verse before he chose that one! I would have had him pick Proverbs 3:4: *"So shalt thou find favor and good understanding in the sight of God and man."* Or better yet, Proverbs 31:28: *"Her children arise up, and call her blessed; her husband also, and he praiseth her."* Well, that might have been a little weird for Preacher's life verse, but it sure is a good one! How about, 2 Chronicles 1:12b: *"…I will give thee riches, and wealth and honour…"*? That is a great life verse! Psalm 21:2, 4 says *"Thou hast given him his hearts desire, and hast not withholden the request of his lips…He asked life of thee, and thou gavest it him, even length of days for ever and ever."* That would not have been a bad choice either. Preacher had any number of verses to choose from, and somehow he picks the one about getting to know God through his power and *suffering!*

I wish we could tell you that living this verse is easy. I would love to say we never struggle with hurt, confusion, discouragement and fear. However, I would not be telling the truth. We are human, and there are many days we wake up and don't want to walk our God chosen path of faith. We would rather give in to our flesh and go back to the way things were.

When Preacher gets up in the night and heads to get a drink of water, normally he has no problem navigating in the dark. He takes the same straight path by the bed, around the dresser, through the door, and into the kitchen. Unfortunately, many more times that I would like to admit I leave my shoes right in the path beside the bed. During the daytime this is not a problem, but in the dark when obstacles (especially high-heeled shoes) are in your way, it becomes a disaster. Once he steps on the shoes and hops around holding his injured foot, things are no longer familiar. He becomes, like most of us do in a dark place, disoriented and everything seems to have been moved. This is the life we are living. We were very comfortable walking by faith because we were familiar with the path. Suddenly God moved all the furniture around and left a very large pair of shoes called cancer in our way. We must now depend on His faithful hand to lead us to places we have not walked before.

On the days we struggle to accept our new path, we stop and read the verses that follow Preacher's life verse. Philippians 3:13–14: *"Brethren, I count not myself to have apprehended: but this one thing I do, forgetting those things which are behind, and reaching forth unto those things which are before. I press toward the mark for the prize of the high calling of God in Christ Jesus."* We have to leave behind what we were and press on to what God wants us to become. This "leaving process" involves grieving the loss of our own plans and the death of many "dreams." We must embrace the unknown future God has for us and trust His loving guidance in our lives. Lucas has a tendency to eat things off the floor. Bugs, dog food, old food from the previous day...you name it; he will try to eat it. I have trained our entire family, (except the awful wiener dog who can't be trained), that if they see Lucas chewing, make him spit whatever is in his mouth out! Boy, does he get mad. He cries and stomps his fat little feet. However, if he would realize that after we take out the dead bug we are going to give him a nice gummy bear or piece of banana, giving up the bug would not be such a big deal. I wonder how many bugs we are grieving over when God wants to provide us with something so much more wonderful. While we forget those things that are behind us, we can find the strength in Christ to press toward the mark. We can press on in the strength of Jesus' name. He alone can make it possible to let go of the past and press on to our future prize of faith.

Like the song says, "When the valley is deep and our body is weary; when we've given our all, In Jesus' name we can press on."

Pressing on,
Mrs. Evona

SEPTEMBER 20, 2006—
Thanks for Sharing... I Think

The first time we had to go to the hospital after the "nightmare MRI," I knew there would be a lot of times when I would want to read. I requested Evona bring me three books: my Bible, *A Bend in the Road*[11] and *Life Wide Open*,[12] both by Dr. David Jeremiah. I had these last two books on my credenza to eventually read and thought this would be a good time. Of course, I read my Bible each day and then decided I'd read *Life Wide Open* first. I began reading the book and was really being challenged about this upcoming battle with cancer. I came to a great story that I asked Evona to allow me to read to her out loud. The story was about Eric Liddell, which was made into the movie, *Chariots of Fire*.[13] I will paraphrase Dr. Jeremiah's telling of the story: Eric was born in 1902 to missionary parents who served in China. Eric attended the University of Edinburgh, where he developed his world-famous running skills. Eric began to feel guilty about gaining global attention through running while his parents served the Lord in China. His father encouraged him by sharing that he could praise God through peeling potatoes if he peeled them to perfection and that he should "run in God's name." Eric continued to run and earned the nickname, "The Flying Scot." He won the gold medal in the 400-meter dash in the 1924 Olympics. Liddell used the opportunities before large crowds to share God's Word and be an impact for Jesus. After his Olympic triumph, Eric Liddell went back to China as a missionary and served God with passion until his premature death from a brain tumor at age forty-three. As I read those words and both Evona and I fell silent. I quietly shut the book and said, "Would you hand me *A Bend in the Road?* Now, *A Bend in the Road* is the true story of Dr. Jeremiah's battle with lymphatic cancer. It is filled with insights from the author and other friends who have faced this disease. I cannot tell you how much it encouraged me and lifted me up right when I needed it.

We have learned that encouragement from others is very important as we travel this rocky road. We have also learned that many people do not know how to encourage and their words can have the opposite effect from what they desire. One lady told Evona the grueling experience of losing her loved one to cancer. They described the looming suffering and the pointless doctor's visits that "simply don't help." I had a young lady come up to me recently and ask prayer for her grandfather with cancer. I asked, "Is he under treatment right now?" She answered, "No, he died yesterday." Even the "you're a goner" looks you get from folks who have seen this kind of cancer before speak volumes. There are times you just have to do like David did when the people spoke of stoning him over the invasion and burning of Ziklag, *".. but David encouraged himself in the Lord his God"* (1 Samuel 30:6). God will always encourage us in times of need, but there are times when we want encouragement from someone we can reach out and touch. It's natural and the Lord knows this. He made Eve for Adam when He could have been Adam's companion. He saw the loneliness of Adam and He provided a human counterpart to be his helpmeet. God even provides us with comfort so that we might comfort others (2 Corinthians 1:1–4).

The key is to surround yourself with encouragers and to be an encourager yourself. This takes human resolve and God's fullness. There's nothing like an "encourager" when you're down and there's nothing like being an encourager to those who are down. May God make us all members of the "building crew" and not the "wrecking crew!"

Encouraged to be an encourager,
Preacher

∽ ∽ ∽

SEPTEMBER 21, 2006—
Double Digits

It seems like you blink and the baby that stole your heart yesterday is now a big boy that is no longer in the single digits. On September 21, Micah turned the big 10! He is now (in his own words) "practically a teenager!" How time flies. Psalm 127:3 says, *"Lo, children are an heritage of the Lord; and the fruit of the womb is his reward."*

From birth to age 18, we only have about 6,570 days to cherish and train our children. On this past Thursday, Micah turned 10 and we only have 2,920 days left! We must love and nurture our children each and every day. Children are a blessing not a burden. Enjoy the "reward" God has blessed you with and make the most of every day. Because of my illness I view time differently. Each day is a gift that I need to make the most of.

From the time we brought him home, Micah has been a startling reflection of me. He looks so much like me that people often ask Evona if she was even there when Micah was born. She loves this! She gained 70 pounds when she was pregnant and vividly remembers the labor pains as proof she was there! (I am absolutely dead for telling how much weight she gained, but there are a few perks to being sick!)

He has become an amazing young man. His heart is so tuned in to God. Not long ago he wanted to know how he could figure out what God's will was for his life. I told him that in time that would come, but he could know God's will for his life right now. God's will for Micah and every other child is to love and honor their parents, love God, love others and work hard in school. Of course this was not as exciting as my telling him a special prayer to pray to have God's will revealed. I think he was pulling for the "professional football player" will of God. Too many times young people surrender to the ministry for the wrong reasons. Just because Micah looks like me doesn't mean God's plan for him will be for him to become a pastor. We are all called to search out God's will and strive to fulfill that part that is clear and listen for his leading in the part that is not clear.

I wrote Micah a poem for his birthday and he said he would not mind if I shared it with you. I hope you cherish your children and thank God every day that you have them to hold.

To Micah on his 10 Birthday (September 21, 2006) from Daddy:

Ten years ago today we brought you home to stay.
As we watched you sleeping in your bassinette,
Our hearts rejoiced that God would let
Two folks like us have a baby boy,
We named you "Micah," what a joy!
You've made us smile for all these years,
And when you're hurt, it brings us tears.
We've watched you grow more like Christ each day,
We love you son…Happy Birthday!

Thanking God for His bountiful blessings,
Preacher and Mrs. Evona

SEPTEMBER 22, 2006—

Hot and Cranky in Frinkville

(From Mrs. Evona)

We send the kids to a school a good ways away from our home. It takes around 35-40 minutes one way. However, the Lord was so good to put another family next door that attends the same school and we are able to carpool. I usually take the kids and our friend and neighbor, Melody, picks up. This week has been a little crazy and we have shifted the schedule around a lot. Wednesday morning Melody took the kids and I picked up that afternoon. As the crew entered Melody's vehicle she announced, "You may talk only if I can't hear you and absolutely no laughing and playing around! I am tired and cranky!" In typical childlike honesty Micah replied, "Don't worry; my mom is tired and cranky too!" Ouch! We teach them to be honest, but we don't mean to be honest about our dispositions or our age!

Of course as soon as Melody dropped the kids off she was on the cell phone calling me up laughing about my "crankiness." I reminded her that the entire subject was only brought up because *she* was cranky. Besides, at least I was only cranky to my OWN kids, not the poor innocent neighbor children! Friends—you can't live with them and you can't live without them.

In all honesty, part of my "cranky issue" has been over-scheduling. I always have two more projects going than I really have time for. However, I love a new project! No matter how many times I vow not to take on something new, I can't help myself when the "new idea" comes to me in the middle of the night! BUT in my defense, we have not had air conditioning in our very hot Florida home for almost a week now. It becomes miserable during the day. I have found that a tired overbooked mom with a sweaty baby latched on to her leg in a hot house with no air (our air conditioner is possessed with an evil devil and will be replaced soon…we hope) is not a great combination! I jump up in the morning ready to tackle the fifty-three things on my "to do" list and then become hot and cranky. I am not sure why my attitude and my temperature are connected but there is no denying the connection. Don't look at me with that pious face; I have heard from very reliable sources that you are the same way!

Paul addresses this issue in his letter to the Philippian church. Paul writes in chapter 4 verse 11, "*...I have learned, in whatsoever state I am, therewith to be content.*" I don't believe he is talking about the state of Florida or Tennessee or California. I believe he is teaching us that in whatever "circumstances" we find ourselves in we should be content. You may be shouting at the computer screen right now, "But you don't know how bad my circumstances are!" Remember Paul wrote this letter to the Philippians *from jail*. Not the best of circumstances for anyone. Yet he still emphatically says "I have learned" to be content. It can be done. Whatever set of circumstances God has allowed to invade our lives, we can be content. How can this be? In this rotten world there are some really bad circumstances that people have to endure. How can we learn to be content? Look further down the chapter and Paul gives us the secret key. Philippians 4:13: "*I can do all things through Christ which strengtheneth me.*" We can't do it on our own. There are circumstances and situations that are humanly impossible to endure with contentment. However, we don't have to do it on our own. Christ will strengthen us for our journey.

Last week I reached down to pick up the baby and realized he was slimy and sweaty. I then began to investigate and found that the air was not cooling like it should. I headed out to the air unit behind the house and did an expert evaluation: I walked around it several times, I peered down into the top of the unit where the fan is turning and last but not least, I kicked it! Sure enough, after this superb evaluation I came to the conclusion that it was *broke*! I then went into the garage and got my "air conditioning tools" and took the air handler apart. Inside I noticed the evaporator on the condenser was not working properly and the coils were loose. After a few minutes of "TLC" with my hammer, all was fixed and we were back in business! *Right*!?! Obviously I know nothing about air conditioners. I even say "turn the air up" when I want it to be cooler in the house! Due to my lack of real expertise, I called an expert. He immediately assessed the situation and ordered us a new air unit. In life we all encounter circumstances that we cannot handle on our own. God has given us his strength to help us deal with situations that are humanly impossible. When I called the "air expert" to help us handle the problem he had the solution, but not the solution I wanted. I would not have chosen to replace the entire air unit and have to wait a week for the unit to come in! I would have had the solution involve a new filter and some duct tape! In our lives when we take our circumstances to the expert, Christ, we must remember that He may give us the strength to endure the circumstance not rescue us from the circumstance. We must turn it over to the Lord and trust his "expertise."

Circumstances should not determine our attitude. We must determine what our attitude will be before we encounter the difficult situation!

Finally cool as a cucumber in Frinkville!
Mrs. Evona

∽ ∽ ∽

September 23, 2006—
God's Unusual Care

I have been blessed to have some great care during my hospital stays. There was one unusual event that happened one afternoon when I went down for my daily chest x-ray. I knew it might be interesting because when the lab tech called my name he had a tone that implied, "If I have to x-ray one more person, I'm going to jump from this floor's balcony and purposely land headfirst on the ground floor." I hesitated for a second as I thought, "Do I really want Dr. Killdare to x-ray me?" "I'm here," I finally said. "You're supposed to be on that side when you're here for a chest x-ray," he snarled, "It makes it where I don't have to walk to this side to get you, I have a very bad back, you know." *I only have lung, bone and brain cancer,* I thought. "Come on," he sighed as he whipped me around and hauled me off to the x-ray lab. He was so rough he almost dislodged my IV! Once in the lab, things got worse. The tech was mumbling under his breath about how overworked he was and how his back couldn't take it and how something would be done or he's outta there! He then kicked a rolling secretarial chair and it went flying across the room. I quietly reached down under my blanket and put the breaks to my wheelchair on. "You know," I began, "you really don't deserve this treatment you're getting." "No, I don't," he replied, "but what do you do?" "You might consider a meeting with the powers-that-be and make them aware of your back situation and how the patient overload is unbearable," I answered, "and I'll pray for you that it has a positive outcome." "Well, thank you, Mr. Frink," he brightened up, "Let me help you get out of your chair for the x-ray…be careful, now." When the x-ray was done and the tech delivered me back to my waiting family, his countenance was bright and he said, "Have a great day, Mr. Frink and I'll look forward to seeing you again." Let me describe the scene for you…Evona, Mom and Cathy in shock. "What did you do, hypnotize him?" one of them asked. "No, I just showed interest." This was not my most unusual caregiving experience but the others are not for publication.

In 1 Kings 17:3–6, God says to Elijah, the Prophet:

> *Get thee hence, and turn thee eastward, and hide thyself by the brook Cherith, that is before Jordan. And it shall be, that thou shalt drink of the brook; and I have commanded the ravens to feed thee there. So he went and did according unto the word of the Lord: for he went and dwelt by the brook Cherith, that is before Jordan. And the ravens brought him bread and flesh in the morning, and bread and flesh in the evening; and he drank of the brook.*

This is an example of God's unusual care for His children. If you are a believer on Christ, you are God's child and He is your Father. Although earthly fathers often disappoint you, your heavenly Father is incapable of failing you. You are *ever in his care*. God's care sometimes takes on a unique and unusual manner. Elijah had just had a face-off with the evil King Ahab, who with his wife, Jezebel, was turning Israel into an idolatrous nation. Elijah declared a famine in the land as God's judgment on their sin. Then Elijah left the king and was guided by God to go to a brook named Cherith and hide there where the Lord would care for him. The manner in which God cared for Elijah was very strange. First of all, God fed Elijah morning and evening by the mouths of ravens. Ravens are the most selfish birds in the bird kingdom. They will let their young starve if there is only enough food for themselves. Yet God used this unlikely source as Elijah's resource. I like to believe that the ravens were flying into King Ahab's kitchen and getting the bread and flesh from his royal table. God does have a sense of humor…look in the mirror. Then God quenched Elijah's thirst from the brook. Because of the famine, water was drying up everywhere, in fact, when God was ready for Elijah to move on, he dried up the brook too (verse 7). Elijah had water when very few did…God's unusual care. God would later care for Elijah through a Gentile widow woman who was ready to die until God worked a miracle, filling her barrel with meal and her cruse with oil. Imagine, one of God's "Hebrew" prophets being sustained by a Gentile woman…God's unusual care.

God unusually cares for us to strengthen our faith in His ability to do miracles. God gives us great testimonies as to His power and goodness from these experiences. God cares for us in ways that are different and unique so that only He can get the glory. If it is something that man can do, then it's "business as usual." When God gets involved in our care, it is "the Father's business as unusual." I love to rehearse the unusual ways God has cared for our family through this trial. It blesses me and challenges me to keep trusting Him to unusually care for me from now on.

We had a great mid-week prayer meeting. We had some songs, the offering and then I preached on "The Church on Their Knees." After the sermon, we had our church-wide prayer time, which we generally do near the beginning of the service. It felt great to immediately apply what we'd received from God's Word. You could see that the church felt this way too. (I couldn't help it...I peeked).

Cared for unusually by God,
Preacher and Mrs. Evona

SEPTEMBER 24, 2006—
What's in a Name?

To the Hebrew people, a name was very important. A name could carry a blessing with it; or it could carry a curse. A name could elevate one to higher status; or it could relegate one to a lowly position in life. This was the way of the Hebrews.

Sometimes, God changed one's name signifying a positive change in his/her life's destiny. "Abram," which means "father of height" was changed to "Abraham," meaning "father of a multitude," "Sarai," which means, "Ja is prince" to "Sarah," meaning "princess," and "Jacob," which means "deceiver" was changed to "Israel," meaning "prince with God."

One time, a woman changed her name temporarily to show God's displeasure in her life. When Naomi returned to Bethlehem Judah from Moab, she said to the people not to call her "Naomi," which means "pleasant," but instead to call her "Mara," meaning "bitter."

When God blessed Hannah's barren womb with a son in answer to her prayers, she named him "Samuel," meaning "heard of God."

The Babylonian rulers attempted to change Daniel and his friend's entire life, especially their allegiance to Jehovah. They started by changing their names. Each Hebrew's name, which pertained to Jehovah, was changed to a Babylonian name which pertained to the Chaldean gods. "Daniel," which means "God is my judge," was changed to "Belteshazzar," meaning "Bel will protect;" "Hananiah," which means " gracious" was changed to "Shadrach," meaning "inspiration of the sun," " Mishael," which means "who is what God is?" was changed to "Meshach," meaning "belonging to Aku" and "Azariah," which means "Ja is keeper" was changed to "Abed-nego," meaning "servant of Nego."

God prompted Pharaoh's daughter of Egypt to give the child she found in the basket on the river the name "Moses," which means "drawer out." This would designate Moses' life ministry of delivering (drawing out) God's children from Egyptian bondage through the Red Sea. To the Hebrew people, a name was very important.

When our boys were born, we decided to give them Bible names. To our first son, we gave the name, "Micah," which means, "Who is like Jehovah?" and "Daniel," which you already know means "God is my judge." To our second son, we gave the name, "Caleb," which means "the dog" (we did not discover this until much later), and "Nathanael," which means "God has given." We thought it would be horrible when Caleb found out his name means "the dog," but he was delighted as he is an animal lover and has said many times that he wants to be a veterinarian when he grows up. To our third son, we gave the names "Lucas" (also known as "Luke"), which means "light-giving" and Samuel, which, again, you already know means "heard of God." Our boys' names are special to us and to them. We love to look at the meanings God has given them. We must be honest, though, we did not give our sons their names with the Hebrew philosophy that their names would help or hinder them in life.

That being said, I am concerned with some of the names people are giving their children these days. A sports enthusiast in Michigan named his son "Espen," after cable's ESPN. A luxury car fanatic named his daughter "A'lexus," after the popular sports car. These infants are being called "brand name babies." Others have been named "Armani," "Dior," "Corvette," "Camry," "Celica." Some have been named after alcoholic beverages ("Hennessy"), while others have been named after office products ("Meridian.") My favorite was the woman who named her son "Lemonjelo" after a box of "lemon Jell-O." He'll probably grow up and name his daughters "Butterscotch" and "Tapioca."

Your name is important. The Bible says in Proverbs 22:1: "*A GOOD name is rather to be chosen than great riches...*" This is not talking about your personal name, though, as much as your personal character. Years ago, men made verbal agreements based on each other's names. It was imperative to keep your name good. I believe it still is. The good or bad character represented by our names will either please the Lord or displease Him. It will also afford us open doors to witness or closed doors to any opportunity the Lord had for us. There are two things to remember in this verse: (1) we choose whether our name is good or bad. We do this by our attitudes and actions. Is our walk consistent with good character? (2) As we choose a good name over a bad name, we are choosing that it will outlast riches. You can't buy good character. The Lord will reward good character at His judgment seat one day.

What do people say when they see you coming? What is your "name?" It's something to consider. Remember, the Bible also says in Acts 4:12: *"Neither is there salvation in any other: for there is none other name under heaven, whereby we must be saved."* Only through faith in the name of Jesus Christ can we be saved. He is the only One who is sinless, who died to pay for our sins and rose from the dead and who can save anyone who will call on *His name* (Romans 10:13).

Making much of His name,
Preacher and Mrs. Evona

September 25, 2006—
Breathing...a Must in Anyone's Daily Routine

I wish I could tell you what a great time I had preaching yesterday at Fellowship Baptist, but I can't because I could not preach. About Thursday of last week, I started having shortness of breath and some breakthrough pain. "Breakthrough" pain is pain that you experience in spite of your regular pain management. You treat it with extra medicine. We think that I overdid it last week. I went in to the office two full days instead of the three half days we said I would start with. I was also deeply involved in creating a treasure hunt for Micah's tenth birthday, which took up a lot of time. We have had good success with this pain patch until I started getting some breakthrough pains in several places where we know there are tumors. This, combined with the shortness of breath, which comes and goes, caused me to go ahead and fill the pulpit with Brother Robert Anders in the morning worship (and before you start worrying and offering to drive me to the ER...my doctor knows about this and has his eye on it) and Brother David Spencer in the evening worship. But you know me...I couldn't stand not preaching! I did attend both services and conducted the welcome and prayer times (and told a joke) so the Lord let me have a small part. Would you like to hear the joke? A woman drove home frantically, ran in the house and yelled to her husband, "Frank! I just won the lottery; pack your bags!" "What should I pack?" Frank asked excited. "It doesn't matter," said his wife, "just get out!" My congregation is used to me after all these years and they never fail to provide a consolation chuckle. We have a member now who can really laugh. You've heard of the "Biggest Loser"...they'd win the "Biggest Laugher" and I love it! I lost a big laugher a few years ago and they have filled the void. Laughter is joy manifested, and believe me, this member has Joy with a capital "J."

GREAT NEWS! We had nineteen first-time visitors in our "Standing Fast In September Sunday School Campaign" bringing our total to fifty-seven first-time visitors in our Sunday School in the month of September! Our average attendance for the month of September increased by sixty due to our campaign! Praise the Lord and thanks to everyone who participated in this great campaign! Campaigns and contests are great tools to get people excited about things, and what better thing to get excited about than Sunday School? It's the place where you can learn more about the Lord with those your own age. Our Sunday School classes also offer social outlets through activities and opportunities to minister through Sunday School special projects. We have a great Sunday School and look forward to watching it grow.

This shortness of breath is no doubt the cancer plus all the things that happened to my lungs because of chemotherapy, such as the clot in the lungs, the fluid build-up in the lungs, the collapse of the left lung and the continual air leak in the lungs. (If they can't fix it at Moffitt, I'm going to "Tuffy's" and get them to plug it for $ 9.99.) The doctors do not want to do surgery and so we suffer with it when it hits. It is very limiting and extremely frustrating so I would appreciate your prayers. One thing is for sure…we're not giving up, we're choosing faith!

"*And call on me in the day of trouble: I will deliver thee, and thou shalt glorify me*" (Psalm 50:15). This tells me that it's a proportionate thing…the more I call, the more He'll deliver me and the more chances I'll have to glorify Him.

Short on breath but long on God's grace,
Preacher

∽ ∽ ∽

SEPTEMBER 26, 2006—
Just Hold Your Peace!
(From Mrs. Evona)

A story is told about a family that had been very rich in the past but fell upon hard times. They were so desperate that there was not even enough food to feed them all. Several years before their change in circumstances, the mother died in childbirth. The grief stricken father now had the responsibility of all twelve of the children. This was a heavy burden and he was not young. Feeling overwhelmed and desperate, the father sent the older of the children in search of food. With great joy the children returned and told their father about a place that overflowed with food. What a relief to this loving father. At last he had the ability to provide nourishment for his starving family. He packed all the family's belongings up and headed to the new city where there were more opportunities and the much needed food. In their new home they prospered and all the children grew strong and healthy. However, there were those who never forgot the poor condition the family arrived in. These people constantly reminded the family that they were only alive because of the charity of others. The same folks that came to their aid began to become bitter that the new family seemed to be getting all the blessings. The town got together and devised a plan to remind the poor family just where they came from. Every day someone would call the house of the poor family and ask them to come over and "help" complete a task. The children of the poor family were asked to clean floors, wash clothes, repair homes, build buildings and other very taxing jobs. Because the father had taught them to be kind and grateful, they willingly worked for others. In time the town's people forgot that the poor family was not doing these projects because of duty but out of thankfulness. They began to expect the children to work no matter what the circumstances. By this time the father of the children had died and they were all alone. Years came and went and the town's people worked the poor family harder and harder. Many times the family was not even given time to worship or serve the Lord. This became a very sad situation for all the children and now their wives and their families. Finally they had had enough and they began praying for a solution to their dilemma. God miraculously allowed them to collect all the back payments for their labors and have opportunity to move the entire clan to a new town. However, moving that many people was not easy and the town's people who had come to rely on the work the poor family provided were not happy. Because of this the family decided that they must move all their belongings and their families during the night. God was in their plan and all went well for several days. Suddenly, a very excited group of families became a very frightened group of people. In the distance they saw dust rising from a caravan of people. It was the town's people chasing after them. The town had decided that they would physically take the family back to their town and continue to make them work. The poor families and their children immediately turned on the few older children who were leading their move. "What a disaster," they cried. "We knew this would never work!" they all said. The orderly group of families suddenly turned to chaos. Children were crying, mothers were weeping, fathers were screaming and all the while the town's people were getting closer and closer. Out of nowhere a voiced boomed and the leader of the poor families cried,

> "…. *Fear ye not, stand still, and see the salvation of the Lord, which he will shew to you to day: for the Egyptians whom ye have seen to day, ye shall see them again no more for ever. The Lord shall fight for you, and ye shall hold your peace"*
>
> Exodus 14:13-14

In an instant the atmosphere changed. Moses, the leader of this "group of poor families" called the children of Israel, raised his staff and the mighty Red Sea parted and the entire group with their belongings walked across dry ground. As soon as the hateful "town's people" (the Egyptians) began crossing the sea, the waters came crashing down and all the pursuers were defeated. When the children of Israel stood still, God took charge!

We can be like this "poor family." So many times we can only trust God when things are going the way we think they should. As soon as the script is changed from the expected and safe to the unusual and frightening, we start running in circles trying to fix the situation. God commands us to *"stand still, and see the salvation of the Lord..."* After we trust God enough to stand still and wait, *"The LORD shall fight for you, and ye shall hold your peace."* Do we dare stand still? Do we have the faith to hold our peace and let God do the fighting? Exodus 14:30 says, *"Thus the LORD saved Israel that day out of the hand of the Egyptians: and Israel saw the Egyptians dead upon the sea shore."* I know God can handle our problems. Will we let Him?

Preacher is feeling better after resting for the last couple of days. Between Micah's party and our air conditioner being broken at our house last week, he was gone off more than normal. He promises that he was gone because it was hot and not because I was grouchy...SURE!

Standing still and waiting on God!
Mrs. Evona

∞ ∞ ∞

SEPTEMBER 27, 2006—
My Ears Are in the Wrong Place!
(From Mrs. Evona)

During the past week, I have found that everything has made me cry: watching Micah play the trumpet in chapel; seeing Caleb standing straight and tall in line with his class; showing up late for practice at church and realizing the baby's socks were lost somewhere between the door to the house and the car. Lying on the couch and resting my eyes for a minute and being hit in the head with a spatula really brought tears to my eyes. During times like this, I find that I talk to myself more often than normal. I begin with the pep talk about how insignificant the specific issue that I am crying over is and how I need to pull it together and get over it. Somehow, when I am this far gone, the pep talk doesn't seem to work. Even now as I write this update the tears keep coming.

I believe this is a sign that I have used up all my own emotional resources and all I have left is God. The beautiful thing about God is that He knows us and doesn't get frustrated over our weaknesses. God was patient with David in Psalm 6:6: "*I am weary with my groaning; all the night make I my bed to swim; I water my couch with my tears.*" Isaiah said in chapter 16 verse 9: "*…I will water thee with my tears….*" In Jeremiah 13:7, the prophet preaches to Israel and tells them, "*…and mine eye shall weep sore, and run down with tear….*" There is even a book of the Bible named Lamentations which means "to sorrow." One of my favorite passages of scripture comes from Lamentations chapter 3. Verse 49 says, "*Mine eye trickleth down, and ceaseth not, without any intermission.*" This has been my theme verse for the week. Earlier in the chapter we are told to "*lift up our heart with our hands unto God in the heavens* (v. 3:41) *…Thou drewest near in the day that I called upon thee: thou saidst, FEAR NOT*" (Lamentations 3:57). What a comfort to know God will draw near in times when our tears will not stop and calm our fears.

When we were first married, Preacher and I had the normal newlywed adjustments to make. We enjoyed this time together, getting to know each other and learning to live together. One thing continued to baffle Preacher however. He did not know how to deal with my tears. He complained that one minute everything was fine and the next I was soaking his favorite shirt. The worst time was on our first anniversary. I had this very romantic idea to wear a beautiful dress (I had specially made for our honeymoon) on our "first year anniversary date." I worked all afternoon on my hair and makeup and then donned the honeymoon evening dress. I proudly walked out, waiting on him to gush over my beauty and fondly remember me wearing that dress our first evening out as a couple. I was sadly disappointed when he said, "You know, do you think you could wear a different dress? I have never really liked that one!" I stood frozen, remembering how much effort I had put into having the dress specially made for our honeymoon. I could barely make it to our room. Knowing he had somehow messed up, Preacher raced after me. I had thrown myself on our bed and was holding my side laughing so hard I couldn't speak. I was imagining our honeymoon dinner and seeing him trying to say nice things about my dress yet hating it the entire time. Somewhere between laughing and trying to explain my outburst, I began to cry. I can still see Preacher's big, brown eyes watching me trying to figure out what to do with a crazy woman laughing and crying at the same time! Well, we weathered that episode and I learned to ask his opinion on my dresses and he learned to never, never say he doesn't like something I have worn already!

We all seem to have difficultly knowing how to deal with tears. But scripture says that God knows just what to do. In Isaiah 25:8 it says that *"the Lord God will wipe away tears from off all faces."* He *cares* about our sorrow and pain. He reaches his loving hand down and gently wipes the tears from off our faces. There will be trials in our lives and there will be tears. God cares and wants to comfort us and "wipe away tears from off all faces" and give us grace to continue trusting Him. One day in the future, Revelation 7:17 says that, *"and God shall wipe away all tears from their eyes."* Our tears will be wiped away one day, but until then God will continue to wipe them off our faces as we walk by faith.

I have always thought that my ears are in the wrong place. I am not sure where I would have placed them, but when I cry in bed the tears slide down my cheeks right into my ears! So not only do I end up with smeared raccoon eyes, a red stuffy nose but also I have two ears full of tears. Once again, God knows just what to do. God takes our tears and keeps them. Our suffering is important to God. Psalm 56:8 says, "*put thou my tears into thy bottle:...*" I have learned to love antiques from growing up with my mom. She loves old things with a story (like my dad! Sorry, that was an editorial comment from the Preacher!) The other day I was standing in front of her antique secretary desk, just looking at the beautiful color and design. My mom rescued this desk that belonged to her father's mother (my great grandmother) after having been left in the weather for many years. She had it restored and now keeps beautiful white earthenware jars and pitchers in the glass front case. The white jars and pitchers against the dark mahogany are so beautiful. I was standing there admiring the jars and bottles when I remembered the verse about God's catching our tears and putting them in His bottle. I think He takes the bottles that hold our tears (I am sure I have thousands just from the past few months) and puts them on a shelf in His beautiful home in heaven and looks at them and *cherishes* our tears. When we go through trials and suffering and "choose faith" in Him, God cherishes our tears. He places them in a bottle and keeps them close.

Psalm 56:3: "*What time I am afraid, I will trust in thee.*" How can we doubt a God who *cares* about and *cherishes* our tears? There will be times that the tears fall, but know that God will wipe your face and put the tears in his bottle and give you grace to face each new day.

Still weepy but trusting God anyway,
Mrs. Evona

SEPTEMBER 28, 2006—
A Time to Weep, and a Time to Laugh
(From Mrs. Evona Again!)

"To every thing there is a season, and a time to every purpose under the heaven...A time to weep, and a time to laugh..."

ECCLESIASTES 3:1, 4a

Yesterday's update talked about tears. We all have times when we can't seem to dry our tears. God understands and even wrote in Ecclesiastes that there is a time for weeping. But *praise the Lord*, there is also a time for laughter. God has a wonderful sense of humor. He enjoys laughter and wants His people to live an abundant life, not endure our time here on earth. Psalm 2:4a says, *"He that sitteth in the heavens shall laugh..."* Psalm 37:13 records that *"The Lord shall laugh at him..."* Psalm 59:8 tells us, *"But thou, O Lord, shalt laugh at them..."* It is very clear that the Lord who is in heaven laughs! Laughter is a good medicine. Proverbs 17:22: *"A merry heart doeth good like a medicine."*

After several weeks of dealing with tears, it was so refreshing to have the Lord send one of his "jokes." He knows just when I need some laughter and sends it in such a way that you *know* it was the Lord and his wonderful sense of humor!

As you know, I love my three boys dearly but have named them the "three smelly monsters." Those of you with boys will know where my inspiration came from, and those of you with only girls just count your blessings that you don't know! I not only have "three smelly monsters," we have a "smelly monster dad" and the obnoxious wiener dog and Houdini the Hamster (really named Q-tip). I am *not* an animal lover. I used to be, and then I became the "monster mom" who had to take care of the terrible rodent and annoying K-9. I quickly realized I really didn't like animals after all. Last week, I inquired about "odor control" from one of my friends whose son has a hamster. To my great surprise she informed me that "her hamster doesn't smell!" I began excitedly quizzing her about what she feeds him and what kind of bedding she puts in the bottom of the cage. *Bingo!* She has the "special odor reducing" pine bedding. I became a woman obsessed. I would find this bedding and then "Houdini the stinky Hamster" would also be odor free like my friend's hamster! I raced to the pet store. My first mistake was going to a small privately owned pet store. They actually like animals there and I stick out like a sore thumb when I just walk in the place. I think the parrot on the owner's shoulder is the one who gave me away. Something to do with the ugly face I made at him after he tried to mess up my "new hairdo!" It went downhill from there. I am opposed to looking for things in a store. Instead of wandering around trying to find what I need, I always ask for help. I politely announced that we have a smelly hamster and I need that special

"odor reducing" bedding that my friend said worked for her. Instead of nicely showing me to the bedding section, she loudly asked (with three other customers standing around) "Well, how often do you clean the cage?" Indignant over this slam on my housecleaning abilities, I assured her we clean the cage at least two to three times a week! "Oh, my," she announces to the crowd at the register. She then turns to me and says, "Does your hamster have a wet bottom?" I stood in shock for several seconds. The loud laughter from the other customers brought me back to reality. *Wet bottom?* How should I know? Does he have fur? Yes. Does he have teeth, yes! (He took a chunk out of Micah and Lucas already with those vicious teeth!) But does he have a wet bottom? This is something I don't care to know! This drama went from bad to worse. She instructed me in detail on how to check the hamster for this dreaded condition called "wet bottom!" Now I am just telling you right now, there is no way I am checking a *hamster's* bottom. I have had to deal with my share of bottoms as a mom, and am still dealing with one as we speak. There was nothing in my job description about hamster bottoms! Needless to say, I did not win the customer of the day award, and I had a message from the Humane

Society on my answering machine saying something about animal cruelty. (I am sure one of those "true animal lovers" at the store turned me in!) Come to find out, wet bottom is a virus that rodents get that causes their stomachs to become upset and thus the terrible, awful, horrendous smell and the "wet bottom" on the hamster. I left the pet store with a fairly expensive bottle of drops that must be given to the hamster several times a day, and an instruction sheet on "Wet Bottom, the Virus."

I sat in the car and laughed so hard that the grocery bag boy asked if I needed medical attention. *Of all people to get a real "smelly monster," it would be me!* God really does have a wonderful sense of humor.

When things are tough and your circumstances seem impossible to bear, remember Ecclesiastes 3:1, 4a: *"To every thing there is a season, and a time to every purpose under the heaven…A time to weep, and a time to laugh…."*

God can lift your heart if you will be open to His consolation. Sometimes it comes in the form of laughter. Just ask me, the official "Smelly Monster Mom!"

Preacher has not been feeling very well this week. We spoke to the doctor today and believe that we have come up with a medicine to help. He has been on so many different kinds of medicines that it has really irritated the lining of his stomach and caused a great deal of pain. They gave us some medicine to help with the stomach pain and coat his stomach lining to avoid any further pain from the medicines. Preacher has also developed a slight rash on his face from the Tarceva, but the doctor said this was good. (Preacher says that the doctor would not say it was good if it was on HIS face!) The rash is a sign that the medicine is working!! Praise the Lord.

Off to give the wet bottom drops to Houdini the Hamster,
Mrs. Evona

SEPTEMBER 29, 2006—

Blessed beyond Measure

> "When Jesus therefore saw his mother, and the disciple standing by, whom he loved, he saith unto his mother, Woman, behold thy son! Then saith he to the disciple, Behold thy mother! And from that hour that disciple took her unto his own home."
>
> JOHN 19:26–27

Since the beginning of May, one of the most difficult things I have had to deal with is watching those I love hurt because of the news we have been given. From the very beginning, my wife and parents have been with me every second possible. This has been comforting to me but very difficult on them.

My mom is broken. Her eyes tell the story. She tries not to cry but I know she does later or before she comes to see me. She and Evona are the two lady loves of my life and I cannot stand to see them hurting.

God has given me a bond with my mother that transcends description. I am so close to her I often do not know where I end and she begins. She has never failed me or disappointed me or hurt me my entire life. I believe she is the single most powerful influence I have had to make me a man of God. She possesses a captivating grace that moves me and I love her with all my heart. I am so blessed to have had such a wonderful mother.

In the verses above Jesus is dying on the cross to pay for the sins of the entire world but he is concerned for his mother. He looks down into her tear-stained face and feels such compassion. He turns to his disciple, John, and entrusts the care of his mother to him. Mary has shown such faith in her life that you would think she would be exempt from further testing. That doesn't seem to be the case. Here, she is having to watch her son die a terrible death. I can identify with the sadness Jesus feels at her pain. However, when I look into my mom's eyes, I see faith and determination to help me fight. It has been so good to be with her during this time. I find myself touching her a lot when I am with her. I guess you are never too old to need your mom.

Today is her birthday. I want to let her know how much I love her and appreciate all she has done for me but most of all for who she is on the inside. I am so blessed.

Continue to keep me in your prayers. I find I am still having some serious breathing issues. I can just walk to my garden and be very out of breath. The doctors are keeping an eye on these issues.

Still a momma's boy at heart,
Preacher

September 30, 2006—
A Dry Spell

In Ezekiel 37, the prophet Ezekiel has the vision of the valley of dry bones. The Lord takes him to a valley where he sees a large number of bones, which Ezekiel says in verse 2 were "very many" and "very dry." The Lord asks Ezekiel a question in verse 3: "...*can these bones live?*" He then had Ezekiel utter a prophecy on the dry bones in verses 5 and 6: "*Thus saith the Lord GOD unto these bones; Behold, I will cause breath to enter into you, and ye shall live: And I will lay sinews upon you, and will bring up flesh upon you, and cover you with skin, and put breath in you, and ye shall live; and ye shall know that I am the LORD.*" As soon as Ezekiel concluded his prophecy, God fulfilled it before his eyes. Ezekiel watched as the Lord assembled an army of men out of the bones (could this be where we get the old song, "The foot bone's connected to the ankle bone" etc.?); covered them with sinews and flesh and breathed life into them so that they stood before the Prophet in the midst of the valley. God reveals to Ezekiel in verse 11 that, "...*these bones are the whole house of Israel...*" This is a prophecy of Israel's national salvation which will take place during the Tribulation period. Israel has been like a valley of dry bones for so long, but the day will come when they will turn to Christ and live!

Have you ever experienced what we would call "a dry season?" You just don't feel close to the Lord and your relationship with Him seems all but "dried up." Your prayers seem to bounce off the ceiling; your Bible seems irrelevant; church seems a waste of time and energy; your Christian friends seem distant and sometimes even judgmental of your condition, and you find yourself not wanting to witness because you are a poor example of what Christianity should be. This is not uncommon to people in the Bible. Elijah had a dry spell when he fled Queen Jezebel's wrath (1 Kings 19); Jonah faced a dry spell when he preached a revival in Nineveh (Jonah 4); Peter faced a dry spell when he denied the Lord the night He was crucified (the Gospels). Even the best of believers face dry spells in their spiritual lives.

The reasons for these spiritual dry spells are because Satan is alive and well and will pour cold water on your fire for God at every turn. He uses people to do his dirty work, too. You've all heard of the "Chairman of the Cold Water Committee," right? There's one in every church, every office, every classroom, every neighborhood, every organization…even the home. They are usually self-appointed and very good at what they do. Try and remember that the devil is truly the one who is behind their discouragements. Resist the devil as James teaches through the armor of God (Ephesians 6) and the Bible promises he will "flee" from you.

Another reason we face dry spells in our spiritual lives is because we get too far from our salvation. When we first get saved, we may as well be a river. We love our time with God and prayer; we love our fellowship with other believers in the house of God; we love to give to the Lord's work and we love to tell others about what Jesus has done for us. But as time passes, and we become "seasoned Christians," we often lose our fervency and drift into complacency and apathy. Just like God counseled the church of Ephesus in Revelation 2, do the "first works." Pray for God to take you back to the place of your salvation that you may taste of those springs of living water fresh and new. Ask the Lord to make you thirsty once again for His presence. Go to church on Sunday and taste of the well of grace as those assembled worship God in singing, praise, rejoicing, giving and the intake of God's Word. Thirsty people generally find relief, and with God's help you will overcome this dry spell and be a "channel" of blessing once again, overflowing God's goodness and grace to other thirsty souls.

Please continue to pray for the shortness of breath and pain I am experiencing. I feel God's hand come over me at times and I believe it is Him answering your prayers and touching my body. I preached on Wednesday night, and even though it was from a chair, it was great to preach God's Word! The Lord allowed me to be free from pain and have no breathing issues as I preached…AMEN!

Thirsty for Him,
Preacher and Mrs. Evona

OCTOBER 1, 2006—
A Character to Be Proud of

What an exciting day today was for me as a father. Evona and I worried that the boys would have a difficult time adjusting to "real school" after being homeschooled all their lives. We have worried about Caleb the most. He is the quieter of the two big boys. He avoids any situation that will bring attention to him. When he was a baby, he would learn to say something new or sing a new song and we would be so excited to show his "trick" to others. We would eagerly assemble the required family members, building up the suspense of the moment only to have Caleb stand quietly and just stare at us. No amount of coaching would solve this dilemma. When he was around three or four, his Sunday School class would sing in church and he would just stand with the other kids and look at the ground the entire time. Evona finally told him that it would be a lot less embarrassing if he would just sing rather than having her come up to the stage and yank him off for serious retribution. This seemed to work. He just doesn't like to draw any extra attention to himself. Kids like this sometimes get overlooked. Because of this, we have been concerned about how he would adjust to his new school environment.

Evona received a call that she should come to chapel this week for a special presentation. Caleb was going to be given the class character award. In Proverbs 10:1 Solomon says just what my heart feels: "*A wise son maketh a glad father:...*" Evona videoed the presentation and I was able to see Caleb get his award. In typical proud father fashion I made everyone who stopped by watch it also.

When we told the boys that I was sick, Caleb was very quiet. However, his mind was working overtime and he came out with the question that had also been on my mind. He said, "How did you get it, Daddy?" I told him that the doctors were not sure. He hugged me and kissed me gently and said, "It's going to be OK, Daddy." What sweet child-like faith. Because of our trial, the Word of God has become a very important part of our family. Recently, Caleb told Evona that if the house was on fire and he was able to save something, he would save his Bible instead of "Puck." (Now, Puck is his teddy bear that he loves and thinks is real.) Once again, we see why God gives children a mother. I would have patted him on the back and

talked about how proud I was at his wise decision. Evona, on the other hand, calmly reminded Caleb that he has *two* hands. One hand could hold his Bible and the other could hold his bear. Caleb is very tender and loving. He is extremely smart and catches everything that is going on but doesn't let on he is listening. I love his clever sense of humor. I am sure he got that from me. When I lost my hair, he came and told me he just had a "great idea." He wanted to take his furry white hamster named Q-Tip and teach him to sit on my head. Q-Tip would hold one ear with his hands and stretch over my head and hold the other ear with his feet. This would solve my bald issue. He wanted to call it "Hamster Hair!" Only Caleb!

One night the boys asked me what my last words to them would be if something were to happen to me. My heart broke at the fear I could hear in their voices. I told them that I want them to love the Lord with all their hearts and love others. I feel such responsibility to help them build godly character. This takes nurture and admonition (Ephesians 6:4). I want them to grow up and be faithful stewards of God's blessings (James 1:17). I will answer to God for the character or lack of it I mold in them. What a blessing it is that they choose to be wise sons most of the time.

Caleb, your tender heart and cheerful disposition make you a joy to be around. I am so glad God gave you to us. I am very proud of you.

From a glad father,
Preacher

OCTOBER 2, 2006—
Life on the Border

The Lord blessed Fellowship with a tremendous Sunday (October 1). We had a great crowd and a family join! I praise the Lord for building and growing the church while I am struggling just to be in the services and preach. I was unable to preach or attend the Morning Worship Service. I had some pain and shortness of breath and some other issues that made it impossible to be there. This week has been a rough one. I experienced a lot of pain, in spite of that "miracle pain patch," and I've had the worst shortness of breath in months. The Lord allowed me to attend and preach in the Sunday Evening Worship Service. I preached a sermon entitled, "Living on the Border of Blessing."

In Numbers 32, the tribes of Reuben and Gad and a half of the tribe of Manasseh requested of Moses that they be given their inheritance of the east side of Jordan rather than the west side, which is the Promised Land. They loved the eastern Jordan territory because it was plush, well-pastured and good for their cattle. It was a selfish request because all the tribes were to cross the Jordan in unity and conquer Canaan together. Then each tribe would be allotted their inheritance in the new land. Moses agreed only on the promise that the two-and-a-half tribes would cross the Jordan with the nine-and-a-half tribes and fight with them to conquer Canaan. Only then could they return to their families and cattle. Moses uttered a very famous verse as he warned the two-and–a-half tribes to keep their word: *"But if ye will not do so, behold, ye have sinned against the Lord: and be sure your sins will find you out"* (Numbers 32:23). The two-and-a-half tribes kept their word but as soon as Canaan was subdued, they returned to the land east of Jordan. The choice these tribes were making was to live on the border of God's blessings. "Canaan" is a type of the fully-blessed life. The two-and–a-half tribes never fully enjoyed the blessings the nine-and-a-half tribes did because those tribes crossed the border and dwelt in the Promised Land.

How often do we make the foolish choice of living on the border of God's blessings? We reside right on the edge of God's abundance. His design is that we live abundant lives (John 10:10). To live an abundant life, to cross the Jordan and live in the land of blessings means selling out to God completely. Yet so many times, we live on the border and watch those living in the land of blessing with silent envy. Why do we live on the border of blessing? Sometimes we do this through not doing consistent daily devotions. We just can't afford to invest the time in meeting with God. Maybe we have "hit and miss devotions"—here a devotion, there a devotion. Maybe we do "fast-food devotions"—we try to get something fast and to go. Maybe we need "spoon-fed devotions"—we get all our spiritual thoughts from a radio preacher on the interstate as we drive to work or when we go to our church. Our schedules won't give an inch for spiritual battery charging. God awaits us on the other side of the border with answered prayers, sweet promises and life-changing truths! There's no border patrol to stop you. Cross over and find the treasure of His Word to you.

There are many other areas of our lives in which we live on the border of blessing: our spiritual gifts and God-given talents; our bodies as God's temple; our finances which God has entrusted us with, etc. There is one area you cannot afford to live on the border and that is your eternal salvation. Jesus Christ is the *only* way to heaven. You must cross the border of sin and unbelief through placing your faith in Him as your personal Savior. Jesus died on the cross for your sins, rose from the dead and waits to give you eternal life as soon as you receive Him. Why trade God's full blessings for a life of half-heartedness and semi-joy? Why remain at the border when all you need to do is cross over and enjoy His fullness? There's no good reason…get crossing! I mean now!

Enjoying life beyond the border,
Preacher

∽ ∽ ∽

OCTOBER 3, 2006—
In the Hospital Again!
(From Mrs. Evona)

After not feeling well for over a week, we talked with Preacher's doctor and he sent us to the hospital. I had to stop by the church office and wait for Preacher to finish his staff meeting before I could take him to the emergency room. He is determined not to let sickness stop him from his "higher calling." Moffitt has an on site ER for their patients and they were very helpful. We were able to walk right in and see a doctor within 15 minutes. Preacher has had severe shortness of breath and stomach pain. We were hoping that the medicine the doctor gave us over the weekend would help the pain, but there was no improvement. The doctor ordered several x-rays and some blood work. Everything came back unchanged from his last set of tests and gave no indication of what was causing his problems. (We know it is Satan, but I am not sure if he would show up on an x-ray!) They felt that it would be wise to conduct some more tests and keep Preacher overnight. We were given a room and more tests were run. After a brief but heated discussion over the hospital gown issue, the nurse and Preacher came to an understanding and we are all doing well.

Our prayers are that they will be able to pinpoint the problem and correct it "speedily" (Psalm 102:2)! Preacher has been very fatigued with not feeling well and not being able to figure out why!

The deepest desire of our hearts is "*that men may know that thou, whose name alone is JEHOVAH, art the most high over all the earth*" (Psalm 83:18). We know that God is paying attention and knows everything that is going on. He is our strength and comfort. "*For the LORD God is a sun and shield: the LORD will give grace and glory: no good thing will he withhold from them that walk uprightly. O LORD of hosts, blessed is the man that trusteth in thee*" (Psalm 84:11–12).

Trusting in JEHOVAH,
Preacher and Mrs. Evona

October 4, 2006—
The Roller Coaster of Life!
(From Mrs. Evona)

I have never been a fan of roller coasters. Why would anyone pay money to stand in line with hundreds of other smelly, sweaty people, only to be placed against your better judgment in a little metal car? Once you are in the car, they make sure they strap you in so you can't make a break for it, and then they smile real big as you fly by their station. The smile is because once again they have duped someone into paying to be miserable. As soon as you are free again, you need a little brown bag to carry all the food you already ate for lunch!

This is a recap of our day yesterday. Our life was a roller coaster of emotions from start to finish. From the early morning until late evening we went from one high peak only to plummet to the bottom and then fly back to the top. Needless to say, by the end of the day we were worn out! As of Tuesday evening the doctors (all fifteen) feel that Preacher has pneumonia on both sides of his lungs (thus causing the severe shortness of breath) and something in his liver. There is also concern about one of his veins that feeds his lungs and heart having a blood clot. He will be having a procedure done on his lungs to get a sample to test. This will determine if the pneumonia is bacterial or fungal. If it is fungal, they will know that what is in his liver is also fungus and will treat him accordingly. If it comes back bacterial, they will have to do a liver biopsy to determine what is going on down there. The liver is what is causing his abdominal pain. We are really not sure what we are praying for. There are so many complications with each scenario that we need to just pray and put it all in God's hands.

What a blessing to know that God understands the situation even when the doctors are baffled and we don't know what to do. He sent his Spirit to intercede for us when we are at our emotional and physical end.

Likewise the Spirit also helpeth our infirmities: for we know not what we should pray for as we ought: but the Spirit itself maketh intercession for us with groanings which cannot be uttered. And he that searcheth the hearts knoweth what is the mind of the Spirit, because he maketh intercession for the saints ACCORDING TO THE WILL OF GOD! And we KNOW that ALL things work together for good to them that love God, to them who are the called according to his purpose.

ROMANS 8:26–28

Thanking God for His Intercessor the Holy Spirit,
Mrs. Evona

OCTOBER 5, 2006—
Ups And Downs Are Part of Life, But How 'Bout a Little Smooth Sailing for a While?

First things first...Happy Birthday Pop! You're a great dad and wonderful grandfather. *We love you!* My dad has been a rock for me during my sickness. He has come to see me every chance he gets, and that is a sacrifice

because he just got a new plasma TV! Dad gave me my roots and then my wings. What a blessing godly parents can be.

On Tuesday, our pulmonary doctors ordered a CT scan of the abdomen to try and get some answers about this pain I'm having in my abdomen. On Wednesday, I had a bronchoscopy and an echocardiogram. You know that I have pneumonia in both lungs and that it has not been determined whether it is fungal or bacterial. After reading the bronchoscopy, an area on my right vocal cord was discovered with some small raised bumps which will be followed up on at a later date. These tests also revealed spots in the liver and a blood clot in the vein behind the liver. Today, I will have a filter inserted above this new clot to prevent it from moving into my lungs. Our doctors will hopefully receive the test results that are pending today. This will help us determine where we go from here.

Amidst all the tests, opinions, medicine and shots that put a frown on my face, God seems to always give me a laugh in the middle of it. Last night, my dutiful wife was helping me get ready for bed. She helped me change my clothes (that even winds me right now); she rubbed my back, legs, arms, head and shoulders with Benadryl cream to help with my itching; she got my bed in the position I love and she brought me my toothbrush freshly loaded with toothpaste. I began brushing my teeth and immediately I knew something wasn't quite right. The toothpaste had an odd taste and consistency and it moved over my teeth with a strangeness I've never quite experienced. I asked, "Evona, this toothpaste tastes a little funny; are you sure it's not expired?" "It's the same one I just used," Evona answered, "Here, let me get it." Evona went into the bathroom to retrieve the toothpaste in question and did not immediately return. I looked in the bathroom and I saw her bent over the vanity holding her side and trying to not let her laughter be heard. "What's going on in there?" I asked. Evona could not speak. She could only laugh at the top of her lungs as she brought me the tube of Benadryl. Apparently, these two very different creams are packaged in the same size tubes and were sitting next to each other on the bathroom counter. At first I started to join the laughter, but then I realized I'd better make sure that there were no skull and cross bones on the Benadryl tube. Once I felt safe I asked my still laughing wife to bring me something to wash the Benadryl out of my mouth. One great benefit of this event…I did not have one itch in my mouth all night (half of my teeth fell out, but who cares).

We are going to spend the day waiting on test results and trusting God. Isaiah 40:31: "But they that wait upon the LORD shall renew their strength; they shall mount up with wings as eagles; they shall run, and not be weary; and they shall walk and not faint." Many of these things like running and walking we take for granted, but in my current condition these things are so important. I would love to be able to run without gasping for air. I would even settle for walking without gasping for air. This verse promises that when we trust God and wait, HE will renew our depleted strength. The ups and downs of these past few days have been physically and emotionally draining, but God will renew our strength and give us what we need to walk and not be weary (or short of breath)!

Checking my toothpaste nightly!
Preacher

OCTOBER 6, 2006—
What Day Is It Anyway?
(From Mrs. Evona)

We have had a very full week! I have had difficulty keeping up with what day of the week it is. Every morning I have to figure out where I am and why there are strangers in my room. After that, I have to compute exactly what day it is and what procedure is scheduled! Preacher seems to handle the confusion better than I do. He just climbs onto the wheelchair and goes wherever they want to take him. I think he just wants to get out of the room!

Yesterday they were able to successfully insert a filter in his vein. The filter is designed to prevent the existing clot from going to his lungs. This was a necessary procedure to avoid the complications we experienced several months ago that involved the two chest tubes. We are still waiting on the results of the bronchoscopy. Hopefully the results will help the doctors determine how to treat the pneumonia. They are still trying to determine what is going on with the liver. They want to biopsy the problem area but have to wait until Preacher's breathing has stabilized.

The boys have enjoyed the week over at the Spencer's house and will spend a few days with my brother, his wife and kids. They were concerned that I was going to come home and spoil their "sleepover" plans! Didn't God make kids great? No matter what the circumstance they are going to have a good time.

Every morning when I wake up, I have to remind myself that no matter where we are or what we have in store the Lord made the day just for us! There is always something that we can find to rejoice in. Even something as small as an open parking space in front of the hospital or as large as a successful procedure can offer us an opportunity to rejoice and be glad. Psalm 118:24: *"This is the day that the LORD hath made; we will rejoice and be glad in it."*

Rejoicing in the day that the Lord has made, (It's Saturday, right?)
Mrs. Evona

OCTOBER 6, 2006—
Calling Post Message
(From Pastor Dave)

Around lunch time today, the doctors told Pastor and Evona that they felt like the problems he has been having are from the advance of the cancer. Dr. Simon agrees with the rest of the doctors that the cancer has advanced to a point that there is no more they can do. However, the only way to be absolutely sure that this is cancer and not a fungal or bacterial infection is to do a biopsy of the liver. Preacher is too weak to undergo any further tests at this time. They will continue to give the antibiotics and anti-fungal medicines even though they don't believe that is the problem. The doctors gave them a choice as to the direction for Pastor's care. They have chosen to go home. This involves Hospice providing an around-the-clock nurse and medical equipment.

Humanly speaking, the doctors expect Pastor to go home and enjoy time with his family and then pass away. We know, however, that God is the healer and we can beg God to intervene and do a miracle. This is the most important time we have ever asked you to pray. Fall on your faces and cry out to God for a miracle for our friend and pastor. We know God is good and no matter what the outcome, *"We Choose Faith!"*

Psalm 30:2–3: "O LORD my God, I cried unto thee, and thou hast healed me. O LORD, thou hast brought up my soul from the grave: thou hast kept me alive, that I should not go down to the pit." We are in the grave part of this verse. Let's pray and trust God that it is time to see Him work a miracle and finish the verse for our pastor and keep him alive!

Pastor Dave

OCTOBER 7, 2006—

(From Brother Derryl Boyette, Evona's Father)

We prayed for Preacher to be able to go home from the hospital and enjoy his garden again. God wonderfully and mercifully answered that prayer and took Preacher home to be with his Savior. He is now looking into the face of the Rose of Sharon and the Lily of the Valley.

At about 8:30 last night (Friday), Preacher went home to be with his Lord. There was no suffering from the ravages of the final stages of cancer. He was very peaceful and not in any pain. What a merciful gift from his loving Lord. In his room were Evona, his mother Kay and his Aunt Carol (mother's sister). His very last words on this earth were to tell Evona "I love you." She responded with, "I love you and I'll take really good care of our boys."

Pray for the family. Pray for Fellowship Baptist Church, and most of all, pray for the hundreds of folks reading these updates that don't know this Jesus and His peace.

Services will be held at Fellowship Baptist Church. Time and date has not yet been determined. We will let you know.

"Precious in the sight of the Lord is the death of His saints."

PSALM 116:15

Derryl Boyette

∽ ∽ ∽

October 8, 2006—
It's Time to Live What I Preach!
(From Mrs. Evona)

My heart is broken beyond words. I can't seem to make my mind believe Cliff is really gone. On Friday just hours before his homegoing, Preacher reached over and wiped my tears and stroked my hair. He had a sad hurt look in his eyes and whispered, "I hate to see my sweetheart cry. Baby, it's time to live what I preach! Do we really love God? Do we really trust His heart? Today is the day we have to live what I preach."

He was loving and considerate to the very end. After the last shot the nurse gave him he thanked her. After the doctor came in and told us that he was not going to make it, Preacher commented on how hard that must have been on the doctor. He talked about his boys and how proud he was of them. He talked about his family and how much he loved them. He talked about his church and how much he wanted them to continue to do right. He talked about his love for God no matter what. Just before he died, I held him close and he kissed me and told me he loved me.

I will never understand why God chose Cliff to be called home. However, I don't have to understand. I just have to "Choose Faith!" Preacher "Chose Faith" until the very end and was rewarded with a peaceful, pain-free entrance into heaven.

The boys and I and his family will miss him every day, every hour, every minute, but we know that he is not suffering and is with his wonderful Savior. Micah said that he is in heaven with Jesus holding our baby that went to heaven in his arms, and that it is probably a girl baby!

One of his last thoughts was to pray for our church family. His last wish was that our church grow and thrive and one day accomplish the vision God gave for Fellowship Baptist Church.

We are going to have a private graveside service. This will be easier on his family. However, we invite you all to attend a wonderful memorial service on Tuesday, October 10 at our own church, Fellowship Baptist Church. We will celebrate a life that was wholly surrendered to the Lord and used mightily for Him. The boys and I and our family will be there at 6:00 to hug and love on you all, followed by the service at 7:00. We ask that instead of sending flowers you give to the Fellowship Baptist Church Building Fund. This will help our church live out Preacher's vision.

> "But without faith it is impossible to please him; for he that cometh to God must believe that he is, and that he is a rewarder of them that diligently seek him."
>
> Hebrews 11:6

With a broken but trusting heart,
Mrs. Evona

October 12, 2006—
A Celebration To Remember!
(From Brother Derryl, Evona's Dad)

God marvelously blessed the services for Preacher. What an outpouring of love and care from more than 1200 friends and family Tuesday evening. The prayers, hugs, tears, gifts, and just plain old love were nearly overwhelming.

The morning gravesite service was a special time for the family. The service was conducted by Rev. Bill Daab, a longtime friend of the family. There were testimonies from Preacher's cousins and brothers-in-law about the influence on their lives and a trumpet solo of "Amazing Grace."

It is difficult to describe the memorial service unless you were there. The ministry in song of the Green family, Pastor's aunt and uncle and cousins from Tennessee, and the church choir and congregational singing set the tone for the messages of Pastor Dave Spencer, Brother David Catlin, Brother Robert Anders and Pastor Scotty Drake.

This was not a funeral. It was a celebration of God's blessings on Preacher's life and ministry. There was page after page on the overhead screen of names of souls who were saved under Preacher's ministry. I would be remiss if I did not say there was sorrow; but there was also joy in celebrating God's blessings.

The reception line, both before and after the service, streamed out the doors. It makes one wonder what the reception line may be like in heaven when Preacher meets all those saved and influenced by his life and ministry. I am sure that just as he always has, he will point them to Jesus.

> "Now unto the King eternal, immortal, invisible, the only wise God, be honour and glory for ever and ever. Amen."
>
> First Timothy 1:17

We love you,
Thanks,
Brother Derryl (Evona's dad)

OCTOBER 13, 2006—
We Will Not Be Bitter; We Will Be Thankful.

Mornings are the hardest. My body finally gives up and finds rest for a few hours, but when I wake up I have to make my mind understand and deal with our loss all over again. There is no way to describe the emptiness and sadness we feel. Our hearts will never be the same.

Last Friday, one week after Preacher's homegoing, I was struggling to find comfort. Everyone has been so loving and kind to me, but there is a large place in my heart where only my husband and best friend could touch. That is the part that needed comfort. I sat in his chair and held his awful "squishy" pillow. (I bet you thought I was going to say his dog! There is still no chance of that!) I cried into his pillow that still smells like him and prayed for strength. Making it through the crisis time of his memorial has been the easy part. It's living without him day to day that is so hard. I reached in my purse for a tissue and felt his wallet. I have had it in my stuff since he went into the hospital. I opened his wallet and saw a picture of our boys. He was so proud of our children. I scanned the rest of the contents of his wallet and brought out a treasure that no amount of money in the world could buy from me. I found a 3 x 5 card filled with what he called his "fighting verses" written in his own handwriting. God knew that only Cliff could comfort me at that moment and he sent me a card full of *wonderful verses especially chosen by my sweetheart. Psalm 91:1: "He that dwelleth in the secret place of the most High shall abide under the shadow of the Almighty."* What am I going to do? Over and over that phrase goes through my head. I need Cliff's counsel. I am going to dwell in the secret place right next to God. Only He can help me through. Second Corinthians 12:9: *"And he said unto me, My grace is sufficient for thee for my strength is made perfect in weakness..."* I do not have the strength to be what my children and church need me to be. Very true, but God's grace will become my strength. Psalm 46:1: *"God is our refuge and strength, a very present help in trouble."* Lord, please give me refuge. I am in trouble. Psalm 73:26: *"My flesh and my heart faileth: but God is the strength of my heart..."* My heart is so broken. I don't see how I can go on. Remember, God is the strength of my heart! Philippians 4:13: *"I can do all things through Christ which strengtheneth me."* I can't do this, Lord. I don't want to live without my best friend. God will help me do the things that seem impossible because I can do ALL things through Christ's strength.

Being at our home is difficult yet comforting. I see Preacher's garden and touch his pictures. The baby keeps pointing at our family picture and saying "Da ee, Da ee." Each day we find new treasures. I had a difficult time finding the original copy of the family picture we had made. I eventually gave up and asked our friend to find the negative. A few days ago I

found the picture in one of Preacher's Bibles. He left three wonderful Bibles. The first was from his early ministry. It has notes about his first wedding and funeral and many godly preachers' signatures, many who have already gone to heaven. The second is his study Bible. This has thousands of notes jotted down in the margins. It has written in the front the salvation accounts of both our big boys and how happy this made him. It also has a paragraph about Baby Lucas, and the joy Cliff felt at his birth, and a prayer for his salvation when he is old enough. The last of his three Bibles is his preaching Bible. This Bible was the one he used in the pulpit service after service. It has quotes and ideas for many new sermons written all throughout. I found pictures of our family in each Bible. I found a note for each boy and myself on sticky notes within the pages—notes he wrote years ago and stuck in there for safekeeping. I found a love note I wrote him tucked in the Psalms. We have boxes of sermons and pages of study materials. I am finding cards that he wrote me as recently as last week lying on our dresser. There are pictures of him holding our babies, kissing me, hugging his dog (unfortunately!), serving the Lord in the pulpit, playing in the yard, making funny faces, and genuinely having a great time. What a lasting impact he will have on all our lives. I will never understand how taking a wonderful husband, devoted father and truly godly man like Cliff home to heaven is for our good, but I don't have to understand. I just have to trust God that He is good and that He is right.

The boys and I don't want to be OK, but we will be! My kids deserve a joyful life, and Cliff would have wanted them to be happy. He planned ahead for us, and our church and family have helped so that I can stay home with our boys and keep our house. We have decided not to be bitter over what we have lost, but to be thankful for what we were given. We have been so blessed!

Preacher would say I need to wrap it up—I am getting "wordy." I am going to make this our last official "Pastor's Health Update." Preacher's health is great! He is walking on the streets of gold not struggling to breathe. He is running around organizing a special service for his grandfathers and other dear friends that have gone on before. He is holding our sweet baby that went to heaven, and he is standing in that "great cloud of witnesses" (Hebrews 12:1) watching to see what we are going to do. Preacher has done his part in all our lives. Now WE must make a choice. Will we take what he has taught us and use it to make a lasting impact, or will we turn aside and become bitter? Preacher wanted to make sure every single one of you will join him in heaven. Don't stand on the threshold of faith. Give your life to God. Trust His Son Jesus Christ to forgive your sins and KNOW that you will see Preacher again!

In the front of Preacher's Bible he wrote, "I thank God for heartaches that lead to blessings." Together the boys and I still "Choose Faith" and will live our lives to make a lasting impact on others. What will you do?

Still *Choosing Faith,*
Mrs. Evona, Micah, Caleb and Lucas

Epilogue

As the sun peeks through my blinds this morning, I rebelliously refuse to open my eyes. Hoping instead the alarm has somehow miraculously malfunctioned and will never go off again. Minutes tick by as I lie here waiting. I am waiting for the inevitable pain that will come to my heart as the cobwebs clear. My mind will recall that life will never be the same. I will realize that my bed is empty and he will never be back. Once again, I will have to come to terms with the knowledge that my three sweet boys have no daddy. The weight and pressure of the responsibility of being mom and dad will come. Maybe if I keep my eyes closed and reschedule today for tomorrow I can escape just one morning of pain. Snuggled deep in my fuzzy blanket with only my nose sticking out, I wait. From a distance I hear a strange noise. The noise is unrecognizable from under three layers of covers. Knowing it is July in Florida and the need for covers is nonexistent, I peel away a layer hoping to improve my ability to hear. Once again I hear the strange sound. Reluctantly, I climb out of bed and peer through the blinds in my darkened room. The sound is louder now and close to my window. Vainly trying to focus my tired, weary eyes, I strain to see what is making the strange sound. Suddenly, I see movement and realize that the strange sound is a bird sitting on the bush outside my bedroom window. A small nondescript brown bird is sitting on the bush my husband planted two summers ago. The bird is celebrating a new day. It has been two years since I have heard birds singing outside my window. Today, I heard the birds sing.

From the day in May of 2006 Cliff woke up with his first debilitating headache until today, I have dreaded the beginning of each new day. I have equated new days with new pain. It has seemed through my eyes of grief that new days bring new hurts. The emotional energy it takes to make myself face reality and function is beyond description. In the beginning, new days brought more bad news from each doctor visit. Days were filled with the sad, scared look in my boys' eyes as they tried to spend as much time with their dad as possible. As time went by, days brought life and death situations and huge decisions. On Friday, October 6, the day brought the worst pain I have ever felt as I held my courageous, kind, loving husband in my arms as he kissed me goodbye for the last time. He whispered loving words of encouragement, telling me he knew I could make it without him and take care of his precious babies. The following new days brought funeral arrangements and thousands of loving friends saying goodbye to my amazing husband and soul mate. Many months have passed and mornings are just as hard. Instead of doctor's visits and funeral arrangements, the days bring history reports and potty training. The past year has brought a new school for the boys and going back to work for the first time since my oldest was born for me. But sprinkled in these unsettling new days are milestones for us all. One new day found the four of us doing the "pee-pee dance" for the baby as he successfully announced the need and made it to the potty in time. Another new day brought the two big boys actually being allowed to walk across the street alone and play at the park. Some days have taught me that though unpleasant, you can clean out the gutters on your house without falling off the ladder even when the slimy green frog jumps down your shirt. We have learned that with a team effort most household fix-it jobs can be accomplished, and the most important tool to keep around is the hammer. Even if it won't fix the problem, you still feel *much* better after you use it! The wiener dog went on an extended vacation to Cliff's sister's house and Houdini the hamster performed his final disappearing act a while back. The big boy smelly monsters did find where I hid all The Three Stooges DVDs and have corrupted the baby smelly monster. I have learned to disregard any information that starts with "Since Daddy is in heaven and can't get in trouble, I guess it will be OK to tell you what we did when we were with daddy and you were not home!" All of the three boys love to flaunt what special part of Daddy they have. One looks like him, one has his sense of humor and one has his sweet chocolate brown eyes that get him anything he wants. Yesterday's new day is over and tomorrow's new day will come. The pain is still here. The loss is still fresh, but...today, I heard the birds sing.

And I said, My strength and my hope is perished from the Lord; This I recall to my mind, therefore have I hope. It is of the Lord's mercies that we are not consumed, because his compassions fail not. They are new every morning: great is thy faithfulness. The Lord is my portion, saith my soul; therefore will I hope in him.

Lamentations 2:18, 21-24

Finding that God's faithfulness is truly great,
Mrs. Evona

Illustration List

Kay Frink, Cliff Frink, Paulette Boyette, Evona Boyette 15

Boyette Family 25

Cliff Frink at radiation simulation at Moffitt Cancer Center 35

Cliff Frink getting his hair cut 41

Cliff, Evona, Micah, Caleb and Lucas Frink 42

Carol Green and Cliff Frink 45

Cliff Frink 47

New Expedition 52

Lucas Frink, Caleb Frink, Micah Frink 54

Dr. George Simon, Cliff Frink 62

Lucas and Cliff Frink 65

Cliff, Micah, Caleb and Lucas Frink 67

John and Cathy Jeter, Kim Allen, Chris White and Cliff Frink 74

Cliff Frink and Curly 75

Cliff and Boys in the pool 77

Dr. Stevens and Nurse Barbara Bertels and Cliff 80

First Grade Sunday School Class at Fellowship Baptist Church 82

Flower from the garden 89

Lucas and his blankie 94

Suzannah, Jenna and Susan Dwyer and Cliff 115

Micah, Caleb and Lucas Frink and Savannah and Jackson Spencer . 122

Dog Card 167

Cliff and Evona Frink 182

Cliff and Dr. Johnny Pope 184

Micah and Caleb Frink on the first day of school	186
Look a like contest done by Angela Cofield	206
Lucas with cookies on his face	210
Micah and Cliff	293
Q-Tip the Hamster	313
Kay Frink and Cliff	315
Caleb and Cliff	320
Cliff Frink Sr. and Cliff	326
Cliff in the Garden	335
New picture of Evona, Micah, Caleb and Lucas	339

Notes

1. McFall, James. "I Still Trust You Lord." Rec. by The Butch Green Family. *As For Me and My House*. Goldmine Recording Studios, 2005.

2. Lister, Mosie. "Goodbye World, Goodbye." Lillenas Resources. Lillenas Publishing Company online (accessed 11 December 2008) http://www.lillenas.com/nphweb/html/lmol/contributor.jsp?contrib=1400.

3. Spafford, Horatio G. "It Is Well with My Soul." (1873). Rec. by Selah. *Greatest Hymns*. Curb Records, 2005.

4. "He Aint Never Done Me Nothing But Good," Rec. by The Crabb Family. Lyrics Mode online. http://www.lyricsmode.com/lyrics/c/crabb_family (accessed 11 Dec. 2008).

5. Osbeck, Kenneth W. *101 Hymn Stories: The Inspiring True Stories Behind 101 Favorite Hymns*. (Minneapolis: Kregel Publications, 1979.) 111.

6. Truett, George W. QuotationsBook. http://www.quotationsbook.com/author/7314/ (accessed 10 December 2008)

7. Wells, Oliver. "God is Still Doing Great Things." Rec. by The Brooklyn Tabernacle Choir. *Be Glad*. (Tennessee: Provident Music Group, 2002).

8. Mohr, John. "You Want To...Now Will You." Rec. by Steve Green. *For God and God Alone*. Sparrow Records, 1986.

9. Siino, Denise Marie. *In Her Steps: Women of Courage and Valor*. (New York: B&H Group, 2005.) 49.

10. Burgess, Dan. "Press On." Rec. by Selah. *Press On*. Curb Records, 2001.

11. Jeremiah, David. *A Bend in the Road: Finding God When Your World Caves In*. (Danbury: Thomas Nelson Incorporated, 2002).

12. Jeremiah, David. *Life Wide Open: Unleashing the Power of a Passionate Life.* (Danbury: Thomas Nelson Incorporated, 2003).
13. *Chariots of Fire.* Dir. Hugh Hudson. Perf. by Ian Charleson and Nicholas Farrell. (Film 1981).